VOICES IN
THE CODE

VOICES IN THE CODE

A Story about People,
Their Values, and the
Algorithm They Made

David G. Robinson

Russell Sage Foundation
New York

The Russell Sage Foundation

The Russell Sage Foundation, one of the oldest of America's general purpose foundations, was established in 1907 by Mrs. Margaret Olivia Sage for "the improvement of social and living conditions in the United States." The foundation seeks to fulfill this mandate by fostering the development and dissemination of knowledge about the country's political, social, and economic problems. While the foundation endeavors to assure the accuracy and objectivity of each book it publishes, the conclusions and interpretations in Russell Sage Foundation publications are those of the authors and not of the foundation, its trustees, or its staff. Publication by Russell Sage, therefore, does not imply foundation endorsement.

Library of Congress Cataloging-in-Publication Data

Names: Robinson, David G. (Researcher in technology policy), author.
Title: Voices in the code : a story about people, their values, and the algorithm they made / by David G. Robinson.
Description: New York : Russell Sage Foundation, 2022. | Includes bibliographical references and index. | Summary: "The critical turning points in our lives are often decided by algorithms— rules carried out by software, on a computer. Algorithms determine who gets scarce seats at top public schools. At a bank or an insurance company, an algorithm mines your data to decide whether you'll get a loan. If you apply for a job at a large employer, an algorithm is increasingly likely to scan your résumé, deciding before any human pays attention whether you're even worth talking to. In each case, there are deeply human questions at the heart of a job that has been given to a machine. Which of a person's traits are legitimately related to her job performance and fair game for her potential employer to consider? How should scarce public resources—be they medicine, housing, or a coveted slot at an elite public school—be distributed? *Voices in the Code* is about choices like these—the ethical trade-offs inside life-altering algorithms—and about how such choices can be made"—Provided by publisher.
Identifiers: LCCN 2022008162 (print) | LCCN 2022008163 (ebook) | ISBN 9780871547774 (paperback) | ISBN 9781610449144 (ebook)
Subjects: LCSH: Algorithms—Social aspects. | Decision making—Data processing. | Computers and civilization.
Classification: LCC HM851 .R628 2022 (print) | LCC HM851 (ebook) | DDC 303.48/33—dc23/eng/20220512
LC record available at https://lccn.loc.gov/2022008162
LC ebook record available at https://lccn.loc.gov/2022008163

The paper used in this publication meets the minimum requirements of American National Standard for Information Sciences—Permanence of Paper for Printed Library Materials. ANSI Z39.48-1992.

Text design by Suzanne Nichols.

RUSSELL SAGE FOUNDATION
112 East 64th Street, New York, New York 10065
10 9 8 7 6 5 4 3 2 1

For Dad,
who taught me that most people, most of the time,
are doing the best they can under the circumstances

Contents

Illustrations |

About the Author |

DAVID G. ROBINSON is a visiting scholar at the Social Science Matrix at the University of California, Berkeley, and a member of the faculty of Apple University. Most of his work on this book took place at Cornell University, where he was a visiting scientist from 2018 to 2021.

Acknowledgments |

THIS BOOK WOULD not exist but for the help and encouragement of many hands.

My gratitude extends first to Meryl Nolan and Nick Farnsworth, who were my students in a 2017 Georgetown Law seminar about the governance of algorithms. They proposed and wrote an excellent term paper about the transplant system, which sparked my interest and began this journey. My colleagues at Upturn, especially Harlan Yu and Aaron Rieke, encouraged my teaching and this project. At Cornell, the AI Policy and Practice Initiative was an ideal home while I did the bulk of the work, and Karen Levy was an incomparable sounding board and guide, especially to the practice of qualitative social science. This project was never easy to classify, and I like to think that it bears the imprint of Cornell's ideal that a university should be a place where "any person" may pursue "any study." The MacArthur Foundation, particularly Eric Sears and his portfolio on AI and the Public Interest, provided through its support of Cornell and of Upturn the patient funding that allowed this project to take shape over the course of several years. The staff of the Cornell University Library, and its formidable collections, helped me pull together an idiosyncratic constellation of sources, some of them quite obscure, and made those sources available wherever in the world I was working. Alex Xu read drafts and gave thoughtful feedback. UC Berkeley's Social Science Matrix and the Algorithmic Fairness and Opacity Group were my community and intellectual home while finishing the manuscript.

No quicker road would have led here. I am grateful to all, more than I can say.

This work has been supported in part by grant 1908-17713 from the Russell Sage Foundation. I appreciate the support and encouragement of the foundation and its able staff, particularly Suzanne Nichols, whose editorial stewardship of this project was ideal. Any opinions expressed in this book are mine alone and should not be construed as representing the opinions of the Russell Sage Foundation.

People throughout the transplant and transplant governance community, whether formally interviewed and quoted or not, gave generously of their time, expertise, and personal perspectives. I am particularly grateful to Clive Grawe, who graciously agreed to share his story and to trust my telling of it. I have deep gratitude as well to James Alcorn, Göran Klintmalm, Darren Stewart, and Monet Thomson, each of whom spoke with me repeatedly, brought me into the remarkable lives that they have led, and provided startlingly thorough, detailed comments on early drafts of this project.

Others gave platforms and feedback on the work, including Berkeley's Center for the Study of Law and Society, the Stanford Institute for Human-Centered Artificial Intelligence, the Data & Society Research Institute, the Privacy Law Scholars Conference, and Microsoft Research.

Special thanks for particular insight and feedback go to Solon Barocas, Josh Cohen, Malcolm Feeley, Marion Fourcade, Joe Hall, Dennis Hirsch, Karen Levy, Deirdre Mulligan, Blake Reid, Alex Rosenblat, Andrew Selbst, Mark Sendak, Robert Sloan, Alicia Solow-Niederman, Kathy Strandburg, Rebecca Wexler, Malte Ziewitz, and the anonymous peer reviewers recruited by Russell Sage.

As this book goes to press, I'm preparing to begin a full-time role at Apple University, which is an internal learning and research organization within Apple. I began teaching at Apple while completing this manuscript. I'm grateful to my colleagues for giving me the time and space necessary to complete this project.

I have always been fascinated by the tools and habits that people bring to their most meaningful intellectual and creative projects. For my work on this book, the critical tools were software: Scrivener for drafting and structuring the manuscript, Zotero for organizing and annotating hundreds of sources, and Aeon Timeline for making tractable a very complex and multi-threaded chronology. The habits, or at least the aspired-to habits, were getting up to write first thing in the morning and meditating in the vipassana tradition. John Lopez, an extraordinary personal trainer, saved me from getting totally lost in the world of ideas, by helping me stay fit and tend to my body. Not only my physical health but the fresh perspective and energy I often brought to my desk are partly to his credit.

My father Jody Robinson and uncle Lew Robinson, physicians of the old school, helped to shape the lens through which I understand the world of medicine, including the matters described in this book. My mother, Meg Robinson, gave perceptive feedback on a draft and moral support throughout. My brothers, Joshua, Micah, and Noah, were at my back throughout this project, as they are in life.

This book draws on many fields, including law, science and technology studies, sociology, computer science, political science, and philosophy. Despite my best efforts, there are likely errors and omissions in its pages. I alone am responsible for these. In particular, footnotes notwithstanding, no accounting for my intellectual debts would ever be complete. I apologize to my intellectual creditors for any inspirations and sources that I have either missed or misunderstood.

Last and most, my wife, Yana Lantsberg, made the creation of this book itself an incomparably happy chapter of my life, even amid the personal and global challenges of the last few years. She was a patient and insightful sounding board throughout. Her encouragement, patience, wisdom, and good cheer make problems smaller, opportunities larger, and life more of an adventure. It's a pleasure always to return that favor as best I can.

David Robinson
San Francisco, California
January 2022

Chapter 1 | The Human Values That Hide in Algorithms

THE CRITICAL TURNING points in our lives are often decided by algorithms—rules carried out by software, on a computer. Algorithms determine who gets scarce seats at top public schools, not only through standardized testing but also through intricate "matching" systems that consider geography, grades, and student and parent preferences. At a bank or an insurance company, an algorithm mines your data to decide whether you'll get a loan, or how much you personally should pay for car insurance. If you apply for a job at a large employer, an algorithm is increasingly likely to scan your résumé, deciding before any human pays attention whether you're even worth talking to. And when you *do* get an initial interview, there's a growing chance that it'll be a cordial chat between you and an algorithm, which may scan video of your face to render an opaque verdict about the kind of employee you would become. In courtrooms and social services offices, algorithms shape vital civic choices, like who will spend time in jail, or when the state should remove children from their parents' home.

You might be tempted to think of algorithms and their design as a purely technical question, a problem for programmers and specialists to worry about. But that would be a mistake. When powerful institutions in the real world use algorithms to make life-altering decisions about people, the algorithms themselves become more than math on a whiteboard. They become the instruments of our values. They are built not on data alone, but also on judgment—*human* judgment—about which values matter most and how to express those values. They are where our ideals collide with reality.

Consider the examples above: in each case, there are deeply human questions at the heart of a job that has been given to a machine. Which of a person's traits are legitimately related to her job performance and fair game for her potential employer to consider? How should scarce public

1

resources—be they medicine, housing, or a coveted slot at an elite public school—be distributed? How should the liberty of an accused and presumptively innocent person be balanced against his neighbors' need for immediate safety?

This book is about choices like these—the ethical trade-offs inside of life-altering algorithms—and about how such choices can be made. I'll focus on systems that you, as a reader and a participant in democracy, have reason to care about: systems that involve either a corporate decision that we've collectively chosen to regulate or a public one carried out in all of our names. In each instance, our shared values are at stake.

Many different ideals are realized—or frustrated—through the algorithms explored in this book. On the private-sector side, we have laws and policies designed to make sure that employers don't discriminate based on race or other protected traits in their hiring. In finance, we enable people to see and correct the error-prone data that banks use to decide about our loan and mortgage applications. In the public sector, values like fairness and legal entitlements such as due process need to be actively protected in courtrooms, public assistance offices, and elsewhere. All of this is equally true, whether the decision-making process happens to involve a computer or not. But when algorithms are involved, the values at stake can more easily get lost.

In this first chapter, we will explore a half-dozen flashpoints where the hard choices inside an algorithm have become a public concern, and where ethical debates are unfolding without a clear road map. Institutions have generally found it much easier to adopt life-shaping algorithms than to design or govern these systems in an accountable and people-centered way. The systems that make key moral choices are often hard to understand, poorly monitored, prone to error, and otherwise disappointing. And the hardest ethical choices inside software—choices that belong in the democratic spotlight—are often buried under a mountain of technical detail, and are themselves treated as though they were technical rather than ethical.

In the heart of this book, we explore an extraordinary story from the world of transplant medicine, where doctors, surgeons, and patients grapple directly with the moral substance of a life-and-death algorithm: the system that allocates donated kidneys to transplant patients in the United States. These efforts are supported by a constellation of institutions and practices that have evolved over nearly forty years, and they are guided by values of inclusion that stretch back even further. Looking at today's debates over other algorithms through the lens of the transplant story, we'll find reason for measured optimism: algorithms don't have to be mysterious, and their moral burdens can be shared—to a point. There is much to learn in transplant medicine, both about *how* to share the moral burdens of a high-stakes algorithm and about the real-world limits of such sharing.

Although they matter in all our lives, algorithms are a particularly popular way to make decisions about people at the bottom or the edges—those who lack wealth and social capital. When people seek welfare or disability support from the government, algorithms analyze each applicant's history to decide on the benefits that person can have. Algorithms run by child protection agencies size up mostly low-income parents to see whether they're a threat to their own kids. And when a person first appears in criminal court, newly accused of a crime and most often indigent, algorithms advise the judge about whether the person is safe enough to send home or so dangerous that they ought to be locked up.

Algorithms bring unique strengths to large-scale decision-making and are increasingly common in government and industry alike. They typically promise to be faster, cheaper, and more consistent than human decisions. When a human being makes a choice, the true reasons for it may be mysterious and might be different from the reasons that person gives. (Such differences are widely studied in psychology and behavioral economics.) By comparison, the mechanical and explicit workings of an algorithm should allow for clarity in decision-making, greater transparency, and a shared understanding of how decisions get made. Seen from a distance, the process of making a high-stakes algorithm—of deciding on rules to answer ethically challenging questions—might appear to be a promising opportunity for policymakers and interested members of the public ("stakeholders," in the jargon of policy nerds) to work through hard questions together.

But all too often, more technology turns out to mean *less* democracy. The unique virtues of algorithms also have a flip side: when ethically fraught decisions move to software, those decisions get harder to understand, and harder to control. Algorithms are intricate, quantitative, and costly to analyze and understand. They act on data—on numbers that have been distilled, inevitably imperfectly, from messy human realities. The data often reflect biases or other problems. Understanding an algorithm's performance requires measurement and technical analysis, including an understanding of the underlying data. These are tasks and knowledge that are not accessible to most people, not even to most policymakers. Deciding how a system *ought* to work, likewise, involves substantial background knowledge.

In addition to these direct, technical challenges, there are also major cultural barriers to governing algorithms effectively. Many people, including those in positions of authority, find digital technology intimidating. This is not only because they lack technical training but also because a mystique surrounds new technology. Asking pointed questions about how a system works can be seen as a sign of weakness, since it may suggest that the questioner lacks understanding. Quantification can serve as a kind of moral anesthetic by seeming neutral and objective, even though, on close inspection, data and algorithms often bear the fingerprints of human passions. Deferring to the numbers can be "a way of making decisions without seeming to decide," as the historian of science Theodore Porter has put it.[1]

WHAT IS AN ALGORITHM?

No matter what our backgrounds are, each of us will need to be bold, to venture a little bit beyond our comfort zone and into the details of how something works—be it a piece of technology, a law, or an ethical principle. Cultural timidity about the human stakes of critical software isn't just a challenge for lawmakers, journalists, and activists. It is also a challenge for you and me, the reader and author of this book.

I said at the outset that algorithms are "rules carried out by software, on a computer." That's how most laypeople, in my experience, use the term, and it is how we'll use the word throughout this book. But there is a little more to the story.

The pioneering computer scientist Alan Turing wrote in 1948 that an algorithm can be "anything that could be described as 'rule of thumb' or 'purely mechanical.'"[2] It is any process that takes in information, transforms it mechanically, and outputs other information. Turing introduced the concept of a "Turing machine," a theoretical object that could read, write, and manipulate an endless list of symbols, using simple rules. An algorithm, in the more precise sense that Turing and his teacher Alonzo Church developed, is any procedure that can be implemented by a Turing machine.

Everything that any of today's computers can do—from the server farms at a place like Google to the phone in your pocket—could in principle be done instead by a Turing machine, if it were given time to perform enough steps.[3] Any program you can run, or any program that can be *written* in modern programming language, is in the same sprawling family as any other program, because both can be done on a Turing machine. The whole process repeats in layers, because one thing a Turing machine can do is read and write new instructions for processing other data in some other, more intricate way.

Algorithms are rigid rules for processing information. A child doing long division with pencil and paper could be described as implementing an algorithm, and so too could a bureaucracy. For instance, if a clerk at the

Department of Motor Vehicles grades a driver knowledge test by comparing multiple-choice answers to an answer key, he is implementing an algorithm, regardless of whether any computer is involved. But algorithms in today's software systems can be so complex that their behavior may be hard for a person, even an expert, to intuit.

In this book, I use "algorithm" the way most laypeople use it: to refer specifically to rigid rules implemented on a digital computer. This lay use of the term is narrower than the official definition, and it irks some scientists, but I think it actually makes sense, for two reasons. First, it's the usage you are most likely to encounter outside of scientific settings, including among policymakers and in the press. And second, as I mentioned above, algorithms-as-software have some specific strengths and weaknesses, as we explore in this book.

In the case of the kidney allocation algorithms at the heart of this book, the algorithm at issue is the set of mechanical rules for compiling a prioritized list of patients to whom a newly available, transplantable kidney will be offered. In other cases, the algorithm might be a set of rules that determine who is eligible for a government benefit, or whose tax return will be audited.

Looking at this very closely, you might notice an assumption I am making throughout the book: I'm assuming that the algorithm described in official policy documents and the one actually running on the computer that generates the transplant offers are the same. That is, I'm assuming that the software code is a faithful expression of the precise rules that some policymaker (or group of people) decided on. This is not always or necessarily the case, especially when the official rules were written without computers in mind. Danielle Citron, who has studied many such systems, has gone so far as to claim that "programmers inevitably alter established rules when embedding them into [software] code in ways the public, elected officials, and the courts cannot review."[4] It was this insight, among others, that led her and other scholars to propose the kinds of governance controls that are described in chapter 2 and that have actually been implemented in the organ allocation system we will explore in chapters 3 and 4. By the time we are done, I hope it will be clear why I feel justified in assuming that the code and the policy of organ allocation match each other.

One important difference between the algorithm at the heart of this book and many other algorithms used in government is that in this case, the policy was designed from the start to be implemented by a computer, so that computer programmers were not placed in the uncomfortable role of adding key details to an underspecified policy. In other instances, such as the algorithms used in welfare and criminal justice systems and explored below, the policy is not fully specified, and so engineers are forced to become quasi-legislators.[5]

What's Special about Algorithms?

Why should governing (digital) algorithms be any different from governing anything else? After all, a building full of bureaucrats can also act as a rigid, consistent, more or less unthinking machine that can be hard to understand. Many laws and regulations could be described, abstractly, as algorithms whose inputs are some facts about the world and whose output is a yes or no: This thing is allowed and that thing is not. You get this, or you don't get it.

We make many such rules through low-tech legislation. A city council can direct that a building be constructed on a certain spot, or that payments be made to certain people in need. Why not, in an equivalent way, simply direct that software be made for a certain purpose and leave the rest to the architects? Sure, one might argue, most elected officials aren't software experts. But they aren't architects or structural engineers either.

From "protecting the best interests of the child" to "making the best use of donated organs," our laws and policies are full of ambiguous standards, partly because vague and imprecise rules are often easier for legislators to agree on than more precise rules would be. When it comes time to turn a law, policy, or regulation into an algorithm (or for that matter, to construct a building or design a form that welfare applicants will fill out), legal rules need to be made concrete in the world. And that will often mean adding specificity to the rules that are being enforced. Filling in details is, in principle, a fine role for professional experts. But answering hard moral questions? That's the role of a broader community, whether directly or through representatives.

This challenge of deciding how to share moral burdens across a community—rather than delegating them to technicians—is by no means unique to software. It extends to many kinds of complex policymaking. It can arise whenever public authorities must act—or must establish rules for how others can act—and yet have not been given clear instruction on important moral trade-offs that their policies must navigate. In that sense, I would argue, algorithms are *not* a special case. The basic impulse to resolve important values questions openly, rather than pretending that such choices are a mere matter of technical detail, arises and in many areas.

In fact, as we'll explore in chapter 2, strategies have been developed in many complex areas of policymaking, from environmental regulation to municipal budgeting to urban planning, for giving the public a stronger voice in shaping the moral trade-offs that policymakers must confront.

We'll look specifically at four types of strategy for sharing burdens: participation, forecasting, transparency, and auditing. With each of these approaches, promising strategies for building software emerge in part from other policy domains.

However, even if the *why* of open policymaking is universal, the *how* is particular to each complex area. The constellation of people to whom decisions matter, the types of expertise needed to understand what's happening, the pace at which decisions are made and revised, and the possibilities for change depend on what kind of decision is at stake.

In the six stories we explore in the following pages, we'll see that software often presents a special challenge and needs its own ways of deciding on how things should be. As we'll see, scholars and policymakers have found a pattern of high-profile cases in which current software-making practices have led to disastrous results. These examples often involve relatively vulnerable people whose fates are being influenced by an algorithm that operates within a powerful institution. Such problems should no longer surprise us, not only because they frequently recur, but also because they are foreseeable in light of how high-stakes algorithms are often made and governed. As Deirdre Mulligan and Kenneth Bamberger note, "Administrative agencies, legislatures, and courts are poorly designed, in terms of structure, accountability mechanisms, and expertise, to take into account the implications of technology design."[6]

A Note on Language

The words we use to describe digital technologies change almost as fast as the technologies themselves do. Choosing words might seem like a scholar's problem, but in this case the stakes are practical. It can be hard to make sense of historical sources, or even to communicate with other people in our own time, when both the things we are talking about and the words we use for them are constantly in flux. One might fairly say that all human communication suffers from some version of this problem. But where both the pace of change and the breeding rate of jargon are high—as they are in digital technology—the challenge becomes particularly acute.

Here, for instance, is a picture of the battle among some popular buzzwords (figure 1.1). The vertical axis shows how often each term appears in published books. The horizontal access is time, with data plotted for each year of publication since I was born.

No two of the terms in figure 1.1 have exactly the same meaning, but the terms overlap, and each one's boundaries are hazy. What to do?

One way forward—a popular strategy in books like this one—is to insist on a single correct meaning for each term in an attempt to bring precision

Figure 1.1   Popular Technology Terms, 1980–2019

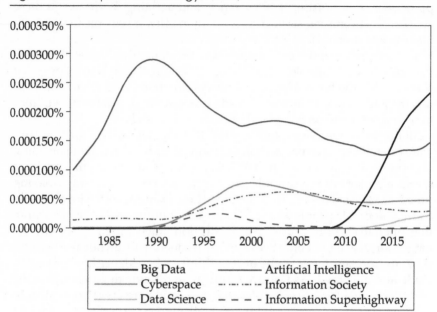

Source: Google Books Ngram Viewer (Google Books n.d.).

to the haze. For instance, all algorithms use *some* data, and if we really wanted to, we could argue about how much data it takes to count as "big." Likewise, algorithms are made by people, presumably to save some other people the work of doing something by hand, so we might say that any such replacement of human by machine should count as "artificial intelligence." Or we might try to draw some other line.

A better way, I think, is to take a step back and focus on the deeper pattern underlying all this language. Digital technology is always changing, and it constantly sparks new ethical and policy challenges. Computer scientists and engineers, who are experts in how the technology works, will naturally employ precise and specialized terms.

But the rules and values for how we live together are a topic for a wider conversation, and that wider discussion does not—*cannot*—belong only to people who are fluent in technological terms of art. For policymakers and the general public, terms like "big data" and "AI" are useful partly because they function as big tents. They stretch to cover whichever uses of software seem worth worrying over. (And even among experts, the precise boundaries that separate AI systems or "big data" from other software are hazy and contested.[7])

Decisions about which software systems to bother governing carefully and democratically cannot depend on whether certain buzzwords rightly apply to the system, such as whether its data is "big" or whether its logic is "artificially intelligent." Such questions lack clear answers. Nor should the decision about how to govern a system depend on the details of its inner workings (such as whether the system uses a particular type of machine learning), because those details aren't visible to the public and policymakers who might do the governing.

Instead, the question of how a piece of software should be governed must depend on what it does—on how its operation affects people. I'll have more to say about that question in chapter 2.

Regardless of what one chooses to call them, the algorithms described in this book work on data about human lives. Almost always, if you scratch the surface of an algorithm that judges people, you'll find a prediction of future human life outcomes: how long a person will live if they get a new kidney, or how well a student will do if admitted to a certain school, or how likely it is that a customer will repay a loan or file a car insurance claim. Data-driven prediction in the social world is an inherently slippery endeavor. Algorithms are based on past patterns, often patterns that social reformers seek to change. Nevertheless, they are often deployed in a way that presumes those patterns will remain the same. Moreover, these predictions actually change what happens and may make themselves come true. We'll come to that theme throughout the book. For now it is enough to know that when you read about the governance of AI, or the rules that surround "big data," the material you are reading is part of the same conversation as this book.[8]

STORIES CHANGED BY AN ALGORITHM

In each of the six stories that follow, the ethical trade-offs made inside of a high-stakes algorithm have attracted public concern. Both the extent of public involvement, and the apparent success or failure of the underlying software, are widely varied.

Aside from ethical contestation, there's one other important feature these stories share: in each one, the people involved lacked an established, structured, proven way of collaborating to understand and shape the ethical trade-offs that a high-stakes algorithm presented.

As we'll discover in chapter 2, a growing community of scholars and policymakers is working to fill that gap, proposing and testing new answers to the question of how an algorithm's moral substance can be brought out from its technical shell so that people beyond the technical team can in one way or another share its moral burden. Spurred on by stories like the ones you are about to read, policymakers and scholars are now proposing a range of new ways to navigate the moral substance of high-stakes algorithms. What they have not done yet, however, is to explore the lessons of the transplant story, which we'll explore in chapters 3 and 4. Finally, in chapter 5, we'll bring everything together and consider how the moral challenge of governing algorithms looks once we have absorbed the experience of transplant medicine.

Interviewing on Camera

In the pandemic autumn of 2020, while working on this book, I taught a class on the ethics of data science for Cornell undergraduates. When it came time for them to write papers about a questionable algorithm, half the class flocked to the same topic: a recruiting system called HireVue, which many of them had encountered that semester while applying for internships. Popular with large employers, including JPMorgan and Unilever, the system was a one-way video job interview: students received a set list of questions and recorded their answers on a webcam. Then HireVue's software automatically analyzed their "employability." Many students, after interviewing with the machine, went no further and didn't get to talk to a human.

HireVue was born as a filing system where human recruiters could store and review video footage of job interviews. According to a company white paper, in 2015 the company began using "artificial intelligence to transform . . . video interviews into a . . . pre-hire assessment."[9] HireVue's chief psychologist told a *Washington Post* reporter that the software would automatically decompose each video clip into specific facial movements—such as a raised eyebrow or a wrinkled nose—and that the rank provided by this analysis "can make up 29 percent of a person's score."[10]

Some students got past the algorithmic bouncer and others didn't, but none found out what the algorithm had seen in their smile. HireVue claimed to be both old and new, purporting to blend cutting-edge AI with a century's worth of research in workplace psychology. And it repeatedly referred to its system as "validated," though company staff seemed more comfortable making that claim in sales brochures than in scientific papers. In fact, as far as I can tell, before 2020 there was no public, transparent, rigorous analysis of the system's accuracy. (A related and tricky question is what exactly it would even *mean* to say that an "employability" algorithm is accurate or not—that might depend on the job. The system's claims to validity were broad and imprecise.) In short, however compelling the evidence available to company insiders might have been, the details of this system's operation were something for regulators, job candidates, and employers essentially to take on faith. My students pointed out that the system might hurt a candidate with an accent, the wrong camera angle, or a different cultural approach to eye contact.

Then, just after my students' final papers were in, the company made an abrupt and mysterious about-face: it had decided "not to use any visual analysis in [its] pre-hire algorithms going forward."[11] Why? Because some very recent internal research, which the company was not making public, had found that "for the significant majority of jobs and industries, visual analysis has far less correlation to job performance than other elements of our algorithmic assessment."[12] (After the announcement, a former member of the company's AI advisory board revealed that he had quit in protest some time earlier, because the company had initially refused to take this step.[13])

By the time it abandoned this AI approach, HireVue had used algorithms to analyze facial movements and decide on the fates of literally millions of job candidacies. The carefully worded blog post left open some chance that facial movements still were positively correlated with job performance, even if they were "far less correlat[ed]" than other factors were. Still, the change wouldn't have been worth making or announcing unless the old algorithm had made some avoidable mistakes. The company was effectively conceding that candidates whose facial movements had most pleased the algorithm had come out ahead—and gotten interviews or jobs that others had lost—even though their smiles weren't the best available signal of their ability to succeed on the job.

On the same day of its sudden change, the company released a third-party audit of one of its default recruiting models, conducted by the auditing practice of Cathy O'Neil, a Wall Street quant turned social critic of algorithms and author of the book *Weapons of Math Destruction*. The audit, which HireVue made public, basically commended the particular slice of the company's software that O'Neil had examined. It's not clear whether the audit process played any role in unearthing the previously unnoticed limits of facial analysis as a job readiness signal.

The audit was one of the first of its kind, a step toward better or different ways of governing high-stakes private-sector software. Yet the audit was narrow in scope, and while HireVue claimed that its results were "public," the report was actually provided only to people who entered into an agreement with the company.[14] "I would quote relevant sections of [the audit]," a reporter at *Forbes* complained, "except that in order to download it, I was forced to agree not to share the document in any way."[15] And the company's about-face on the value of analyzing job applicants' faces — awkward for a firm whose name sounds like "hire view" — remains largely mysterious.

All of this suggests that, while voluntary audits by technology vendors may have a valuable role to play, setting the audits' scope and terms will be a challenge, and such audits may never provide a complete picture of how hiring algorithms work. Upturn, the civil-rights-and-technology NGO that I cofounded in 2011, recently investigated the hiring algorithms in use at fifteen large hourly employers, including Walmart, Amazon, Starbucks, and McDonald's. Its research found that "it is simply impossible to fully assess employers' digital hiring practices from the outside. Even the most careful research has limits. It is critical that regulators, employers, vendors, and others proactively assess their hiring selection procedures to ensure that all applicants are treated fairly."[16] At the same time, the report argued, existing laws are inadequate and "employers lack incentives to critically evaluate their hiring processes."[17] To ensure that hiring is fair, these algorithms apparently need to be regulated. And for that to happen effectively, the algorithms and their underlying data need to be clearly understood, not only by the companies who make them but more broadly.

Driving toward Greater Fairness

As a second example, consider the price an algorithm sets when you try to buy car insurance. The sociologist Barbara Kiviat has done a pathbreaking study of these algorithms and their moral logic.[18] Car and other property insurance are commercial products and might seem to be just a matter of numbers, but there are ethics hiding in those numbers. The major credit bureaus keep dossiers on the financial lives of most Americans, and we are accustomed to thinking about that data as the basis for our credit score, which determines our access to borrowing by predicting the risk that we'll default on a loan within the next two years. What many people don't know is that other algorithms use that same "credit file" data to generate *other* scores and to inform other decisions. These can include whether to lease someone an apartment, whether to offer certain types of jobs (such as a bank teller position), and how much to charge for car insurance — or even whether to offer insurance at all.

There's a basic moral trade-off when pricing insurance: the more the prices are individualized, the less policyholders will share risk. We each should pay a price that reflects our choices, but on the other hand, some-times bad things happen that are out of our control. Algorithms that use our credit data to price insurance threaten to break this balance: they make insurance pricier for people who have worse credit histories. (As it turns out, people with worse credit histories tend to file more insurance claims, partly because they can't afford to take care of things like minor car repairs on their own, while wealthier policyholders often self-fund repairs to avoid making claims and having to pay higher rates.) Bad credit can sometimes reflect bad choices, like refusing to pay a loan back, and sometimes it simply reflects bad luck. For instance, a natural disaster, a divorce, or being deployed in the military all lead to worse credit and increase the risk that a person will file a car insurance claim. But are those really fair reasons, we might ask, to charge a person more for their car insurance? Even if a disaster survivor *does* have a higher chance of filing a car insurance claim, it might be the kind of risk we as a society ought to share through the premiums we all pay, rather than shifting the cost onto the unlucky individual.

The case for sharing more risk—rather than pricing based on all the available data—gets stronger when you consider that people are legally required to carry car and other property insurance, and that in many places one can't keep a job unless one is able to commute to it by car. Of course, people often disagree about where luck ends and responsibility begins. The question is a moral one, and yet its answer inevitably will be encoded in the algorithms that insurers use to set prices.

When insurance scores based on credit data began to be used in the 1990s, the insurance companies said it was fair to use any data that their algorithm found predictive of claims, regardless of any choices the customer had made. (The idea, as Kiviat has summarized, was that, "if it predicts, then it's fair."[19]) And even though some people might have disagreed with that idea at an intuitive level, there was no established or structured way to debate which risks ought to be shared among policyholders. But then, in a "rare case of extended public debate" over the ethics of an algorithm, there was a wave of legal and policy intervention in these systems that started with state insurance regulators and extended to state legislatures, ultimately including full-scale investigations in seventeen states, as policymakers probed the code to examine, and ultimately change, how these systems worked.[20]

"Because credit behavior is recorded and interpreted as a sequence of individual choices, the vagaries of harsh circumstance . . . which powerfully structure how, where and when people borrow and repay . . . magically disappear from view" in a credit file.[21] But lawmakers thought that some of these vanishing differences—like the difference between a deadbeat and a deployed soldier, each of whom might have defaulted on a loan for the same amount—needed to be brought back into view, a process that Kiviat calls "de-commensuration."[22]

Today all fifty states restrict the factors that companies can use to price or deny car insurance. Typical exclusions—factors that can't be counted against someone, even if they do predict more claims—include natural disasters, "serious illness or injury" of the policyholder or a family member, divorce, identity theft, military deployment, and long-term unemployment.[23] Kiviat explains:

> In writing such lists into law, policymakers codified situations in which they thought the market ought not hold people accountable for their data. People may feel constrained in the decisions they make, but they do ultimately choose to get divorced or join the military knowing that deployment follows. The inclusion of these situations shows that policymakers were concerned not only with how people might be disadvantaged for circumstances over which they had no control, but also with how people might be disadvantaged for making morally justified choices.[24]

The insurance case was extraordinary. Yes, hard ethical choices were buried inside an algorithm, as they often are. But in this case there just happened to be a constellation of leaders—including a broad spectrum of state legislators who were prepared to devote their scarce legislative time to this specific issue—who had the right constellation of authority, expertise, and incentives to force a public reckoning with those trade-offs and to make hard choices about how the system could work.

This debate over the ethics inside of an algorithm was extremely unusual. But the underlying situation—an algorithm doing the kind of thing that *ought to* get debated—was not. The resolution of the ethics of algorithms proves that such resolutions are possible, but the seventeen state investigations of these algorithms do not represent a scalable or repeatable method for applying ethical deliberation to high-stakes algorithms. Legislative attention, in particular, is a scarce resource that cannot realistically be applied to *each* algorithm that makes hard and publicly significant moral trade-offs.

To repeat the governance success that happened here, we will need to find methods that are more scalable and repeatable.

The Doctor Won't See You Now

If your doctor thinks you need opiates for pain relief, there's a growing chance that, before you receive medication, the doctor or pharmacist will check your "NarxScore"—a proprietary, commercial algorithm that claims to describe your "overall risk" of abusing prescription opiates with a number from 0 to 999.[25] It's made by a company called Appriss Health and draws mainly on state-managed databases that collect information about every opiate prescription. The score goes up if, for instance, the same person got multiple prescriptions for opiates from different doctors at the same time; in principle, this is a useful way to check for risk. The company has suggested that its NarxScore might also include other data, such as the distance between a person's home and the various pharmacies where their past prescriptions have been filled, though a spokesperson recently claimed that it has not yet added any of its own data to what the states provide.[26]

How does this score balance the risks of opiate abuse against the hazard of wrongly denying care to people who really need painkillers? No one outside of Appriss appears to know what the algorithm actually is—or when or how it changes—and most of the limited public evidence about its workings and accuracy comes from the company's own publications, which have not been peer reviewed.[27] A company-produced training manual warns medical staff that high NarxScores are "intended to trigger a *discussion*, **not a decision**" (emphasis in original).[28] But an investigative report by *Wired* magazine found that high-scoring patients have been summarily cut off from care—and treated with hostility and suspicion in health care settings—without getting the chance to tell their side of the story. One woman with painful ovarian cysts was admitted to the hospital, treated for a couple of days, and then suddenly cut off from further treatment—and "terminated" by her gynecologist—owing to a high score. She eventually figured out that her two aging dogs, whose veterinary painkillers and sedatives had been prescribed in her name, had likely caused her high score, but most doctors and pharmacists didn't want to hear her story. Appriss offers no way for people to correct, or contextualize, a misleadingly high score.

This seems like an unsolved governance problem: somehow, ethically fraught choices are happening inside an algorithm, but they aren't getting the right amount, or right kind, of public attention in order to be handled wisely.

Screening Opportunity

In New York City, 20 percent of all the public middle and high schools use a screening algorithm to pick their students. Each participating school has a unique formula, based on numerical factors such as grades, test scores, attendance, and punctuality, and uses it to produce a rank-order list of the students it wishes to admit.[29] Students, meanwhile, rank their choice of schools, and then a separate "matching" algorithm assigns each student to one school.[30]

Unlike many other cities, New York "has a large base of middle-class families that attend the public schools," according to the education scholar Richard Kahlenberg. "Screened schools are a way to appeal to them and keep their children in the public schools, especially in a city where public housing projects sit beside million-dollar apartments," he has explained.[31] Each school's criteria are unique, and until very recently, the specifics were hard for parents or others to find. The criteria generally involve academic performance, but the details for a given school might only be revealed on prospective parents' nights, and thus only to parents with the resources and motivation to appear in person. This advantage, in turn, enabled more-involved parents to be more strategic in composing their children's rank-order list of schools to apply to. In 2019, in response to a freedom of information request, the city's Department of Education disclosed that it itself could not provide a full report of each school's criteria, because the screening criteria for each school were "generally maintained at the individual school and . . . not centralized."[32]

Critics argue forcefully that these algorithms are immoral and unlawful because they amplify racial segregation. The investigative journalism organization *The Markup*, which focuses on the social impacts of algorithms, gathered demographic and admissions data from the city and showed that the students at the most competitive schools were much more often Asian and white than was the case across the school system. Black and Hispanic students who applied to highly competitive screened schools were generally much less likely than their white and Asian fellow applicants to gain admission.[33] In November 2020, a group of teenage student activists who attend city schools filed a complaint with the U.S. Department of Education, arguing that the city's screening algorithms were illegally discriminatory.[34] A month later, Mayor Bill de Blasio, who was generally critical of competitive high school admissions, announced that a citywide website would henceforth publish each school's admissions criteria.[35]

Publishing the criteria for each school is a positive step, but outside observers are still up against a sharp limit: for privacy reasons, none of them can see any data about the academic performance of the student applicants. Members of the public can only see overall patterns in the race of the students who apply and the race of those who are admitted. *The Markup*'s report noted that its reporters did "not have access to data on the students' test scores, grades, attendance, or other academic measures used to assess their qualifications . . . but the admission rates show clear racial trends."

Similarly, the civil rights complaint filed by student activists gave the racial breakdown of applicants and admitted students, identifying several schools where black or Hispanic students made up 40 percent of applicants but less than 10 percent of those admitted.[36] But the complaint can't say how particular factors within the rubric contributed to racial disparities. Instead, the students argued that a different approach should be used, one in which each school would automatically enroll a representative complement of average, above-average, and below-average students—an approach that would rely, somewhat paradoxically, on the very same standardized tests that the litigants simultaneously argued were racially biased.[37]

If an auditor or analyst with the incentives to ask tough questions were given more intimate access to the data and audited the system under careful conditions to protect student privacy, then a more nuanced conversation might unfold. For instance, to what extent does the use of attendance data, as opposed to grades or test scores, amplify or dampen a discriminatory effect? Maybe a disproportionate number of high-performing nonwhite students miss class or are late because of relatively challenging home circumstances, but are nonetheless ready to thrive in a rigorous school and are being needlessly screened out. And how well do these screening factors actually predict success, anyway? Among the students who do get in, which factors seem to matter for their success, and to what extent? Answers to questions like these could help advance the conversation.

Setting up an analytics office that's close enough to the data to use and understand it, but far enough from the politics of school selection that its analyses would be rigorous and tough, would certainly be a delicate balancing act. But as things stand now, critics and interested citizens are flying partly blind.

Computer Says "Go to Jail"

Before starting work on this book, I spent years in Washington, D.C., as a technology adviser to civil rights organizations. I saw firsthand how hard it can be for people to understand algorithms' role in the criminal legal system. A growing number of criminal courts, often acting under legislative direction, have adopted pretrial "risk assessment" software. This software is supposed to help judges by estimating the chance that each newly arrested person would stay out of trouble if set free until their trial. (Judges assess such risks at a "first appearance hearing," because it's the newly arrested person's first time in a courtroom.)

These predictions deserve to be taken with a big grain of salt thanks to limits in the underlying data.[38] For instance, a judge or magistrate is usually most interested in predicting the risk of violence—such as the risk that an accused person, if allowed to go home, might threaten or hurt a witness or commit some other violent crime. But risk assessment algorithms usually don't assess that risk because the court doesn't have access to specific or complete data about violence. What the court does have data about—and thus what algorithms can be trained to predict—is how likely the defendant is to be arrested in the future.

Unfortunately, this information is of little use for the questions that actually matter most at a first appearance hearing. Most arrests are not related to violent crime, and a significant fraction of violent crimes never lead to arrests. A person's risk of being rearrested can thus reflect their living in a heavily policed neighborhood more than any real threat of violence that they personally pose. No one should be sent into a cage for carrying this risk. And this risk falls more heavily on racial minorities and those with lower incomes, as it has from the time our legal systems were first established. Indeed, in criminal law and in many other areas, the most complete and best-maintained administrative data often reflects and reinforces unjustified racial disparities.

The racial impacts of data-driven systems are not the central focus of this book, but they are an important part of the story that follows.[39] (Such injustices are also a focus of my own prior work.[40]) Racial injustice and the fantasy of escape from it through technical means can be an important part of the tacit appeal of data-driven approaches to social problems in areas ranging from criminal law to medicine. As Ruha Benjamin has written, there has been a long pattern of "the employment of new technologies that reflect and reproduce existing inequities but that are promoted and perceived as more objective or progressive than the discriminatory systems of a previous era."[41]

The statistical predictions made by pretrial risk assessment algorithms are often based on training data from past time periods and distant jurisdictions, reflecting an outdated picture of police conduct and social services. Paradoxically, these algorithms are often introduced at the very same moment when patterns on the ground are changing, thanks to drug treatment programs, prosecutorial policy shifts, and other changes. The result can be "zombie predictions" where an still describes people as dangerous and suggests sending them to jail, even after new reforms have reduced the true risks.

Court staff often aren't software experts, commercial vendors puff up what these software tools can do, and busy judges don't want to see a bunch of complicated numbers or carefully worded caveats. Engineers or court staff, lacking a clear process to follow, often end up radically simplifying things: sometimes, they distill the results into high, medium, and low risk and direct the "high-risk" cases straight to jail. One system I encountered in New Jersey literally showed judges a stop sign in certain cases (as in, "STOP—do not let this person go free"). But who had decided how much risk should count as "high" and cost a person their freedom? How did anyone know if the system's predictions were accurate? Were the predictive models even up-to-date?

My own and others' work has shown that these courtroom pretrial algorithms are frequently implemented with little input from the people they will judge, opaque, configured in ways that violate controlling law, not adequately tested, and too rarely monitored or updated in response to changing ground conditions.[42] Many observers—including scholarly critics, machine learning experts, and advocates of criminal law reform— have concluded that in their present form, such tools should not be used at all.[43] Similar challenges arise with algorithms used in criminal sentencing, where algorithms claim to forecast risk but do not even attempt to measure how different defendants will *respond* to time in prison (for instance, whether imprisonment will make them more or less likely to commit crimes after release).[44]

A national coalition of more than one hundred U.S. civil rights organizations (whose work I helped to coordinate before starting this book) argued for a series of changes to how such algorithms are made and used. They argued in the first case that the tools should generally be avoided in favor of presumptive release and went on to say that, if used at all, such systems should be "transparent," "independently validated," "developed with community input [and] revalidated regularly by independent data scientists with that input in mind." Such input should come from a newly created "funded and staffed community advisory board, supported by data scientists to understand how algorithms work . . . and how pretrial decisionmakers use the algorithms in real decisions."[45]

False Accusations of Fraud

In government programs that provide benefits to poor families and children, software that decides who gets what has acted in ways that contradict the law—such as denying services to people who actually qualify—and has in some cases falsely accused beneficiaries of fraud owing to stark misunderstandings of the available administrative data. One system in Colorado "issued hundreds of thousands of incorrect Medicaid, food stamp, and welfare eligibility determinations and benefit calculations. . . . Many of these errors can be attributed to programmers' incorrect translations of hundreds of rules into computer code."[46]

An algorithm used in Australia accused welfare beneficiaries of fraud, declaring many of them to be in debt to the government for ill-gotten payments (sometimes tens of thousands of dollars' worth) without human review. The methodology of the algorithm itself was riddled with flaws. It sought to compare incomes that people reported to the welfare office with those their employers reported to the tax office—but it assumed, incorrectly, that each person received income evenly throughout the year. The system "fail[ed] to accurately account for the fluctuating fortunes of casual or contract workers, which often results in variations between the two figures."[47] An inquiry by the Australian Senate later concluded that "a lack of procedural fairness [was] evident in every stage of the program," and that the program had gratuitously inflicted "emotional trauma, stress and shame" on wrongly accused program recipients.[48]

These denials are often mysterious, not only to the beneficiaries who lose service or are wrongly accused of fraud but also to program staff.[49] In other high-profile instances, problems like these have been traced to programming mistakes and engineering practices far below the standards of the private sector, suggesting ineffective supervision and understanding of the technology by responsible public servants.[50]

And yet the life-altering details of software systems are very often left to programmers to decide—existing institutional arrangements simply do not provide sufficient guidance or review, so that programmers "inevitably engage in rulemaking when they construct an automated system's code."[51] From Colorado to Australia, new governance practices appear to be needed in order to create software that comports with existing understandings of fairness.

LOOKING AHEAD

These six stories were drawn from different domains—the first three commercial, the latter three civic. Yet each involved a struggle to shape the moral trade-offs in a high-stakes algorithm. Regardless of whether the hand of the state fit inside the algorithmic glove, in each of these cases a broader community struggled to resolve hard moral trade-offs rather than leaving those trade-offs to the technical experts to decide.

In some of these stories, like the criminal justice and HireVue examples, the key trade-offs seem shrouded in mystery, not yet subject to a robust public debate. In other cases, a meaningful public debate over the values of an algorithm did take place, for instance, in the insurance pricing story or the ongoing debate over New York City school screening. But even in these cases, the participants still seemed to lack good tools for understanding the algorithm and its alternatives, and for collaboratively deciding among those possibilities.

In chapter 2, we'll turn toward the scholars and policymakers who are proposing, and in some cases actually trying out, new governance strategies that are specifically intended to address this challenge. Specifically, we'll explore four strategies for making the moral choices contained in algorithms easier to understand and change: participation, transparency, forecasting, and auditing.

Then, in chapters 3 and 4, we'll delve into a story that can shed light on all four of these strategies: the development of the Kidney Allocation

System, a new algorithm to match transplant patients to donated kidneys in the United States. KAS, as it's known, was developed with extensive public consultation and input. Forecasts of the algorithm's possible impact played a pivotal role in helping people understand the stakes and ultimately helped lead to one approach being scrapped and another approach being adopted. The system's decision logic, and the factors that determine each patient's fate within the system, were transparent—not only publicly disclosed, but explained in lay terms that made it feasible for patients themselves to understand. And the system's performance is audited annually by an independent expert organization that publishes not only extensive data but also helpful analyses of the system's performance, fairness, and other factors.

In other words, we will be examining a case where an algorithm that makes hard choices about life and death seems to be working relatively well. We will be exploring a case where people have found ways to navigate and negotiate the moral substance of an algorithm—an algorithm whose moral stakes could hardly be higher—in a participatory, collaborative, understandable, and mutually tolerable way. It is a story that concretely illustrates the benefits (as well as the limits) of each of the four dimensions just mentioned.

Interlude: Dallas, 2007

FOR CLIVE GRAWE, it was a matter of life and death—not only for him, but for his daughter. He had flown from Los Angeles, where he worked as a traffic engineer, to the ballroom of an airport Marriott in Dallas, Texas. It was February 8, 2007, and the room was packed full of transplant professionals—doctors and surgeons, nurses and social workers—who had gathered to consider and debate a potential rewrite of the U.S. kidney allocation algorithm. This software decides who, out of the more than 100,000 Americans waiting for kidneys, will be offered each newly donated organ.

These decisions—for better and worse—totally transform people's lives. If your kidneys fail and you don't get a transplant, then in order to stay alive you'll probably have to rely on hemodialysis, which is usually a thrice-weekly, hours-long ritual in which a machine cleans toxins out of your blood.[1] This process carries significant health risks, so that after just the first year of treatment, one in every five patients have died.[2] Under ideal conditions, dialysis can continue for decades. But the daily experience of being a dialysis patient is bitter: each week includes some days of feeling relatively healthy and some days of feeling fatigued and ill.

If you are not chronically ill, it's worth pausing to imagine what that routine would actually feel like. I hadn't tried to imagine this myself until I was finishing the book you're reading now, in January 2022, and caught a mild case of Covid-19. It was just headache, lethargy, and the sniffles, coupled with the loss of my sense of smell, which I hope may soon come back. But even this "mild" experience left me no good for writing, thinking, or planning out anything important. Imagine if you had to spend a couple days like that every week. Objective data tell part of the story: 60 percent or more of dialysis patients are unemployed.[3] But more than those numbers, an offhand remark from a transplant surgeon I spoke with sticks in my mind. Once they receive a transplant, she said, most of her patients "tell me they'd rather die than go back on dialysis."

22

Back to that ballroom in Dallas: Following three years of careful work, the doctors and scientists were unveiling their first draft of the new allocation algorithm. Called LYFT (Life Years From Transplant), this new system would seek to match each available kidney with the patient whose life would be prolonged the most by receiving that particular organ. In practice, this meant giving higher priority to patients who were relatively young and, apart from their failing kidneys, relatively healthy. It would be a big change from the previous system, which had emphasized how long each patient had been waiting for a transplant. The new algorithm would consider the blood type, immunology, and ages of the organ and of the recipient. It would also factor in logistics, like how long the organ would need to spend in transit in order to reach each potential recipient, after removal from the donor. The system was very appealing to surgeons and other medical professionals, who hate to miss any opportunity to save or prolong a life.[4]

All morning a series of physicians and surgeons, together with a professor of biostatistics, had carefully laid out the rationale for the new system, including simulations of how it would work and the additional years of life that it would save if it were allowed to replace the current regime. Now the time had come for meeting attendees to respond to the proposal. All of this was part of the process; the new algorithm could not be adopted without extensive and careful public vetting.

Clive Grawe was the first person without an MD or a PhD to address the group.[5] His qualifications were more personal. He had polycystic kidney disease (PKD), a rare genetic condition that causes cysts to form inside the kidneys, so that the organs grow larger and gradually break down over time. People with PKD can live with their natural kidneys—and delay their need for a transplant—often for many years, and the disease could take decades to run its course. But eventually PKD patients who live long enough will need a transplant, or else have to rely on the risky and life-dominating ritual of dialysis to stay alive from one day to the next.

Clive explained that he was fifty-four years old and in generally excellent health. But his kidneys were a different story. Doctors describe a person's kidney health in terms of how fast their kidneys filter the toxins from their blood, a rate called the estimated glomerular filtration rate (eGFR).[6] A score of 60 or higher is normal, 15 to 59 means kidney disease, and 0 to 15 means kidney failure—an immediate need for transplant or dialysis. As he stood onstage, Clive's eGFR was 16, and he was on the transplant list. Patients who need a kidney often seek a donation from a family member. But PKD is a genetic disease, and Clive explained that all of his living blood relatives—two sisters and his only biological daughter—had likewise inherited the condition, and so none were eligible kidney donors.

Clive argued that health, not age, should be the dominant criterion in selecting candidates. He argued that a healthy patient in their fifties would be a better transplant candidate than someone in their forties with serious underlying health conditions, such as heart disease. His slides put the question starkly: "Should my daughter be penalized for living a healthy life?"

"If you have an easier time getting a kidney in your forties," he asked the assembled group, then "what's the incentive to take care of yourself and prolong your kidney function" into your fifties?

Indeed, as the morning's technical briefings had illustrated, the LYFT proposal would bring about a massive shift of organs from older to younger recipients. The fraction of transplants offered to people in their twenties was slated to triple, and people over fifty would have less than half the chance they did before.[7] By midafternoon, when "breakout groups" of attendees around the ballroom took their turn offering feedback, it became clear that sentiment was overwhelmingly against the LYFT proposal. It simply seemed unfair to older recipients.[8]

This was a truly remarkable moment: the people responsible for a high-stakes algorithm had opened it up to public debate, with detailed transparency, simulated consequences, and explanations. Then an impacted person had intervened in that debate, helping shift the conversation so that ultimately LYFT was rejected and a totally different algorithm was adopted.

Was that different algorithm really a better choice than LYFT? It depends on what counts as "better." Assume for a moment that the experts in Dallas had prevailed: LYFT really would have saved more years of life than any other system. But that's not the end of the story. The proposal would have changed not only *how many* years of life were created, but also *who* got to live those years. Some people—likely older ones, some like Clive Grawe, ready and eager to take great care of themselves and their transplants—would actually live shorter lives under LYFT, because they would lose out on the opportunity to receive an organ at all. I'm not sure whether LYFT's trade-off would have been worth it. But I do know something else.

The choice was really about ethics, not technology. The ethical trade-off wasn't a question for surgeons or data scientists. It was a question for a wider community, including non-experts and laypeople who care about the issue because they need a kidney. And in this case, laypeople had a voice, and that voice mattered.

How did this moment come about? And what can we learn from this story that Clive Grawe was part of, about how we can raise our voices to shape the ethics of the algorithms that decide so much in our lives?

Those questions are at the heart of this book. In the pages that follow, we'll venture into the still-unfolding debate about digital technology's civic impact and pick up a basic intuition for how digital decision-making actually works along the way. Then we'll dive into the remarkable history of kidney disease and kidney transplantation—a context that has become an ideal laboratory for the sharing of high-stakes medical, ethical, and data-driven decisions. And finally, we'll extract some lessons for the road ahead.

Chapter 2 | Democracy on the Drawing Board

How SHOULD HIGH stakes algorithms be made, and used? Scholars and policymakers from many disciplines, and many parts of the world, now find themselves asking this question. Much of their work has understandably focused on things that seem to have gone wrong, as in the stories from chapter 1. Such cases show the real human impact of poorly governed algorithms—and sometimes the haphazard nature of good governance when it does emerge—and thus motivate the search for better ways of doing things. "Taken together," Ryan Calo and Danielle Citron have written, stories like these present "a disturbing picture of unforced errors and gaps in understanding and accountability." People worry urgently about opaque and unreliable decisions, stealth value judgments cloaked in the language of expertise, and ineffective and confused oversight of software systems by non-engineers. These problems seem "all the more perverse as they take place amidst the perception that we live in an age of technical wonders."[1]

Thanks to the scholarship and policy efforts of the last fifteen years, a foundation has now been laid. People largely agree that important problems exist in this area. The conversation is increasingly turning toward the question of *what to do* about those problems.

We will explore four broad strategies in this chapter and throughout the book: participation, transparency, forecasting, and auditing. These can be used separately or together. The people who made the new Kidney Allocation System—the characters at the heart of this book—used all four methods. In examining their story, we'll learn something about how each approach can work in the real world. By the end of the book, we'll return to this broader discussion and ask how the story of transplant might inform hard choices about other algorithms.

Before we can explore these ideas about how to do things better, we need to address a couple of framing questions. First, what might we mean by "better"? What leads us to say that one high-stakes algorithm was made and used well, and that a different algorithm was made and used badly? Second, *which* algorithms are "high stakes," in the sense that they deserve the kinds of careful and costly governance that we're considering here?

THE VALUE OF FACING HARD CHOICES

As we saw in chapter 1, many people have had their lives upended by an algorithm's mistake: the pain patient falsely accused, and denied relief, because of her pets' veterinary needs, or the welfare recipient falsely accused of fraud because his work is seasonal. Cases like these remind us that it is important to be sure a system actually works as intended. No human-made system will be perfect, but when the stakes are high, we should aim to build systems that get things wrong only rarely, and in which errors are easy to find and to remedy.

The question in this chapter is not just what makes a good algorithm, but what makes a good *way of making* an algorithm when the stakes are high. One part of the answer must be that a well-made algorithm will do what it was made to do. So a good way of making algorithms will be a careful way that follows best practices and avoids obvious mistakes and design flaws where possible. Such a process will also be alert to the possibility of surprise, rather than presuming, unsinkable *Titanic* style, that the newly built system will never hit an iceberg of serious and unanticipated problems. I'll refer to this basket of basic virtues as "competence." There is no doubt that competence matters.

But for our purposes here, competence can't be the whole story of what it means for a high-stakes algorithm to be well made and well used. If all that mattered were making sure that nothing was broken, then technical experts could handle things all on their own.

The strategies described in this chapter are after something more. It matters not only whether algorithms work as planned, but also what the plans are, and where they come from.

The most important question about how algorithms are made is who decides on their *moral* logic. Who answers—and how do they go about answering—the human questions that make the stakes of this technology so high in the first place?

By the time someone's life actually gets changed, it may be an algorithm that mechanically and unthinkingly determines which school a student can go to, or which risks will count against a person when pricing insurance, or what it will mean to call a job candidate "employable," or who should have priority in the allocation of transplantable kidneys.

But for each decision of this kind, there are people somewhere whose choices determine the moral shape of the software. Sometimes those people are lawmakers or business leaders who provide engineers with very specific instructions: each taxpayer gets a $600 stimulus check, or library fines are doubled next year, or the job of transcriptionist will be offered to whichever candidate can transcribe a page of text in the shortest amount of time with the fewest mistakes. And then it falls to programmers to carry out those instructions, albeit with some inevitable filling in of details. But that's not always how it goes.

Often, when software is made, technical experts are left to decide central moral questions. For instance, thinking back to the stories we encountered in chapter 1, let's consider a few of the moral questions that the technical experts were apparently left to resolve:

- How should a newly arrested person's future be forecasted and described to the judge who will decide about that person's freedom? Is a vague "high-risk" label ever appropriate? What about a big red stop sign that says, in effect, "Do not allow this person to go free. Send them straight to jail"? How much risk—and risk of *what*, exactly—is enough to justify sending someone to jail?

- Suppose a company wants to make software to analyze people's faces and thereby winnow the pool of job applicants. What, if anything, should that company first have to prove to the public about its software?[2] Suppose the data it uses about past employee performance is tainted by sexism or racism. How, if at all, should an algorithm built with such data be checked for bias?

- How important is it to desegregate the public schools? If a particular screening algorithm tends to amplify segregation (or to miss out on the chance to *reduce* segregation), how should that cost be weighed against the benefits of whatever else the algorithm achieves—such as a complete school orchestra, or a critical mass of students for a school to offer a particular foreign language or science course?

- When checking welfare programs for potential fraud, how important is it to avoid falsely accusing legitimate recipients versus to catch each case of fraud? When people do get falsely accused, what does society owe them?

These are moral questions at least as much as technical ones. I believe they belong to a wider community than just the people who make the software.

The big problem here is the relationship between technical expertise and moral authority. Who is an expert, and who gets a voice? With questions like the ones just mentioned, a certain amount of technical expertise, which most people lack, really is indispensable. You need to know what's possible, and how the business or government bureau works, and what the trade-offs are. An informed judgment may also require that a new algorithm be prototyped and tested, or that data be analyzed in certain specific ways, and those tasks are indeed the work of technical experts. But in none of these cases will technical judgment actually *provide* an answer. Moral judgment is needed too. And it is often unclear who will—or who *should*—make that judgment.

Sometimes technical experts can imperiously take over moral choices. This may have been especially common, for instance, in medicine as it was practiced fifty years ago. A medical ethicist named Robert Veatch, writing in 1973, defined a previously unrecognized disease that can afflict medical professionals: "'As-a' Syndrome."[3] It occurs when a doctor, surgeon, or other expert claims the moral authority to decide which of the medical treatments available to the patient is wisest to pursue, even over the patient's own objections. When the doctor begins to claim, in other words, a moral role that, Veatch says, may belong to the patient, the family, or the public. Veatch writes that when a doctor gives a moral opinion "as a physician," "the gratuitous clause has a way of sneaking in special pleading for [the doctor's] moral arguments." Of course, as Veatch admits, there may be good reasons to give special weight to the moral opinion of a technical expert. Doctors have watched the emotional journey that many patients go through and may be well positioned to predict which moral choices a patient or family will later be glad they made and which they will regret. But even when an expert's moral opinion does deserve special weight, that doesn't mean it ought to be the last or only word.

More recently, the social scientists Jenna Burrell and Marion Fourcade have pointed to the rise of a "coding elite" for whom "mastery of computational techniques" brings "cultural, political, and economic" power, buttressed by the seemingly objective and apolitical world of numbers. They observe that information technology in particular, long before computing, can be read as "a more or less continuous drive to refine control" over people, materials, and markets.[4]

At other times, the issue seems to be not that experts grab the moral microphone but rather that the rest of us fall silent, effectively dodging hard choices that must, in the end, be made. When this happens, people often end up pretending that moral questions are technical. Just letting the experts decide can bring a kind of relief for the rest of us—the public, the lawmaker, the anxious patient, the busy executive, or the general public. Technical intricacy can act as an escape hatch from moral challenges.

In setting up the organ transplant system, for instance, Congress vaguely directed that organs be shared according to "medical criteria," indirectly denying a hard truth: medical judgment cannot fully resolve the organ allocation quandary. Medical criteria can't tell you which of two patients who both need an organ is more deserving than the other. We could, of course, decide that the moral thing to do is just to give each organ to whoever would gain the most "medical benefit" from it (perhaps defined as the most quality-adjusted years of life). But the decision to use that criterion would itself be a moral choice rather than a medical one. Such an approach would ignore the question of *who* gets the medical benefit. As we saw in the Dallas interlude (and as we will explore in greater depth in this chapter), such a path was ultimately rejected on moral grounds. But in other settings— courtrooms, school screening, job candidate triage—the moral trade-offs are not necessarily as thoughtful or explicit.

Bureaucracy itself can serve as a way of converting hard moral problems into boring technical ones, a process that long predates computers.[5] But software-based systems can accelerate and amplify this trend. Quantification can be a moral anesthetic, and computers make that anesthetic easier than ever to administer. In the book's final chapter, I'll briefly consider the claim that such anesthesia might sometimes be for the best, even though it is seldom chosen openly. But for now I'll say that the pattern of abdicating important moral choices to technical experts often seems both accidental and unwise.

Precisely what ought to be done *instead* of abdicating hard moral choices to the technical experts is hard to say. It's a question on which many people have valuable perspectives, not only experts and scholars from many disciplines but also the people whose lives are at stake in each particular hard decision.

In a certain light, the question of how best to make software code that will govern people is just a special case of how best to make laws. We might wonder about the relationship between process and result. About which values matter most, and how they fit together. We might ask what vision of people's lives together ought to guide our choices about which software to make and how to use it.

People disagree about the merits of different ways of making high-stakes software, just as they disagree about the merits of different ways of making laws.

Some focus on the governance process itself, apart from the algorithm it may produce: words like "democratic," "accountable," "open," "legitimate," or "inclusive" appear in the algorithmic governance literature as procedural virtues.[6] (Meanwhile, empirical social scientists are studying public beliefs about these virtues, such as whether people think that a particular algorithm is legitimate or accountable.[7]) These ideals align with a concept in political philosophy that has been called "democratic proceduralism," which says that laws should be compared based on whether they are "the result of an appropriately constrained process of democratic decision-making."[8]

Proceduralists think that the best way of making laws is best for an intrinsic reason, such as that it gives all adults an equal voice, rather than because it necessarily leads to a wiser result. (After all, who can say ahead of time, and apart from the debate, which result is really wiser?)

Traditional laws are often judged based on how they were made. People might think that a new law is valid and ought to be obeyed because, for instance, the lawmakers who approved it were duly elected. Likewise perhaps for the software that shapes our lives: maybe we should trust software to assign students to public schools only if parents and teachers and (dare we imagine?) students themselves have had a voice in its design.[9] To generalize slightly, we might say that for any high-stakes system, important "stakeholders" —those to whom the system matters most—should be consulted. On the other hand, the mere claim that students and teachers "gave input" to an algorithm's designers might not be enough. Putative consultation could turn out to be a mere fig leaf for a situation where people aren't really heard out and don't really end up having reason to agree with an algorithm's decisions.[10]

An opposing approach claims that we should judge an algorithm-making process based totally or mostly on the algorithm that it leads to, rather than the path that was followed to reach the outcome. We might ask whether the algorithm's decisions are fair, whether those decisions tend to make people on average better off, or whether they tend to make the worst-off better off.[11] This approach aligns with a school of thought in political philosophy called "democratic instrumentalism," which "take[s] it as a premise that there is an ideal outcome that exists independently of the democratic process," and then says (in the strongest version of this argument) that democracy is valuable only insofar as it gets us to this right outcome.[12] People who hold such views may be confident about their ability to define "better off" ahead of time, and for everyone. In any case, to them a lawmaking (or algorithm-making) process is "justified inasmuch as it is necessary to serve the well-being of people [and] relies, for its legitimacy, on its ability to deliver sound decisions," where soundness refers to a good rule, not necessarily a particular method for making one.[13]

On that theory, to return to the example of school assignments, we might ask whether a new algorithm for assigning students to schools reduces racial segregation, whether it leads to more students becoming proficient in math, or whether it supports strong neighborhoods. In other words, who cares how we get there, as long as we land in the right place?

I feel torn about this results-driven approach. On the one hand, like most of us, I've got my own strong views about what (some) laws should say, and about how (some) high-stakes algorithms ought to operate. On the other, it seems shortsighted to pick a method based on an expected outcome. You never can tell what people will do once they get together. And there's a kind of hubris implicit in saying, the right way of deciding things together is whichever way will get us to the decision that I want. It seems to lack a true commitment to the "together" part of deciding together and to show a distrust and disregard for the interests of others. Then again, maybe that's always how politics works.

On closer inspection, there is no sharp line between virtues-of-the-process and virtues-of-the-resulting-algorithm. The process and the landing place may both be important, and good processes and good results may be mutually reinforcing. Many political theorists advocate deliberation: a careful public debate, a reasoned and well-informed comparison of alternatives in which members of the public can and do realistically participate.[14] They argue that deliberation is *inherently* valuable because it treats people respectfully as equals, regardless of where it may lead. And yet at the same time they also claim that deliberation *tends* to lead to better results. This may be both because a system developed in this way will tend to work better (having been carefully vetted) and because the people to whom it matters will have more reason to tolerate the hard choices the system makes, even when they are disappointed or frustrated by a particular decision. Moreover, a transparent process may lead to better results because it allows the public to understand what the system's consequences actually are, and to challenge or improve them.

The policy proposals for algorithm-making in this chapter are built on a range of ideals, explicitly or tacitly. Some are focused on procedure, some on results, some on a mixture of the two. A single intervention, such as publishing audits of a high-stakes system, might be needed under several different theories of what makes a high-stakes algorithm (or the process used to create it) a good one.

I will not provide a grand unified theory of what makes a great method for making laws, or for making algorithms. My argument in this book is simply that when it comes to high-stakes algorithms, it's better for political communities to face the hard moral choices together than to abdicate and ignore those choices, abandoning them to the technical experts.

Of course, for a community to face some choice together does not necessarily mean that every member of that community should understand, pay attention to, or even care about that choice. One of the threads running through this book is that most people won't want to wade into the technical details of most systems. Even when the moral burdens of an algorithm are shared with a wider community than just the people who build that system, it may be a few rather than a multitude who ultimately make the hard choices.

Existing democratic institutions go some way toward representing everyone's interests with respect to high-stakes algorithms. We might argue that the stories recounted in chapter 1, insofar as they reveal unsolved problems, simply show that new laws should be enacted using the same legislative methods as in any other area of life. If that's so, then no new governance strategies specific to algorithms may be needed.

And yet, existing legislative practices are struggling to regulate algorithms effectively in many different domains, and the struggles seem to be more similar than the domains are. Moreover, if we take it for granted that collective self-rule *must* involve something like today's national legislatures, we are ignoring much of history, as Hélène Landemore has recently argued.[15] Juries, citizen assemblies, and other forms of representation throughout history have been integral to making democratic values real. Apart from whatever is special about technology, a "deliberative wave" of new governance ideas is sweeping across the world.[16] This is not limited to open comment processes (which Landemore terms "spatially inclusive" because they welcome whoever shows up) but also includes deliberative polls, citizen juries, and many other types of participation and engagement by non-experts, carefully constructed to represent those who aren't present, build consensus, and achieve other deliberative goals. More on these below, but for now: an educated, resource-intensive conversation that is well informed won't necessarily be one where vast numbers of people take part. I do not object in principle to letting small groups decide important questions on behalf of broader groups. But wherever that happens, the relationship between the few who decide and the many who are governed should be careful and intentional.

WHICH ALGORITHMS ARE "HIGH STAKES"?

So far, we've been talking about how to govern "high-stakes" algorithms, yet have not defined the category.

We've looked at some cases where algorithms are making very important decisions with very little effective oversight. But in order to do some algorithm-making much more carefully, we would need a way of knowing when to take such care. Regardless of whether the point is to embrace democratic or deliberative procedures or to strive toward results that are "better" in some other sense, one needs to know when to do the embracing or the striving.

The conceptual problem we first encountered in chapter 1—what counts as an "algorithm," or "AI," or "big data"?—becomes a practical challenge for any would-be legislator or scholarly critic. If government has to follow a careful and expensive process whenever it makes something, and if regulated businesses must follow special rules whenever they create something, then it may be very important to define what the something is. Draw the lines too broadly—*any* algorithm?—and we risk imposing new bureaucracy before a city clerk can fire up his spell-checker. Draw them too narrowly, and life-altering software might end up being exempt.

An experience in New York City illustrates that this problem is both hard and practically important. On December 11, 2017, the New York City Council approved a local law to create an "automated decision systems task force," which was tasked with advising the mayor on what should count as an automated decision system, how to enable residents to receive explanations and raise objections about decisions reached by such systems, how to identify and address concerns about disparate impact, and how to make such systems and decisions more transparent.[17] The focus of the effort was on things that mattered to people and might go badly wrong, including systems used in social assistance, health care, and law enforcement. But as the task force approached its one-year anniversary, it emerged that members couldn't agree on what an "automated decision system" even was.[18] Earlier drafts of the New York ordinance would have compelled specific steps—such as publishing the source code of covered systems—but those ideas were shelved partly *because* there was no clarity about which systems such new mandates might cover.[19]

A more encouraging precedent comes from Europe. In April 2021, the European Commission proposed a legislative framework, commonly termed the AI Act. (This new framework could have global reach, since even non-European companies doing business in the EU might find it easiest to follow these new rules everywhere.) The AI Act would define a new legal category of "high-risk AI" so that such systems could be subject to heightened requirements across the European Union. It would define "AI" so broadly that nearly any software might be covered.[20] But while the proposal is vague about what counts as AI, it makes a serious and detailed effort to define "high risk."[21] So the proposal is, in effect, a new way to govern high-risk software. I am using the term "high stakes" where this proposal uses "high risk" because, to me, "high stakes" feels like a better-fitting label: it draws attention to both the important risks and the potentially life-transforming benefits of algorithms such as the ones described in this book. In any case, the EU framework follows the approach I suggested in chapter 1: it governs software based on what the software does—that is, on how its operation impacts people—rather than on its technological specifics.[22]

The proposal identifies eight new categories of "high-risk" systems:

1. Biometric identification and categorization of natural persons
2. Management and operation of critical infrastructure

3. Education and vocational training (including specifically "assigning natural persons to educational and vocational training institutions")

4. Employment, worker management, and access to self-employment

5. Access to and enjoyment of essential private services and public services and benefits

6. Law enforcement

7. Migration, asylum, and border control management

8. Administration of justice and democratic processes[23]

I gathered the six stories in chapter 1 before seeing this EU proposal. But when I put the pieces together, I find that each of the six stories contains what the Commission's proposal might consider a "high-risk AI" system.[24] The proposal would also empower the Commission to designate *new* categories of high-risk AI wherever some other system "pose[s] a risk of harm to . . . health and safety, or a risk of adverse impact on fundamental rights" that is "equivalent to or greater than the risk of harm or of adverse impact posed" by the systems already listed.[25] Elsewhere the proposal describes how the Commission should decide on new categories to add to its list. Among other factors, AI is more likely to be considered high-risk when:

- governments have received reports of "health and safety" or "fundamental rights" getting hurt or being put at risk by this kind of algorithm;

- people judged by the system have no practical way of opting out of it; or

- people judged by the algorithm "are in a vulnerable position . . . due to an imbalance of power, knowledge, economic or social circumstances, or age."[26]

This framework raises tricky questions of its own: What makes a "private service" count as "essential," for instance? It also leaves out some concerns: the European Evangelical Alliance, for example, wants to see more consideration of the ethical risks of computer-brain interfaces, and other commenters have argued for carbon footprints to be included as part of the risk calculation.[27]

The proposal is likely to change before implementation, and even if it does ultimately become law, the list of "high-risk" systems is written on a whiteboard, not chiseled in stone. Still, the process reflects extensive and careful thought and illustrates some of the tensions inherent in any such line-drawing exercise.

Something like the European Commission's process, picking out some essentially similar basket of "high stakes" systems, will likely be needed wherever the moral burdens of high-stakes algorithms are to be shared.

FOUR GOVERNANCE STRATEGIES

Scholars have explored at least four governance mechanisms for algorithms: strategies for broader participation in an algorithm's design, transparency practices that would be specifically tailored to the context of software (such as disclosure of source code or of an algorithm's decision logic), forecasting processes to consider how new or changed algorithms would make a difference in the world, and methods to audit algorithms after deployment and adapt them to changing conditions.

Most of these proposals for innovative governance mechanisms for algorithms are still on the drawing board. Some scholars take inspiration from other cases in which a special-purpose governance mechanism was created for a particular kind of decision, such as environmental impact assessment, or participatory municipal budgeting. Others imagine new ways to protect long-standing legal and philosophical commitments, such as due process rights or transparency ideals, in the light of new (or newly pervasive) technology. Still others are experimenting with new governance practices in laboratory settings. Meanwhile, policymakers have begun to craft legislative and policy initiatives, a few of which are starting to be implemented.

A recent review distinguishes two complementary strands of thought in this algorithmic accountability literature.[28] The first strand focuses on individual cases or decisions and suggests ways to apply the legal doctrine of due process to automated decisions,[29] or else to introduce due process–inspired protections in commercial or other settings where the existing constitutional right does not directly apply.[30] The second strand emphasizes "systemic accountability measures," which "include public disclosure of source code, agency oversight, expert boards, and stakeholder input."[31] Scholars frequently commend both approaches, even while focusing principally on one or the other.[32] Other work, including some of my own past work, focuses on new and specifically technological means of achieving governance goals, such as cryptographic "zero knowledge" proofs that a decision was reached using an approved procedure.[33]

At the individual decision level, due process operates both as a directly applicable constraint on some algorithm-based decisions and as a useful analogy for the potential regulation of other decisions. Likewise, at the systemic level, a broad range of existing legal requirements already provide both a binding constraint on some algorithm-based decisions and a potentially useful template for managing others.

For instance, federal administrative law, including the requirements of the Administrative Procedure Act, sometimes compels federal agencies to engage in certain kinds of planning, formally consider input, and make certain disclosures *about* their use of algorithms in certain contexts.[34] Scholars and litigants have harnessed existing open records laws to shed light on public-sector applications of algorithms.[35] And in Europe, the General Data Protection Regulation (GDPR) provides a suite of new methods that may compel or motivate new algorithm-governance practices across a broad range of contexts.[36] In addition, legislation is pending in both the United States and the European Union that contemplates more directly regulating algorithms.[37]

The construction and application of existing law to the governance of algorithms could fill a treatise of its own. I reserve those important analyses for other writers. Here I ask, what systemic governance practices do scholars and practitioners believe *should* apply to the governance of algorithms?

Many of these proposals seek gains from trade with other domains in which there is a struggle to democratize the understanding or governance of something complicated: environmental impact statements, standardized accounting metrics in finance, or nutrition labels, for instance. I focus the discussion here on four dimensions of algorithm governance where new proposals are currently proliferating, and where I believe that the experience of kidney allocation may be able to shed some light:

1. Participation by stakeholders

2. Transparency measures

3. Forecasting of system impacts

4. Auditing of what actually happens once the system is turned on

This is a rough-and-ready categorization designed to make the literature (and the space of governance possibilities) more navigable. These four approaches are also particularly useful for us in this book, because the story of the kidney transplant algorithm illustrates each of them. Actual and proposed governance practices do not necessarily confine themselves to just one of these dimensions, nor should they.

My goal in discussing each of these four dimensions is to illustrate the range of governance practices currently on the drawing board, not to exhaustively inventory the literature. I will also say a few words in each section about how the case of governing transplant algorithms—the case at the core of this book—can illuminate the debate on each dimension.

Participation

Recent governance literature has often advocated crafting or adapting new governance practices to ensure that certain perspectives will be incorporated into the development of an important algorithm. Such proposals often focus specifically on the interests or needs of vulnerable groups that have, in the past, borne the brunt of poor system design, errors, or other problems.

Just as the question of how to make important algorithms parallels the broader question of how to make important laws, so too the question of how people can participate in the making of important algorithms parallels the question of how people can participate in the making of important laws. Software and statutes benefit from different kinds of expertise and analysis. But in both contexts, when the word "important" means "morally fraught and salient to many people," the basic challenge is the same. Lurking within a thicket of questions that experts must answer is a question that laypeople should help to answer.

Earlier in this chapter (in the section "The Value of Facing Hard Choices"), we briefly touched on the global trend toward participatory and deliberative ways of making laws (and important legal decisions). It is worth taking a closer look now. "Deliberative institutional experimentation," say the authors of one recent review, "is flourishing throughout the world."[38] Scholars who study deliberation and participation often seem to assume that we already know what those words mean, and many specialists probably *do* know what they mean, but I did not. Joel Fishkin, the inventor of a technique called "deliberative polling," provides what I find to be a very helpful definition. Fishkin and a colleague say that deliberation ideally aims to be:

- *Informed* (and thus informative): Arguments should be supported by appropriate and reasonably accurate factual claims.
- *Balanced:* Arguments should be met by contrary arguments.
- *Conscientious:* The participants should be willing to talk and listen, with civility and respect.
- *Substantive:* Arguments should be considered sincerely on their merits, not on how they are made or who is making them.
- *Comprehensive:* All points of view held by significant portions of the population should receive attention.[39]

Deliberative polling exposes "random samples [of members of a political community] to balanced information, encouraging them to weigh opposing arguments in discussions with heterogeneous interlocutors, and then harvesting their more considered opinions. It is a way, at least in miniature, of serving both deliberation and equality."[40]

Hélène Landemore has recently written that "representative democracy, the model of democracy with which we are so familiar, may not be the only possible way" of giving power to the public. She finds vivid examples in history that prefigure the "deliberative wave" of experiments over the last fifteen years or so. Classical Athens was ruled by a council of "500 citizens randomly selected from among the willing and able," for instance.[41]

Today this strategy of randomly choosing citizens to deliberate over contentious questions is enjoying a revival in democracies around the world. Ireland used randomly chosen citizens' assemblies, which met and deliberated over time, to revisit its laws on gay marriage and abortion; ultimately the country authorized gay marriage and decriminalized abortion.[42] In Iceland, a carefully managed process of random selection (from groups of people balanced by gender, age, and geography) led to a new constitution.[43] This kind of random selection is known to political scientists as "sortition" — the same strategy that we've long used in the United States to create juries for criminal trials. But randomly choosing people is just the beginning: as with juries, these assemblies typically meet repeatedly face to face, receive careful briefings about the matters they must decide, and deliberate carefully before they reach a decision.

Another way processes can be differently democratic is to give power to whoever shows up, an option Landemore calls "self-selected representation." That's what happened in the transplant case. As she writes:

> The self-selected aspect of this kind of representation comes from the fact that there is no gate at the door and the status of representative is open to anyone willing to participate, even though there is no expectation that the entire population of persons with affected interests will show up. For the most part, such democratic practices do rely on just a fraction of the eligible population actually showing up or participating. . . .
>
> The main advantage of self-selected representation is that, at least in theory, everyone is able to participate. There is no qualification for inclusion, whether social salience and ambition or luck. All it takes, if we temporarily set practical constraints aside, is the will to participate. Self-selected representation can be usefully contrasted against elected assemblies, which are at best accessible to the willing and ambitious, and against lottocratic bodies that are only open to all over time (at least with sufficiently frequent rotation).

Not everyone who thinks about participation is comfortable with this open-door method. Edward Weeks, for instance, fears that "citizens with a special interest in the subject matter [will offer] policymakers a skewed representation of the views of the general public and, worse, [convey] to citizens the impression of special interest domination of the policy agenda." Thus he claims that participation should be *both* widespread *and* representative. This is different from other processes that might be democratic without seeming to be widespread and representative (because, for instance, they hear more from those most affected by a contemplated policy).[44]

Today a similar family of participation strategies is being proposed for algorithms in particular. "Rather than allowing tech practitioners to navigate the ethics of AI by themselves," writes one group of scholars, "we the public should be included in decisions about whether and how AI will be deployed and to what ends."[45] Algorithms should be subject to democratic control, says another, because "the problem of algorithmic fairness is first and foremost *political* and the technical task only comes as secondary."[46] Danielle Citron has suggested that public agencies might establish "information technology review boards that would provide opportunities for stakeholders and the public at large to comment on a system's design and testing."[47] Dan McQuillan proposes that social applications of machine learning could be governed by "people's councils" modeled on grassroots organizations of psychiatric patients and of factory workers.[48]

Policy practitioners have also explored steps in this direction.[49] In the criminal law context, a coalition of civil rights organizations recently argued that jurisdictions adopting actuarial risk assessment algorithms should create "community advisory boards" that would play a central role in determining the values choices implicit in the algorithm.[50] These boards would be empowered to "pause or roll back" the use of such an instrument if the board found that it was not achieving "decarceral or racially equitable goals."[51]

Researchers have also begun to conduct laboratory experiments about engaging people in the governance of algorithms. For instance, a team at the University of Washington recently partnered with a local nonprofit that routes leftover food to charitable organizations and led a yearlong participatory effort to redesign the matching algorithm that decides which food goes where.[52] The researchers worked with the organization's staff, recipients, volunteers, and food donors, and tried several different ways of eliciting and combining stakeholder preferences. In one approach, they used pair-wise comparisons between different allocation alternatives to build a model of each participant's preferences and then took a "vote" among the respective models representing different opinions to make allocation decisions. Along similar lines, participatory approaches to algorithm-making have become a topic for several recent workshops.[53]

These efforts are part of a broader "participatory turn" in technology design, which also includes ideas such as user-led innovation and feminist human-computer interaction.[54] Such efforts are rooted in part in the disability rights movement, which coined the phrase "nothing about us without us." In the broadest sense, participatory approaches to designing algorithms could be one part of the movement toward design justice, an "effort to imagine how all aspects of design can be reorganized around human capabilities, collective liberation, and ecological sustainability."[55]

There is also an important, skeptical countercurrent to all the recent enthusiasm for having laypeople help make important algorithms. Johannes Himmelreich agrees that "AI governance has a democracy gap," but he argues that recent proposals to broaden public participation in the design of high-stakes algorithms should nonetheless be rejected.[56] Whatever makes the stakes high, it usually involves a context where we already do things carefully, such as a court or a social services office. *Those* contexts should indeed be subject to democratic control (and they often are), but not because they happen to rely upon software. Getting lots of people involved in the software-making, Himmelreich thinks, is redundant with these other controls, costly for all concerned, and very optimistic—perhaps baselessly optimistic—about how much wisdom the new participants will add to the mix, when compared with whatever the experts would have chosen.[57] (This argument reminds me of public surveys involving organ transplant scenarios, which imply that many people's first intuitions tend harsh rather than compassionate: work by Peter Ubel and his colleagues found that many members of the public are inclined to tacitly punish former alcoholics, even if those people are at no risk of relapse, by denying them access to liver transplants.[58]) Insofar as people care about the unjust consequences of high-stakes software, the thing they are really trying to change is injustice, not software, he argues. In a similar spirit, Ngozi Okidegbe argues that in order to be truly meaningful, participatory governance needs to reach beyond the technology that a powerful institution may or may not be using, to exercise control over the substance of that institution's decisions, whether software-driven or otherwise.[59] Another critique points out that there is a risk of "participation-washing," where a powerful institution exploits participants without actually listening to them.[60]

In the final chapter, we will assess criticisms like these in light of the transplant story. For now, suffice it to say that although participation is no panacea, I believe the evidence gathered here confirms its potential as one part of a useful approach.

In the transplant context, public engagement is a central component of the governance process. As we will see below, throughout the development of the new Kidney Allocation System, there were a series of windows where the people designing the new algorithm sought and received public input. The traditional notice-and-comment approach was the backbone of this input process: the relevant committee would publish a written description of the algorithm design or strategy that it was considering, then seek and receive written feedback from a broad spectrum of stakeholders, including both interested individuals and advocacy groups. Seeking written comments, however, was not the only method used. As we saw in Clive Grawe's story—and as we'll explore further in this chapter—the in-person "forum" in Dallas in February of 2007 became a critical turning point in the development of the new algorithm. A second public forum took place in St. Louis two years later and also provided important feedback.

The idea of "participation" also shaped the transplant story in more fundamental ways. The committee that developed the new algorithm *itself* included participants from a variety of specialized backgrounds, including not only transplant surgeons but also nephrologists, statisticians, and others. It may not have included anyone who served in their capacity as a patient or an organ donor. But the body that ultimately approved the new algorithm—the Organ Procurement and Transplantation Network (OPTN) board of directors—is required under its bylaws to reserve at least a quarter of its seats for "transplant candidates, recipients, organ donors and their family members."[61]

Transparency

One of the most frequently sought systemic virtues in the governance of algorithms is transparency, which can take many forms. Decisions about an algorithm, even when they have high moral stakes and are deeply contingent, can be hard to understand and often "appear inevitable or apolitical."[62] Many scholars are calling for tailored transparency practices to avert these risks.

The engineers who develop software always have some method of deciding how to use it or when it is ready; no matter how advanced or complex the algorithm may be, it is always in at least that sense understandable, at least to its architects.[63] On the other hand, source code and other technical details are often informative only to specialists.

A commonly proposed element of a transparency regime is to disclose the actual source code of an important algorithm, though it has long been a consensus position among scholars that such disclosure alone is insufficient to achieve the governance aims toward which it may contribute.[64] Important limitations include that code can be hard to read, and the operations of a system can be difficult to predict without the corresponding input data.[65]

Other observers have highlighted ways in which transparency can be actively counterproductive, pointing out that mandated disclosures sometimes create a formal but inaccurate presumption that the public effectively understands or participates in a decision.[66] And in some cases transparency mandates may be a "Trojan horse" that lawmakers use to undermine the agency on which such mandates are imposed.[67] Such arguments, at the very least, highlight the need for an understanding of institutional and social context in creating or evaluating particular transparency mandates.

Beyond the disclosure of source code, a growing number of authors propose that governing authorities create and publish more accessible documentation or description of the data being used,[68] or the decision logic being followed,[69] for an important algorithm. A related family of proposals and policy initiatives would provide explanations for and with each individual decision.[70] But some scholars point out that the reasons behind an algorithm's decision, even when they are disclosed, may not be the kinds of reasons that make intuitive sense to a human being.[71] Some such material may be newly generated as part of the recommended accountable design processes.[72]

In the transplant context, transparency is extensive: the algorithm itself and plain-language descriptions of how it works and how it might change are published, updated, and widely debated. This does not necessarily mean that the situation as a whole is easy to understand—more on that below—but it is, as these discussions suggest, a valuable ingredient in the governance recipe at the heart of this book.

Forecasting

Many scholars and advocates argue that, when an important algorithm is under development, the planners should be required to create "impact statements" that describe the new system's benefits and risks.[73] If you're new to this discussion, the wording may be a little confusing, as it was for me at first: here, "impact statements" generally are *not* descriptions of the impact that an algorithm had. (That kind of after-the-fact, backward-looking analysis is usually called an "audit," and we'll consider those in the next section.) Usually, instead, impact statements are predictions: the algorithm has not been deployed yet (so it has not actually had a chance to have impact), and the idea is to forecast the consequences of a new system in order to decide whether to build it the proposed way, some other way, or perhaps not at all.

One proposal argues, for instance, that police departments should be required to "evaluate the efficacy and potential discriminatory effects" of crime-prediction algorithms by producing "algorithmic impact statements," which would be patterned after the environmental impact statements demanded by federal environmental law, and would also allow opportunities for public comment.[74] Other authors have called for "human impact statements," or for federal legislation to create "human rights impact assessments" that would "focus agencies on the competing values and unintended consequences of technological regulatory tools."[75]

At the start of this chapter, we briefly considered how hard it is to precisely define *which* algorithms, exactly, any new policy process should cover. All these "impact statement" proposals raise additional questions: "Decisions about what type of effects count as an impact, *when* impacts are assessed, *whose* interests are considered, who is invited to participate, [and] who conducts the assessment," among others, all need to be resolved.[76] The research team posing these questions calls for "multi-stakeholder collaborations" to come to consensus on these points,[77] but I wonder if these questions will ultimately be resolved by trendsetting pioneers who pick something and just do it, much as these researchers indicate that Canadian public officials have already begun to do. Such early efforts are unlikely to fully satisfy anyone, but they will at least give the rest of us something to criticize or improve upon, insofar as their outputs are public.

In some cases, these requirements could apply not only to government authorities but also to private companies engaged in sensitive activities like selecting people for employment or credit. Competence and incentives become tricky in such cases: the company knows its technology best but is unlikely to apply careful regulatory scrutiny to its own activities. As a result, it may be very important for regulators to hire people who understand how companies make software and to design reporting requirements that align well with existing steps in the development process.[78]

In the United States the 2019 Algorithmic Accountability Act would have required companies over a certain size, when using data from a regulated domain like credit or health, to proactively forecast the discrimination impact and other risks of their systems but would generally not have required the assessments to be public.[79] This would perhaps reduce the impact of such statements, but might also make them more tenable.

Statements of this general kind may already be required for some systems under European law. When data are processed using "new" technology that is "likely to result in a high risk" to the rights of data subjects, Article 25 of Europe's recently implemented General Data Protection Regulation requires a "Data Protection Impact Assessment." Lilian Edwards and Michael Veale, parsing the GDPR, emphasize that such assessments will be compulsory wherever "there is a 'systemic and extensive evaluation of personal aspects relating to natural persons' . . . based on automated processing." Taken together, they argue, these and other new measures in the GDPR "offer exciting opportunities to operationalise" earlier due process proposals from Danielle Citron, Kate Crawford, and Jason Schultz, albeit while also carrying "a real danger of formalistic bureaucratic over-kill" that may be ineffective at protecting important rights.[80] An exercise mandated by a different part of the GDPR may also provide an opportunity to proactively assess an algorithm's impact, and Margot Kaminski and Gianclaudio Malgieri argue it should be approached as such.[81] At the same time, European observers are keenly aware that outside efforts by journalists and activists will be another important part of the puzzle.[82]

Another branch of this work approaches the governance of algorithm-making as part of professional ethics for system designers.[83] Robert Brauneis and Ellen Goodman, investigating the use of algorithms in the municipal context, found in part that "publicly deployed algorithms will be sufficiently transparent only if . . . governments generate appropriate records about their objectives for algorithmic processes and subsequent implementation and validation."[84]

In the transplant context, forecasting the impact of proposed changes to the kidney allocation algorithm was one of the most important things the policymaking committee did. As we saw in our brief visit to Dallas, a forecast about how LYFT would impact older patients played a pivotal role in dooming that first proposal. That forecast, with admirable candor, showed that older patients would receive far fewer transplants under the proposed change. The forecast was conducted by the Scientific Registry of Transplant Recipients (SRTR), an analytical office separate from the main organ-allocating organization. SRTR also conducts audits of the allocation regime after deployment.

Auditing

Finally, most scholars and practitioners interested in the governance of high-stakes algorithms agree that a system's actual consequences should be rigorously and publicly monitored once the system is in use. Some of the most widely read policy literature on governing algorithms emphasizes the auditing approach.[85]

Many commentators have suggested that public agencies and private companies operating in sensitive contexts ought to internally audit their algorithms, yet only a few agencies or companies have actually done so. Precise ideas about how to conduct an audit, the infrastructure necessary to carry one out, and the standards to use in judging audit results are still nascent.[86]

In some cases, outside researchers have managed to conduct "adversarial audits" of commercial systems—including, for instance, facial recognition systems that are relied upon by police—in which they probe a system without access to its code or the cooperation of its operator.[87] Such audits have led to concrete improvements in system performance—for instance, in better gender recognition performance for black faces after Joy Buolamwini and Timnit Gebru's landmark Gender Shades study.[88] But auditing an algorithm in the more typical sense of the word, where an organization would retain outside experts to conduct a confidential analysis of its own systems, is not yet a widely standardized practice in high-stakes public-sector software.

Part of the question is what to audit *for*. Citron suggests that agencies should design automated systems to "generate audit trails that record the facts and rules supporting their decisions," so that in individual cases due process can be honored and mistakes corrected.[89] Others have focused on how the hunt for discrimination in algorithms would benefit from an audit-based approach.[90] There is an emergent interdisciplinary scholarly field of Fairness, Accountability, and Transparency, rooted in computer science, where researchers compete to devise computational metrics of various kinds of fairness—for instance, comparing the performance of a credit decision-making system across different demographic groups.[91]

Both scholars and practitioners have suggested that financial auditing could provide a useful template for post-deployment reviews of high-stakes algorithms. These proposals often focus primarily on private-sector applications. In their book *Big Data*, Viktor Mayer-Schönberger and Kenneth Cukier propose the concept of "algorithmists," who would function as accountants do.

> They could take two forms—independent entities to monitor firms from outside, and employees or departments to monitor them from within—just as companies have in-house accountants as well as outside auditors who review their finances. . . . They would evaluate the selection of data sources, the choice of analytical and predictive tools, including algorithms and models, and the interpretation of results. In the event of a dispute, they would have access to the algorithms, statistical approaches, and datasets that produced a given decision.[92]

Some companies that specialize in ethically sensitive uses of software—such as the hiring platform HireVue that we met in chapter 1, or a rival named Pymetrics—have begun to commission their own audits.[93] It is unclear, however, how rigorous and independent such audits are; for instance, Pymetrics describes its audit as "collaborative" rather than independent.

After asserting the need for "algorithmic audits" of high-stakes systems in her book *Weapons of Math Destruction*, Cathy O'Neil entered into a business partnership with KPMG to provide such audits to companies, including HireVue.[94] Professionals at Accenture have promoted similar steps.[95]

In the transplant context, the independent Scientific Registry of Transplant Recipients has a federal contract just to keep track of outcomes in the transplant system. It operates independently of the organization that actually designs and operates the transplant algorithm. Not only does SRTR keep track of each kidney transplant that happens in the United States, but it also publishes extensive annual reports that describe the system's performance, complete with graphs visualizing contentious performance metrics such as the relative performance of the system for patients of various ages, races, and other characteristics.[96] Much of that work informs the discussion that follows in this book. The material is wide-ranging, it's carefully designed to be easy to understand, and it's longitudinal, reaching back decades to describe progress over time.

Perhaps inevitably, there are limits to (and debates about) the data that SRTR curates and the analyses that it conducts. For instance, there is much more information about the medical condition of each patient and organ than there is about social determinants of health, such as patients' access to in-home care or their ability to pay for immunosuppressive medications and other costs. And the system places strong emphasis on one-year survival of each organ and patient after transplant. Some critics argue that this emphasis gives too little weight to the difference between short- and long-term success. The emphasis on one-year survival also discourages surgeons from taking on hard cases and may lead to more organs being wasted.[97] I recall a surgeon's remark from a public meeting I attended: "I can't be a 95 percent surgeon in a 97 percent world," lest the hospital's program be shut down for underperforming.

OFFICIALLY OPENING THE ETHICS: ALLEGHENY COUNTY

The child protective services agency of Allegheny County, Pennsylvania—an area that includes Pittsburgh—has built a high-stakes algorithm and at the same time pioneered best practices for algorithmic governance. To my knowledge, the system that the agency has created is by far the most careful and most thoroughly documented real-world exploration of potential best practices for high-stakes algorithmic governance, apart from the events described in this book.

Instruments that predict child abuse or neglect and inform denials of parental rights frequently involve statistically invalid combinations of data that reflect divergent or shifting definitions of "abuse" and "neglect," do not differentiate parentally inflicted abuse from other abuse, and, again, ignore the impact of services in reducing risk.[98]

Unlike the medical challenge of keeping a patient alive, the social ills of child abuse and neglect are extremely difficult to define and measure. Three-quarters of the calls to the hotline allege neglect, not abuse, and "nearly all the indicators of child neglect are also indicators of poverty: lack of food, inadequate housing . . . utility shutoffs [and] lack of health-care," for instance.[99] The definition of neglect changes over time, may vary from one investigator to the next, and is vulnerable to distortion from racial bias.[100] And no matter how careful and disciplined public servants may be, the incoming data on which they must base their decisions are badly biased, for two reasons: members of the public who call the hotline in the first place are likely to reflect whatever biases are present in the larger community; and low-income children, who are also disproportion-ately nonwhite, tend to have much more contact with "mandatory report-ers," such as teachers and social workers, who face draconian penalties if they do not call the hotline each time they have any reason to.

The Allegheny Family Screening Tool (AFST) is used by call screeners who answer the phones at the county's child abuse and neglect hotline. Callers are alerting the county to possible child abuse or neglect, and call screeners must decide which calls the agency should investigate, since it cannot pursue all of them. The AFST provides "decision support" to the call screeners by predicting the chance that, if the call is not investigated, the child will end up needing to be removed from the home within the next two years.[101]

Unlike the governance of transplant algorithms, the events in Allegheny County have already received wide attention from scholars, policymakers, and journalists who are interested in the larger challenge of governing automated decision-making. The system's creation, and the ethical debates that surround it, were described in Virginia Eubanks's landmark book *Automating Inequality* and written up in the *New York Times Magazine*.[102] Just as importantly, the officials and scientists involved in building the system have published extensive reports, held community meetings, and even analyzed their own performance as they attempt to build trust with the communities where this algorithm is used.

An ethical analysis of the new tool, commissioned by the county, found that although its predictions risked amplifying biases, those risks could be controlled (for instance, by making sure investigators do not know the algorithm's risk score, for cases they are sent to investigate). Overall, the analysis found, the tool was likely worth implementing because it had a meaningful chance to save lives.[103] The county adopted the ethicists' recommendation to blind investigators to risk scores. Later, after the tool had been deployed, an impact analysis found that it had not widened racial disparities. Also, after the tool was adopted, the investigators who were sent out found reason to open a case more often, which implies that the tool may indeed have succeeded in improving the call-screening process.[104]

The people involved in developing this tool published a thoughtful study of their own engagement with the local community, which included conducting focus groups to gather further opinions from the impacted populations. They found, in essence, that people's perceptions of fairness depended on larger issues, such as perceived unfairness in the child welfare system as a whole, rather than on details of how the algorithm was deployed or developed.[105]

FRAME-MAKING AND FRAME-BUSTING

Some scholars, advocates, and policymakers argue that it's a mistake to focus too much on improving how we make or use high-stakes algorithms. They say this effort skips past the most important question: not *how* to build high-stakes algorithms, but *whether or not* to build them in a particular case.[106] When, in other words, should algorithms be trusted with high-stakes authority at all?

These critics say that discussions about how to improve an algorithm can encourage people to think too small and may even make things worse by taking discussions of more fundamental changes off the table. I saw this firsthand in debates about criminal justice policy. As I described in chapter 1, many jurisdictions are implementing new algorithms to advise judges about which defendants to send to jail. Many civil rights advocates condemn this as a misguided approach. They say that the current U.S. jail regime is morally untenable and constitutionally indefensible, and that the whole idea of jailing a substantial fraction of newly arrested people is unacceptable.[107] More than a hundred civil rights organizations have urged an outright rejection of pretrial risk assessment systems in a statement I helped coordinate while working at Upturn.[108] Research and policy efforts meant to *improve* algorithms that steer some people to jail arguably undermine this effort, even if the "improved" algorithms really do show less racial bias or really are easier for judges and accused people to understand.[109] The legal scholar Ngozi Okidegbe argues that pretrial algorithms "reinforce and entrench the democratic exclusion" that the racially marginalized communities most affected by these algorithms "already experience in the creation and implementation of the laws and policies shaping pretrial practices."[110]

This pattern is not limited to courts. In Los Angeles, for instance, there has been some ethical debate about an algorithm that allocates beds to the homeless. One could ask whether the algorithm is fair in its allocation of the scarce supply of beds. But no matter how the algorithm is made, the underlying problem is that there are far too many homeless people and not nearly enough beds. As Virginia Eubanks put it in an interview with the socialist magazine *Jacobin*:

> We are creating these tools that just split up this pie that's made of s—t. We can create the most sophisticated tools to share out that pie, but it's not going to change the fact that the pie is s—t. I want a different pie. I don't want a s—t pie.[111]

Even in the Allegheny County example described above, the carefully built algorithm is acting on data that embed significant racial and class-based biases. Eubanks continues:

> The thing that's so challenging about that case is, in Allegheny County, they have done every single thing that progressive folks who talk about these algorithms have asked people to do. There is participatory design in the process. They are completely transparent. They publish everything. They've been working on racial disproportionality for a long time.
>
> And so this is the case that I kind of think of as the worst best-case scenario. Because at the same time, I still believe the system is one of the most dangerous things I've ever seen.[112]

A growing range of scholars and activists are explicitly naming "refusal" of algorithms or data as their scholarly theme or policy aim. In 2020, a scholarly conference on "technology refusal," organized by my colleagues at Berkeley, pulled together many of these voices.[113] The authors of a "Feminist Data Manifest-No" described their determination to "refuse any code of phony 'ethics' and false proclamations of transparency that are wielded as cover [to] let the people who create systems off the hook from accountability or responsibility." They wrote in that they would "refuse tech solutionism as a moral cover for punitive data logics like always-on facial recognition systems, default capture of personal data, and racist predictive policing." In contrast to an ethos of centralized power and remote, authoritative, disembodied data, they propose "centering the needs of the most vulnerable" and "valuing the expertise of community-engaged practitioners."[114]

Refusal is also gaining at least some ground among policymakers. A second panel at the Berkeley event featured activists and scholars who had sparked several cities—including San Francisco, Oakland, and Boston—to forbid the use of facial recognition algorithms by city departments, including the police. And in Europe the proposed AI Act would "ban some forms of AI entirely, including real-time facial recognition in some instances."[115]

A discussion about refusing to make or use algorithms might seem out of place in a book about *how* to make and use algorithms. But I believe the question of what should not be built is essential. Sharing the moral burden of high-stakes algorithms is vital, wherever such systems are made. But just because it may be feasible to involve software in navigating a particular morally fraught question does not make it wise to do so. The refusal conversation reminds us that algorithms tend to make the world seem and be a certain way—flatter, more regimented, more uniform, more abstract. People judged by machine may themselves come to seem more coglike, or even to *be* more coglike. As James C. Scott has written, it is worth asking, "What kind of person does this sort of institution foster?"[116] These efforts push everyone to consider a wider range of civic possibilities and to hold the door open for more fundamental changes. More subtly, they also remind us all that every algorithm makes assumptions, and every algorithm treats some parts of the status quo as fixed.

Even once you decide that *some* algorithm will or may be created, the system that seems most obvious to build may not be the wisest. The way a problem and its solutions are imagined can have a sweeping effect, and these assumptions can be locked into place before the first line of code is written.[117]

A recent body of scholarly literature has emphasized that "problem formulation" can be among the most important phases in any data science project.[118] These early phases of data analysis and algorithm development are often informal and undocumented. Some researchers are pioneering new work practices so that these subtle choices, along with the data and algorithm itself, can be recorded and shared, analyzed and criticized.[119]

Sometimes, a project that starts out as an effort to build a new algorithm may turn into something else entirely, if it is appropriately attentive to the social problem that it aims to resolve. Such attentiveness is an essentially human, empathic quality. If it exists at all, it must be found in the people or organizations that address social problems, rather than in software code as such.[120] For example, when a city's data scientist was brought in to develop a new dispatch system for the city's ambulances, further investigation revealed that the real problem was that ambulance crews were responding to social crises for which they were poorly equipped and trained, such as homelessness and mental illness. Rather than build a new algorithm, the city decided to train and equip a new unit to respond to these challenging situations that did not require an ambulance.[121]

On the other hand, the rhetoric of refusal can mask the fact that there are some contexts where an algorithm really is needed. Even if we hope for a world where kidneys aren't scarce, we currently inhabit a world where they are, and rapid decisions must be made at all hours—in a context with hundreds of thousands of transplant candidates and many complex factors that are relevant—in order to prevent organs from going to waste. Likewise, when students need to be sorted into schools in an area as large as New York City, automation is an indispensable ingredient; hundreds of thousands of exercises of human discretion would likely be less consistent, less fair, less reviewable, and far more costly to administer than the existing system. I find it telling that, for instance, even the student plaintiffs who seek to disrupt the existing algorithm for student screening proposed their own alternative algorithm—one that relied, as the existing systems do, on the imperfect quantitative signals readily available.

TURNING TOWARD TRANSPLANT

In the pages that follow, we will explore the algorithm that decides, out of the roughly 100,000 Americans who are waiting for a kidney transplant, which person will be offered the chance to receive each newly available organ. There are never enough organs to go around, so the choices that this algorithm makes are bound to be sources of elation to some patients and caregivers and, by the same token, sources of desperate lament to others.

The algorithmic allocation of kidneys has for decades been governed in ways that accord with many recent proposals for how to share the moral burdens of an algorithm. It thus offers a rare chance to watch how such practices can really work.

In the kidney allocation story, the governance process is expressly concerned with achieving a public interest—namely, the wise use of a scarce supply of donated organs. (Whether the "wisest" approach is to maximize total benefit, to give similar resources to each patient, or to do something else again is a big part of the debate.) The institution governing the algorithm has decades of experience doing so. Stakeholders representing many different perspectives have the resources and motivation to participate in governance debates, partly because the stakes are so high. The basic values of health and fairness are readily identifiable, albeit contentious in their particular application, and are richly explored in the professional literatures of medicine, bioethics, and philosophy. And the algorithm will be used by a single organization, for a single, unchanging, highly specific purpose. At the same time, different conceptions of fairness are in play, the tensions among these are sharp, and tragic trade-offs are inevitable. In other words, by the time a donated organ actually needs to find its way into a transplant recipient, there's no escape from making a hard choice.

Taken together, these factors make the transplant context a rare laboratory for watching four different governance strategies play out—participation, transparency, forecasting, and auditing.

To build my understanding of organ transplantation and organ allocation policy—and specifically to understand the new Kidney Allocation System that debuted in 2014—I canvassed scholarly and official sources about transplantation and organ allocation, including historical and biographical sources, the medical literature, statutes, federal rules, litigation filings, and the proposals, comments, explanatory materials, and actual allocation policies published by the United Network for Organ Sharing. I obtained more than 1,500 pages of documents directly from the UNOS archive. I read extensively in the scholarly and lay literature, from the early days of transplantation throughout the period over which the new kidney allocation algorithm was being developed, and I examined unofficial sources such as webinars for transplant professionals and podcasts and other materials for kidney patients. Finally, I conducted semistructured qualitative interviews with eleven people who are knowledgeable about organ allocation, several of whom played key roles in the pioneering of transplant surgery and the development and approval of the new kidney allocation algorithm.[122] In addition to Clive Grawe—the patient we first met in Dallas earlier in this book—these include the surgeon who chaired the UNOS kidney advisory committee during the period when that committee created and approved the algorithm that was deployed in 2014 as well as the research scientist from UNOS who was detailed to the committee and helped it analyze the impacts of various competing proposals.

I approached this work out of an interest in how algorithms and the public policy that surrounds them are made and revised. I have tried to convey some sense of the feelings and human experiences that surround this software code, but those were not my principal focus. Thus, this book touches on but does not centrally explore the experiences of people who try and fail to obtain a transplant, or who are deterred from seeking a transplant, or who do not even know that they could seek a transplant, or who do not know that their existing organs are failing. Those absences are undoubtedly limitations of this book, and they point to opportunities for future work, including both qualitative investigations and quantitative clinical and survey research.

I am by nature an optimist. I like to find things in the world to admire. I have tried to present the story that follows warts and all. I point out significant limitations of the algorithm that allocates kidneys, and also flaws in the processes by which that algorithm is made and revised. Still, through researching and writing this book, I confess that I have come to admire the field of transplantation medicine in the United States, the people who make up that field, and the algorithms and algorithm-making processes that live at the center of the whole ongoing drama. I hope through this work to make the experiences and accomplishments of clinicians, advocates, and patients alike more legible and usefully instructive to all who care about the design and governance of high-stakes software.

Chapter 3 | A Field of Life and Death

WHEN CLIVE GRAWE used his perspective as a patient to weigh in on the design of the kidney allocation algorithm, he was part of a deep tradition. Collaborative decision-making about hard ethical choices in kidney medicine began before the digital revolution. It began before there were many kidney transplants. It started, in fact, with Teflon, and the work of a pioneering doctor, a man his friends called "Scrib."

Without a working kidney or medical help, no human can live for long. The kidneys filter your blood, help maintain the necessary balance of salts and fluids, and supply hormones, such as erythropoietin, that are essential to other life processes.[1] Kidneys are a "paired organ": a typical adult has two of them, but only one is necessary for normal health. Physicians and surgeons who specialize in kidneys (a field known as nephrology) had long dreamed of transplanting a kidney from a healthy person into a sick one, allowing both people to live normally. They understood that if transplantation could be made reliable, living donors could provide "physiologically ideal live donor kidneys" without imperiling their own health.[2] (It is also possible to recover kidneys from newly deceased donors, which is the only way of obtaining hearts, for instance.) The mechanical part of kidney transplant was first accomplished in the early 1900s: removing a kidney and then connecting it to blood vessels in the recipient's body. But as the *New York Times* reported from a 1914 conference of surgeons, there was a crucial problem:

> The surgical side of the transplantation of organs is now completed, as we are now able to perform transplantations of organs with perfect ease and with excellent results from an anatomical standpoint. But as yet these methods cannot be applied to human surgery, for the reason that [they] are almost always unsuccessful from the standpoint of the functioning of the organs. All our efforts must now be directed toward the biological methods which will prevent the reaction of the organism against foreign tissue and allow the adapting of [transplants] to their hosts.[3]

In other words, the real barrier to transplanting kidneys was the immunology: getting the recipient's body to accept and use the new kidney rather than attack the new arrival as a foreign invader. For decades, the pioneers of transplant had honed their craft on dogs and other animal models, while the science of immunology gradually made progress toward unlocking the secrets of biological compatibility between donor and recipient.[4]

The first long-term success in human kidney transplantation was achieved in December 1954, with a donor and recipient who just happened to be genetically identical twin brothers, making their immune systems perfectly compatible.[5] A year after that surgery, with the transplanted kidney still going strong, the Boston-based surgeons reported their success in the *Journal of the American Medical Association*, writing that "transplantation ... of a functioning kidney appears to be a feasible procedure in identical twins, but to date successful permanently functioning [transplants] appear to be limited to such individuals."[6]

In the meantime, doctors also looked for ways to keep patients alive even when they did not have working kidneys, largely by using machines to filter toxins from the patients' blood. That process was known as hemodialysis.[7] The first external dialysis of human patients took place in Nazi-occupied Holland during World War II.[8] These early efforts, and others like them, showed success in removing toxins from blood. Doctors always struggled, however, to get the blood in and out of the patient's body: each treatment required inserting large needles into the body and then removing them, and this could not be done in the same place twice.

> It took only about a month before all of the body's vascular access points were exhausted. Unless the patient took a turn for the better within that window of time, the patient would die. It was heartbreaking for physicians and loved ones to see patients' Lazarus-like recoveries from the effects of renal failure, only to lapse back into a uremic coma and die once their arteries and veins had been used up by the dialysis procedure.[9]

Thus, in 1958, when a physician named Belding Scribner became chair of the Department of Nephrology at the newly established University of Washington Hospital, kidney medicine was in a tantalizing state of suspense. If a patient entered kidney failure, surgeons knew how to transplant a healthy kidney into them—but unless that organ came from an identical twin, the recipient's body would usually reject the transplant within a few weeks. And without transplant surgery, nephrologists knew how to filter blood and keep the patient alive—but they could only do it for a month or so before they lost access to the patient's blood.

Scrib, as he had been known since childhood, knew a thing or two about transplant. In fact, he was a walking advertisement for the procedure: he had terrible eyesight and was one of the first people in the world to benefit from transplanted corneas, the clear lenses inside of each eye.[10] But Scrib also knew that transplantation was not feasible for most of his kidney patients.

The spark came in March 1960. Scrib and his colleagues designed a tube from a synthetic material called Teflon that could be permanently inserted into the patient's body (figure 3.1). Unlike a glass or rubber tube, the Teflon tube allowed blood to flow through it without clotting, at least when the patient was being treated with an anticoagulant drug called Heparin. The tubing could thus remain in place indefinitely, in the patient's arm, for repeated rounds of dialysis.[11] "With the first surge of blood through the shunt, it became possible for [kidney failure] to transform from an inevitably fatal disease into a chronic condition."[12] Initially each patient's blood was dialyzed as infrequently as once every three weeks, but it quickly became clear that dialysis every few days kept patients in better health.[13]

But with the possibilities opened up by this smooth plastic tubing, Scribner had also created a sticky moral challenge. Within his own clinic in Seattle, Scribner had the facilities to treat only a few patients at a time.[14] Although patients paid some of the cost, treatment was unaffordable for most, and Scribner funded these efforts partly through research grants.[15]

Scribner and his team were inundated with pleas from dying patients and their physicians.[16] Perpetual dialysis had become possible, but the machines and expert personnel necessary to provide this service remained scarce and costly. Richard Rettig, a leading historian of kidney policy, writes that Scribner was "persuaded that the treatment was efficacious [but] nevertheless quite conscious of the limits that scarcity imposed on access to care."[17]

Faced with this quandary, Scribner and his colleagues chose to do something extraordinary: they shared their moral burden with the community they served.

The medical team established a two-step screening process: Patients were first screened by a team of physicians, who determined eligibility for the program based on what Scribner and his colleagues considered medical criteria, including being "a stable, emotionally mature adult under the age of 45" who was ready to comply with the dietary and other constraints of the program.[18] From today's perspective, it may seem that a group of medical doctors deciding which patients were "emotionally mature" enough for treatment were not engaging in a truly *medical* decision, so much as making an inescapably difficult ethical choice on nominally medical grounds. In any

Figure 3.1   Diagram of Dr. Belding Scribner's Original Dialysis Shunt

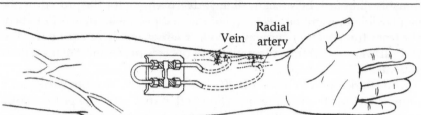

Source: Quinton, Dillard, and Scribner 1960. Reprinted with permission by Wolters Kluwer Health.

case, there were many more medically eligible patients than available dialysis spots. Scribner therefore decided to establish a second screening step: a committee of laypeople, who would make the non-medical decision of how to allocate available slots among the medically eligible patients. The committee members were given some basic education about kidney medicine, but they were not told how to choose which of the medically eligible kidney patients should receive lifesaving dialysis treatments.

This approach reflected several important principles. First, even though the technology of dialysis might be complex and new and fully understood only by experts, the moral questions that it raised belonged to a wider community, not just to the technical experts. Second, hard ethical questions should be faced directly, rather than buried in medical or other technical jargon. And third, the onus was on the physicians to educate laypeople about the new technology at least enough so that appropriate input could be obtained.

"They Decide Who Lives, Who Dies," was the headline of a 1962 *Life* magazine article about this committee.[19] Its members, who were anonymous, were photographed in shadow. A clerical collar can be seen on one; the lone woman of the group clasps a pair of reading glasses in her folded hands. The committee was grounded in "acceptance of the principle that all segments of society, not just the medical fraternity, should share the burden of choice as to which patients to treat and which ones to let die."[20]

Formal criteria for decision-making were not actually used by the lay committee. But in making its decisions, it considered the following: the ability of a housewife from eastern Washington to move to Seattle; the relative importance of saving a parent with two children compared to one with six; the prospect for rehabilitation and return to work; the potential of "service to society" based on education; the candidate's "character and moral strength" based on church membership; and the probable opportunity of the surviving spouse to remarry.[21]

In its first thirteen months of operation, the Seattle Area Kidney Center "considered 30 candidates, of whom 17 were judged medically suitable. . . . Of the medically suitable, ten were selected for treatment; the other seven died."[22]

The approach was controversial. One pair of legal scholars captured the mood of skepticism:

> The magazines paint a disturbing picture of the bourgeoisie sparing the bourgeoisie, of the Seattle committee measuring persons in accordance with its own middle-class suburban value system: scouts, Sunday school, Red Cross. This rules out creative nonconformists, who rub the bourgeoisie the wrong way but who historically have contributed so much to the making of America. The Pacific Northwest is no place for a Henry David Thoreau with bad kidneys.[23]

And yet, for all these faults, I think the Seattle committee gave us much to admire. It was profoundly, even uncomfortably, honest about the hard choices at the center of kidney medicine. And it was profoundly, even uncomfortably, democratic. The Seattle physicians and their lay colleagues were rationing a scarce supply of dialysis treatments, but the issues they faced were a preview of the dilemmas that would later appear in the rationing of transplantable organs. Later policymakers—including Congress— would take shelter behind the claim that all these rationing decisions can, and rightly should, be made solely on the basis of "medical criteria." But when a lifesaving treatment is unavailable to all the people who need it with similar urgency, and who could benefit from it to a similar degree, calling the choice among such people "medical" amounts to mere semantics. It is an ethical decision. And a simply articulated rule such as "maximize life-years saved" might provide a comforting ring of objectivity—saving policymakers from having to make explicitly qualitative decisions about whose lives were worth saving—but as Clive Grawe would one day point out in Dallas, such a rule would also have perverse effects. The Seattle committee, somewhat radically, insisted that ethical questions be faced as such, rather than disguising them as technical ones.

Other early dialysis centers used less overtly qualitative methods, including in some instances a first-come, first-served approach.[24] "What did change in the wake of the Seattle 'Life or Death Committee' was that patient selection committees now comprised physicians and generally excluded lay people, while being less explicit about making judgments regarding human worth."[25] Criteria that were outwardly medical, however, often masked other values: "Poorer people were understood to lead more chaotic lives, making compliance with dialysis schedules and dietary restrictions less certain, and they often suffered additional medical conditions assumed to undercut the effectiveness of dialysis. [A] utilitarian definition of medical suitability meant that the socially disenfranchised were almost guaranteed to lose."[26] In other words, when the community shifted away from grappling explicitly with ethical trade-offs and chose instead to construe the problem of choosing patients as a purely technical matter, the result was arguably less fair. That same pattern—of technical experts making underexamined moral assumptions that might in fact amplify inequality—would recur across the history of transplantation. Even today pessimistic beliefs about the social lives and behavior of low-income patients—beliefs that are not measured or analyzed anywhere near as carefully as matters of blood type or immune system matching—often lead to patients being excluded as transplant candidates.[27] Like most burdens associated with poverty, in the United States, this one falls disproportionately on nonwhite patients.

A MORTAL WAITING ROOM: CONGRESS SIGNS A BLANK CHECK FOR DIALYSIS

From the beginning, the federal government played a central role in funding treatment for kidney failure in the United States. The early dialysis experiments of the 1960s in Scribner's lab and a range of other places were funded by National Institutes of Health (NIH) research grants. Meanwhile, the Veterans Administration (VA) was among the first major health care providers to embrace dialysis. The VA sought funds as early as 1966 to construct dialysis units for its patients—a request whose enormous cost prompted the federal Budget Bureau (the precursor of today's Office of Management and Budget) to impanel a Committee on Chronic Disease.[28] The committee determined that dialysis and transplantation alike—once surgeons began, in the early 1960s, to have occasional success with transplants among close relatives—were no longer experimental. It recommended that ongoing treatment be funded by Medicare.[29] "The Budget Bureau, upon receipt of the report sought to minimize its impact and its distribution and did nothing to implement its recommendations."[30]

But then, on November 4, 1971, a kidney patient named Shep Glazer turned the tide at a House Ways and Means Committee hearing on federal funding for kidney dialysis.[31] He brought with him five patients who, like himself, relied on dialysis to stay alive, including a homemaker and a medical student. Glazer explained that "we live in constant terror that if these treatments are taken away from us because our money has run out, death will come in a matter of weeks." While the testimony was happening, Glazer's wife—who oversaw his in-home treatments—hooked him up to a dialysis machine that had been borrowed from a nearby Georgetown hospital for the occasion and filtered his blood in full view of the committee. "The idea of bringing the machine was not for shock value or publicity," she said, but "to prove and inform. . . . It can be done anywhere if it could be done here in the hearing room." Glazer and the other patients argued that if funding were provided, dialysis could be moved out of the high-cost hospital context and more economically and agreeably provided at home or in outpatient centers. One congressman in attendance said, "I don't know of any testimony that I have heard in such a short period of time that has made a more dramatic impact on me."[32]

Glazer's pitch to Congress included an escape from hard moral choices. "Because of presently limited finances," he explained, "dialysis raises many moral issues. Selection committees are forced to choose who shall be allowed to survive. This moral dilemma can be eliminated," he argued, if dialysis is provided for all in need.

On October 30, 1972, Congress responded to the stark human impact and cost of dialysis by passing section 2991 of the Social Security Amendments Act, a provision that introduced a disease-specific Medicare benefit—the only one of its kind—that funds dialysis treatment for everyone, regardless of whether the patient is old enough to qualify for Medicare.[33] Medicare covers 80 percent of dialysis costs, and state-level Medicaid and other programs typically cover the remaining 20 percent for patients who cannot afford to pay it.[34] At its inception, the program covered dialysis starting three months after treatment itself had begun, as long as it was needed. Support for transplant-related medical costs was more limited: the program initially covered just one year of postoperative care, even though transplant recipients typically require extensive follow-up care and immunosuppressive medication throughout their lives.[35] The federal program remains in place today (and now covers three years, rather than one, of postoperative costs for transplant recipients).[36]

If Scrib's Teflon shunt had created a hard moral problem at his own Seattle clinic, the federal decision to fund dialysis effectively took that problem national. Dialysis keeps people alive, but it is no substitute for a transplant. The basic approach, which became widespread once the spigot of federal funding was opened, remains in place today. Dialysis typically happens three times a week, in an outpatient clinic, for four hours per session.[37] It is expensive, albeit to the government rather than to patients. It is also dangerous: "After one year of treatment, those on dialysis have a

20–25% mortality rate, with a five year survival rate of 35%."[38] Under ideal conditions, though, dialysis can continue for decades. Quality of life on dialysis can be difficult. The sessions are disruptive (60 percent of patients on dialysis are unemployed), and the patient's level of energy and sense of wellness will seesaw over the course of each week.[39]

"Now that long-term dialysis is available to nearly everyone with renal failure, it is organs that are in scant supply. . . . Organ shortage is the paradoxical product of increased access to long-term dialysis."[40]

That paradox—the suddenly vast numbers of surviving kidney patients, many of them eager for a transplant—added pressure to the drive for transplantation, especially to enabling more transplants among strangers.

WHAT WE ARE WAITING FOR:
CYCLOSPORINE ARRIVES

"Only a few diehards went into transplantation in those days. In 1976, the [one-year] mortality rate for kidney transplant patients in the U.S. was 30 percent. . . . You had to be a diehard to be in this field because it was gruesome; it was hard work."[41]

That's how Göran Klintmalm, one of the modern pioneers of transplant surgery, describes the landscape he found when entering the field as a surgeon in the late 1970s. Dr. Klintmalm—who shared his perspective with me over several long interviews and gave feedback on the manuscript that became this book—has been a leader in transplantation ever since he flew from his home in Stockholm to Denver in August 1979 to train as a protégé of Thomas Starzl.

Sixteen years earlier, in 1963, Starzl had effectively launched the field of organ transplantation by showing that a "cocktail" of immunosuppressive medications could reverse patients' rejection of transplanted kidneys and induce tolerance over time so that the medication could be reduced and the transplanted organ could continue to function.[42] This work "transformed kidney transplantation from a clinical experiment to an incipient clinical service using both cadaveric and live donors [and] led to a steady proliferation of transplantation centers of excellence in the United States and Europe."[43] But the survival odds facing each patient remained grim.

Starzl, Klintmalm, and their colleagues pressed on with a relentless work ethic. "Starzl slept only three or four hours every night. He came in about 5:00 a.m., he got home about 1:00 a.m., seven days a week."[44] Early in his time on Starzl's team in Denver, Klintmalm says,

> We had just done a liver transplant and I was so tired I was nauseated. The fastest liver transplant I ever experienced when working with Starzl was 15 hours, and the longest one was 25 hours! It normally took about 20 hours.

I had fallen asleep on this bed waiting for the next shoe to drop when I got a phone call from the operator about another donor. The thought of doing another transplant after just completing a marathon transplant surgery was insane to me. Of course, we couldn't do another transplant! Everybody was dead tired. I returned the call and said, "No. I don't think so. We are out. We just finished and we can't do another one," and hung up. Of course Tom was aware of everything that went on. The next day Tom chewed me out— left, right, up, and down—because I had turned down a potential donor. I explained, "We just did a transplant; we couldn't do another one." He said, "We can always do another one. If we have a donor, we can always do another one."[45]

Klintmalm spent two years with Starzl—he would return to Sweden in the summer of 1981—during a critical inflection point in the history of kidney transplantation. Just as Scribner's Teflon shunt had done for dialysis, Starzl and Klintmalm's breakthrough work on immunosuppressive drugs was about to unlock enormous benefit and at the same time to open ethical challenges that we are still grappling with today. The new drug would make many more transplants possible—and thus would one day make the algorithm that chooses among such transplants a devilishly hard piece of software to design.[46]

A Swiss biologist working for the pharmaceutical company Sandoz had first found the compound in 1969 in a soil sample in Hardangervidda, Norway—about 450 miles west of Stockholm, as it happened.[47] The drug that the world would come to know as Cyclosporine had immediately shown strong immunosuppressive potential in the lab and in animal models, but the first physicians who had tried to use it in humans—particularly in Britain—had struggled.[48] The drug showed some promising signs but seemed toxic to patients. By late 1979, Sandoz was seriously considering pulling the plug on further development.

Then, in December, Sandoz's medical director arrived in Denver bearing a gift for Starzl and the team. "When he came to Denver," Klintmalm recalls, "he took us to the Rodeo Restaurant. He had brought with him a tin coffee can. In it was a plastic bag full of some sort of white powder. We later learned that it was crystallized cyclosporine. He placed it on the table and said, 'This you can have for your dogs,'" meaning to use in animal experiments. Within a few weeks, Starzl and his colleagues got approval and "performed the first human kidney transplant using cyclosporine. . . . The day before Christmas Eve."[49] Over the ensuing spring of 1980, Starzl and Klintmalm reached a crucial insight: by combining Cyclosporine with just the right amount of steroids, they were able to keep their patients, and transplanted organs inside those patients, alive. They established that the new drug worked for kidney transplants and also for Dr. Starzl's primary interest, livers.

The new survival numbers looked so good that when Starzl's team submitted them to the upcoming international conference of the Transplantation Society—slated to take place that summer in Boston—the team's abstracts were all rejected: the reviewers evidently found them hard to believe. But Starzl was still allowed to address the group in person. Klintmalm told me what ensued: "He gave the talk. . . . And it was a scene—it was almost riot police had to come, because results were so incredible. We had an 80 percent graft survival in kidneys, and . . . [the response] was better than a volcanic eruption."[50]

After the conference, Cyclosporine, previously a nonstarter, became a kind of salvation for the field of transplant medicine. "The increases in graft and patient survival when cyclosporine was part of a multidrug immunosuppressive regimen across all categories of existing solid organ transplantation" were "nothing short of stunning in the 1980s, when 1-year graft survival rates exceeded 89% in kidney transplantation recipients."[51]

Ever since those early days, outcomes have continued to improve. Of the nearly 60,000 kidney transplants performed between 2008 and 2011, more than 78 percent of the transplanted kidneys were still functioning, inside a still-living transplant recipient, five years later.[52]

A SCRAMBLE FOR LIFE

"This is the girl's only chance."

It was Saturday, December 22, 1984.[53] The voice on the phone was Dr. Tom Starzl's, and he had begun his story without preamble or even introducing himself. He had telephoned Baylor University Medical Center in Dallas, knowing that his old protégé Dr. Göran Klintmalm was there.

Klintmalm still lived in Stockholm and was wrapping up a two-day visit to Baylor, where he had agreed to move in order to establish a new transplant program that would handle kidneys and livers. He was planning to leave Dallas later that afternoon, clothed in his last clean shirt—it was such a short visit that he hadn't even brought checked luggage.

Starzl told Klintmalm that there was a four-year-old girl "sitting in an aircraft on the tarmac in Peoria, Illinois, waiting for instructions on where to go."[54] She was dying, and a donor liver that was a match for her had been found in Canada. Neither Starzl (who by this time had moved to Carnegie Mellon in Pittsburgh) nor any of the other programs then transplanting livers had the multiple teams of surgeons ready that it would take to perform the intricate operation.

Could Klintmalm and his brand-new team at Baylor take the girl?

At this point there were no algorithms in place to match patients with organs, just hard-driving surgeons searching for a way. The same relentlessness that had driven these pioneers to surmount medical and biological barriers was now coming to bear on social, organizational, and financial ones.

Starzl confided something else to the Baylor team: this patient, Amie Garrison, was a celebrity. She was one of a series of children whose desperate need for a liver transplant had drawn national attention.[55] Unlike with kidneys, there was no equivalent of dialysis for liver patients: those who did not get a transplant when they needed one would typically die. The distant but nonzero likelihood of a transplant, especially for children at death's door, made for gripping public drama.[56] The issue had so captured President Ronald Reagan's attention that he had designated a member of the White House correspondence office, Michael Batten, to coordinate the requests for a transplant; that office, which came to be known as the "body shop," had received more than 325 requests by April 1984.[57]

Amie Garrison was one such case—just a few weeks earlier, she had lit the White House Christmas tree. And cases like hers were shifting the national debate. As one commenter wrote at the time, "Congress, driven by an emotional desire to provide lifesaving therapies to children afflicted with liver disease and by legislators who believe that government should intervene more aggressively to help, is moving rapidly to enact legislation aimed at improving the nation's capacity to procure human organs for transplantation."[58]

Klintmalm happened to be at a meeting with hospital leadership when the call from Starzl arrived. He recounts:

> It sounded like this little girl's only chance was an emergency liver transplant. But at the same time, we were not yet set up at BUMC. We were not ready, and if she died it would be bad public relations. The pros and cons were discussed back and forth and finally they all, including Boone [the hospital's CEO], turned to me and said, "This must be your decision. Should we do it or not?" I paused for a moment and said, "Yes. Let's go."[59]

Several teams of surgeons engaged in an intricate choreography over the next seventy-two hours. Starzl called the Garrison family, who flew to Love Field, near Baylor. Klintmalm pulled his team together in Dallas while Starzl flew to Canada with another team, surgically removed the donor's liver, and flew it back to Dallas. That return trip needed to be quick, because the donor liver could survive only eight hours outside a human body. As Starzl's team and the liver were flying back, the pilot informed them that they would have to land at Dallas–Fort Worth instead of Love Field and pass through customs, since they were arriving internationally from Canada. Starzl knew that this would likely delay their arrival and doom the transplant. He called the White House from the plane and received presidential authorization (conveyed, in some versions of this story, by First Lady Nancy Reagan, who had met Amie Garrison at the Christmas tree lighting) to skip customs and land at Love Field. They arrived in time, and the operation—the nascent Baylor program's first transplant—succeeded. Klintmalm, now wearing borrowed clothes, left Dallas in triumph before he had even formally begun. Young Amie, celebrated in the media, grew to adulthood and had children of her own.

Even as livers predominated in the headlines, kidneys remained the most important organ from an allocation perspective. Ever since Congress had made dialysis a universal entitlement in 1972 through the Medicare End Stage Renal Disease Program, dialysis sustained a large population of patients who would benefit from a kidney transplant. The immunosuppressive improvements of the early 1980s had made many potentially suitable recipients available for each donor kidney.

As one commentator wrote in 1984, "Although the problem of obtaining livers for children . . . has generated the bulk of the publicity, the people who stand to benefit the most in the short run from any effort to improve the system are the estimated 6,000 patients with renal disease who are awaiting kidneys for transplantation."[60]

That effort to improve the system—and to bring some sense of nationwide coordination—began with the National Organ Transplant Act (NOTA).

AUTHORIZING A NATIONAL SYSTEM, WITH NATIONAL ALGORITHMS

The National Organ Transplant Act of 1984 established a federal statutory framework for organ transplantation. People have always been free to donate a kidney to, or receive a kidney from, a family member or friend— these are known as "directed" donations. But the hard policy problem was, what about a donor who does *not* choose a specific recipient? Most organs come from people who have opted in to organ donation and then died without choosing who should receive their organs. Given the shortage of organs, some form of rationing was and still is inevitable.

The most important part of the new federal law, for our purposes, was that it called for the creation of a "national system, through the use of computers and in accordance with established medical criteria, to match organs" with patients who were waiting on nationwide lists for each organ.[61] This would be accomplished through a federally designated nonprofit organization, the Organ Procurement and Transplantation Network, which would "have a board of directors which includes representatives of organ procurement organizations . . . transplant centers, voluntary health associations, and the general public."[62]

In calling for the general public to decide how this computerized rationing system—that is, this algorithm—should work, Congress was following in the footsteps of the lay committee that Scrib had established in Seattle in the 1960s to select dialysis patients. And, it was charting a course that would one day lead to the 2007 Dallas meeting where Clive Grawe and other members of the public would reject the expert-made algorithm that proposed to favor young kidney recipients over older ones.

One major advantage Congress would gain, by allowing the public to shape the allocation algorithm, is that it would relieve physicians and surgeons of the need to decide which of their patients should be favored with a scarce organ. Immunosuppression was constantly improving, and at the same time, technologies for preserving organs outside the body were also getting better. This meant that more patients were potentially medically suitable for each organ and more could get to the operating room in time. Before NOTA, physicians and surgeons had increasingly been forced to route available organs among their competing patients. This role was in conflict with the tradition of the Hippocratic Oath—often summarized as "first, do no harm"—which requires the physician to care equally for every patient.[63]

The need to ration organs through an algorithm came in part from the decision not to allow an open market in organs. Before the federal law was enacted, there had been an open question about how, if at all, incentives might be used to increase the supply of organs. A physician in Reston, Virginia, named H. Barry Jacobs drew national publicity for his plan to establish a business that would buy kidneys from economically disadvantaged people overseas and transplant them into Americans in need. In a 1983 op-ed explaining his views, Dr. Jacobs wrote that "compensating the donor for blood or a kidney is the American way. . . . When it comes to deciding what to do with our bodies, Congress is not a better judge than the individual. . . . Only in the Soviet Union do human organs belong to the State."[64] These remarks and others like them triggered outrage in public debates and in Congress, where Dr. Jacobs sparred at a hearing with then-representative Al Gore. After the hearing, Gore added a provision to the pending legislation that would bar organ purchases, and it eventually became part of the statute.[65] Other ethicists urged that organs should not be commercialized, warning of risks that the poor might not only lose access to needed care but also be exploited or demeaned by selling parts of their bodies.[66]

DESIGNING THE FIRST ALGORITHM:
THE MEDICAL AND MORAL DEBATE

Two schools of thought emerged in the 1980s about how to ration organs, especially kidneys. The first approach, which Dr. Starzl favored and had pioneered in Pittsburgh, was to use waiting time—a "first come, first served" philosophy, at least when choosing among viable candidates.

A rival approach focused on a medical rationale for prioritization, known as tissue typing (also referred to more specifically as antigen matching or HLA matching): a laboratory assessment of biological differences between a donor's tissues and a recipient's immune system to predict which patient's body would be least likely to reject the transplanted organ.[67] The precise relationship between tissue typing and transplant success has always been fiercely debated. It changes over time as standards of care evolve, differs for different subsets of the patient population, and is a perennial controversy in transplant medicine.

As David Hamilton puts it in his authoritative history of transplantation:

> Tissue typing provided an objective way of choosing between patients from the pool of those waiting. This absolved and removed the doctors from the difficult choice in judging between the patients waiting for a kidney, and it preempted any allegations of allocation bias by local doctors. But this scheme rested in its entirety on the assumption that tissue typing mattered in routine cases.[68]

In other words, whatever its clinical merit, the use of tissue typing was a moral expedient for doctors, policymakers, and others, since without it, they might be left to ration organs on more directly moral, nonscientific grounds.

"What unexpectedly became clear over time . . . was that . . . a single or multiple antigen disparity in [tissue typing] did not create an unsurmountable hurdle for graft survival."[69] Strangers scarcely ever have identical antigens, and "mismatched" donor and recipient antigens are broadly correlated with organ rejection, so that transplants involving many mismatched antigens generally have a less favorable prognosis than transplants with few or no mismatches. But this does not necessarily mean that every mismatch is an equal—or a meaningful—reason to be more pessimistic about how well a given transplant will go. In many cases, it was (and remains) unclear how much difference specific mismatches make to the likelihood of transplant success.[70]

The debate carried a strong racial subtext because, in addition to being a predictor of compatibility between donors and recipients, antigens are also statistically correlated to race. African Americans are much more likely to experience end-stage renal disease than the population at large (their risk is approximately triple that of white Americans) owing largely to social determinants of health. However, donated kidneys from white deceased donors—the majority of deceased donors, reflecting the U.S. population—tend to be closer tissue typing matches for white recipients than for black recipients. Thus, the more importance is given to antigen matching in allocation, the less access black patients will have to kidneys.

Under the new federal law, the question of how to design the new algorithm (or really, how to set up the organization that would design it) was delegated to a new national task force. The U.S. Task Force on Organ Transplantation held a series of public hearings in 1985 and 1986, and it ultimately supplied much of the specific character of the federal organ transplant regime.[71]

The task force was charged by statute to produce "recommendations for assuring equitable access by patients to organ transplantation and for assuring the equitable allocation of donated organs among transplant centers and among patients medically qualified for an organ transplant."[72] Its report called for "a single national system" of organ sharing and "broke new ground in recommending 'that each donated organ be considered a national resource to be used for the public good.'"[73]

It further recommended that "the public must participate in the discussions of how this resource can be used to best serve the public interest."[74] Specifically, the task force recommended that allocation criteria should "be developed by a broadly representative group that will take into account both need and the probability of success."[75] Ultimately, the task force urged that "a single national system for organ sharing" be created with "uniform policies and standards," and that "its governance include a broad range of viewpoints, interests, and expertise, including the public."[76]

The task force's eagerness to involve the public in developing an allocation algorithm could be interpreted as a continuation of a pattern that Congress had established by deferring allocation questions to the task force itself. The task force members, like the legislators who impaneled them—and also like Dr. Scribner in Seattle, who had faced the same problem before Congress did—eschewed final responsibility for deciding how to allocate organs among the waiting patients.

The task force "recognized that heavy reliance on HLA matching could potentially disadvantage minority patients," particularly if close matches were used as a rationale to move organs from one geography to another.[77] Empirical work in immunology had found that "the frequencies of certain HLA phenotypes are different in black, Hispanic, and white populations."[78] And "in cities or regions with large black and Hispanic populations, a disproportionate number of the potential transplant recipients are black or Hispanic, while most of the donors are white," so that "a system of sharing based on histocompatibility may result in more of the kidneys procured in such a city or region being assigned to white recipients elsewhere than can be matched to local nonwhite patients." Similarly, nonwhite patients would be less likely than white ones to receive an ideally matched kidney from *outside* their local area, since more of these organs were donated by, and were likely to match with, whites.[79]

The task force argued that the allocation system should "be based on medical criteria that are publicly stated and fairly applied." Where patients were equally "medically qualified" for an organ, the choice between them "should be based on length of time on the waiting list."[80] It further recommended that only one organ procurement agency be certified in each geographic region—in effect recommending the end of competition among such agencies.[81]

Congress responded to the task force's recommendations in the Omnibus Budget Reconciliation Act of 1986, which effectively gave the Organ Procurement and Transplantation Network itself compulsory power to regulate many aspects of transplantation practice across the United States.

The United Network for Organ Sharing (UNOS) received the federal contract to operate the OPTN in 1986, and it has held that role ever since.[82] In 1988, Congress formally confirmed the OPTN's power to set allocation policy, requiring it by statute to "establish . . . *medical criteria for allocating organs*, and provide to members of the public an opportunity to comment on such criteria."[83]

It's worth pausing to wonder whether allocation criteria for organs—which inevitably incorporate a range of medical, logistical, and moral considerations—can fairly be summarized as "medical." It may be that the temptation to describe the overall system as a medical one stems from a desire to emphasize its objective, scientific aspects rather than the value judgments it will also, inevitably, contain.

UNOS deadlocked for years over how much weight to give tissue typing. By October 1987, UNOS had decided to follow the path preferred by Starzl, and in fact adopted wholesale the allocation algorithm he used locally in Pittsburgh, which was the first multifactorial point system that credited patients for waiting time, antigen matching, and medical urgency, among other factors.[84] However, in February 1989, UNOS reversed itself and switched to the more antigen-focused approach favored by Dr. Paul Terasaki, a professor of surgery at UCLA.[85] Antigen matching was based on testing both organs and recipients for six different types of antigens, leaving a range of outcomes between a (best-case) zero-antigen mismatch and (worst-case) six-antigen mismatch.

Starzl and his colleagues complained after this change that "a small group of determined lobbyists" were creating "a presumption that typing counts, despite mixed evidence."[86] Starzl and his colleagues argued that

> typing itself, while perpetuating the dreams and ambitions of a few hundred thousand typers or transplant surgeons and physicians, will become an instrument of social injustice to the extent that the distribution patterns are distorted. The first question to be asked is if ethnic minorities, specifically blacks, will be placed at a disadvantage by the new emphasis on matching.[87]

After the 1989 changes, popular press accounts highlighted the disadvantages that tissue typing created for nonwhite kidney patients. For instance, one *Wall Street Journal* account described how "a growing number of scientists believe that tissue-typing has proved to be medically insignificant in most cases, as well as racially discriminatory."[88] Scholars, likewise, explored the issue. One debate was about how much additional survival could be gained if *all* kidneys were sent to the "best" matching recipient or group of recipients; in 1991, Terasaki and his colleagues made the eye-catching claim that a national system based on HLA matching would "improve long-term results to the same extent as cyclosporine" and urged its adoption.[89] Others claimed such a system would improve outcomes only marginally.

The inspector general of the U.S. Department of Health and Human Services (HHS) reported in 1991 that "blacks on kidney waiting lists wait almost twice as long as whites for a first transplant. . . . Such a differential remains even when blood type, age, immunological, and locational factors are taken into account." Relatedly (prefiguring another of the fundamental fault lines in kidney allocation), the OIG report found that "patients at some transplant centers wait much longer than those of others," with then-typical waiting times at particular hospitals ranging from less than six months to more than eighteen months.[90]

The debate over how heavily to weight these lab tests in making allocation decisions was also, indirectly, an argument about geography. Better antigen matches are more common over larger populations of kidneys and recipients. Those who believe the impact of antigen matching to be relatively important therefore tend to favor sending organs longer distances so they can be shared with more compatible (but distant) patients. Those in sympathy with Starzl's view, on the other hand, object to geographic redistribution, especially since (as the task force itself had noted), nonwhite recipients are disproportionately unlikely to find themselves well matched to a distant organ.

Sending kidneys longer distances, so they can be given to people with closely matched antigens, also requires those organs to spend a longer period outside the human body—medically termed "cold ischemic time"—during which their quality deteriorates. "Patients who receive an organ [that has spent] more than 36 hours" outside of the donor's body "may not benefit from HLA matching."[91] Additional concerns with broader sharing included its expense: organs must move quickly and can require dedicated air travel when the distance from donor hospital to recipient hospital is more than a few hundred miles.

Meanwhile, prior to the advent of UNOS, a patchwork of local territories had emerged around major transplant centers. These were effectively catchment areas within which, if an organ became available, that center would do the removal surgery. In the rules that emerged, there was a strong preference for keeping organs local unless the match with a distant recipient was exceptionally good. But the results were sometimes arbitrary, since the rules applied by zone to the arbitrary zones—known as Donation Service Areas (DSAs)—that had existed before the national regime began. So it would sometimes happen that an organ went to a relatively distant recipient who happened to be in the same zone instead of a relatively nearby recipient who happened to be separated from the organ by a district boundary.

TISSUE TYPING FADES, WAITING TIME BECOMES DOMINANT

During the 1990s, as immunosuppressive regimens continued to improve, critics of antigen matching gained force. As one influential group of critics wrote, although zero-mismatched transplants did last longer than other transplants, the evidence for a meaningful survival difference was much weaker when it came to intermediate degrees of antigen compatibility.[92] One review found that over the period 1994 to 1998, "with each successive year, ever-increasing degrees of HLA mismatching were required to have a statistically significant adverse impact" on transplant outcomes.[93] (However, while this may be the case for transplant recipients as a whole, mismatches have a greater impact among highly sensitized patients.)

As one influential critique in 1993 argued, "technological advances have made antigen-based allocation less critical to transplant success." Normatively, then, "the equitable claims of black dialysis patients for cadaveric kidneys outweigh the marginal improvement in transplant outcomes currently associated with matching."[94]

Persuaded over time by arguments like these, the UNOS advisory committees and governing board made a series of changes throughout the

1990s that reduced the role of antigen matching in the kidney allocation algorithm and left the system more focused on waiting time.[95]

A technical issue with the data may be one significant contributor to the controversy over antigen matching. Dr. Klintmalm told me that although modern immunosuppressive therapies are indeed powerful, and outcomes are favorable even with mismatches for the first few years after transplant, latent conflicts between a patient's immune system and a donated organ tend to surface after a few years.[96] That is, for the first few years, mismatching makes little if any difference, but at the five-year mark or the ten-year mark, differences are more pronounced.[97]

Arguments over the clinical significance of tissue typing continue to this day. As a current reference source for practicing physicians summarizes the literature: "The weight of overall evidence suggests that HLA matching still has a significant impact on allograft survival. The main effect can be observed between a zero antigen mismatch versus a six antigen mismatch." However, "some studies have challenged the importance" of such matching overall.[98]

A COLLABORATIVE PROCESS WITH MESSY RESULTS

The OPTN, as it had developed by 2003, was a collaborative organization characterized by "transparency, consultation and voting."[99] Today multiple committees, organized both by organ system and for cross-cutting purposes such as the representation of general and minority patient interests, discuss rule changes in meetings open to the public. The committee chairs routinely participate in the meetings of related committees. Proposals originating in committees receive comment from all other committees, and public comments are also solicited. Proposals for major rule changes are often presented in public forums to inform stakeholders not directly involved in governance and to obtain feedback from them. Although the process seeks consensus, proposals are adopted based on majority-rule voting by the OPTN board of directors, a feature that allows at least incremental change, despite the challenge that most changes in allocation rules create losers as well as winners.[100]

Relatedly, this policymaking process has a robust infrastructure both for monitoring outcomes and for simulating the potential results of alternative policies. Such efforts are led by the Scientific Registry of Transplant Recipients (SRTR), which, among other functions, provides simulations to UNOS committees that attempt to model the likely impacts of proposed policy changes.[101]

James Alcorn, the current policy director at UNOS, explained to me that simulation plays a vital role in committee debates. SRTR maintains models that simulate the consequences of differing allocation choices and can simulate policies as the committee requests. "They will typically actually simulate multiple options because the committee usually debate between several options. So they have a pretty good track record. It . . . gives a pretty good sense of what the overall direction of this policy is going to be before we actually implement it."[102] The SRTR's formal replies to the committee— reports of simulation results—themselves become public documents.

LASTING DEBATES

In 2003, a ten-year process to redevelop the Kidney Allocation System began. Several long-standing controversies in kidney allocation helped form the backdrop for debates over a new allocation system.

Race and Access

As described above, antigen matching was controversial not only because of debates over its medical significance, but also because emphasizing such matches in the allocation formula tended to disadvantage black transplant recipients. Changes in 1994 and again in 2002 reduced the role of antigen matching and narrowed the racial gaps between white and black patients.[103] These changes were motivated both by the racial equity concerns and by clinical evidence that "the largest gains in graft success from genetic similarity" were in cases of zero-mismatched HLA. "The new allocation rules give preference primarily to no mismatches rather than to partial matches."[104]

Transplants generally need to be matched based on blood type in order to be successful; if blood types are not matched, the recipient's immune system will attack cells from the donor organ. The same compatibilities are required as in blood transfusions, with type O as the universal donor and type AB as the universal recipient. This presented a somewhat parallel problem to tissue typing: types A and O are most common in the U.S. population, but nonwhite kidney patients were more likely to be blood type B, so there was a disproportionate demand and longer wait in this group.[105] "Historically, blood group B candidates awaiting deceased-donor transplantation, the majority of whom are African American and Hispanic patients, are less likely to be transplanted than candidates of any other blood group."[106]

However, pioneering treatments in the 1990s, first developed in Japan, "[overcame] the ABO antibody barrier" and allowed surgeons to perform transplants across conflicting blood types.[107] This increased the likelihood that, where a kidney patient had a living donor willing to donate, transplant between the two would be medically feasible. It also raised the question of whether the deceased-donor allocation algorithm should ever allow for transplants across conflicting blood groups. Lab tests have found that blood types A2 and A2B provoke less of an immune response in blood type B recipients than those of the A1 type.[108] Experiments in Minnesota had established that transplants from blood type A2 and A2B donors to blood type B recipients, although not fully compatible, have particularly favorable results.[109]

The OPTN Minority Affairs Committee sought between 1994 and 2001 to explore whether such transplants could be allowed in the deceased-donor algorithm, thus reducing the access gap for minority patients, who were disproportionately from blood group B.[110] In 2002 a "national variance" to the kidney allocation algorithm was introduced, and a select group of blood type B patients from across the country were provided with deceased-donor transplants of A2 and A2B kidneys.[111]

A related debate, which became a focus of committee activity in 2002 and 2003, concerned how patients got onto the waiting list in the first place. The Institute of Medicine found in 1999 that "much of the [racial] disparity appears to be due to the fact that African Americans are not placed on waiting lists as quickly, or in the same proportion, as their white counterparts."[112] As described above, a landmark 1998 study had found that earlier steps in the process—such as learning about transplantation, choosing to seek a transplant, and getting the preliminary workup necessary to join the list—were a more important source of racial disparity than the algorithm itself. Moreover, black patients who did join the transplant list tended to do so later in the course of their disease, often after they had been on dialysis for several years, relative to white patients, who statistically tended to have better access to medical care and could be listed as soon as—or in some cases shortly before—they began to need dialysis. Thus, not only were white patients more likely to be well informed about transplant, but they also accumulated more waiting time relative to black patients who were later arrivals on the transplant list. As a way to correct for this disparity, it was proposed in 2002 that waiting time be calculated from the time a patient either joined the list or began dialysis, whichever was earlier. This proposal could not get consensus in the kidney transplant committee, however, and was not acted upon.

Efficiency

One prominent critique of the pre-2004 system was that it was failing to "make the most" of available organs. For instance, the algorithm might allocate a kidney with a long usable life to an elderly transplant recipient, while sending an older and likely shorter-lived kidney to a young and healthy transplant recipient. In such cases, the older recipient might die with a still-healthy kidney inside him, while the younger one might outlive the older kidney and become a candidate for retransplant. Whenever that happened, opportunities for transplant success—years of life and health— were wasted.[113] This old regime was also criticized on several grounds for its racial equity impacts.

Second Chances

A related long-standing problem was the issue of "highly sensitized" patients. Sensitization occurs when, even before receiving a transplanted kidney, a patient's immune system has *already* produced antibodies to target a particular foreign antigen that can be found on some kidneys. This commonly occurs among women who have had several pregnancies, people who have received multiple blood transfusions, and transplant patients who have had a previous transplant that failed.[114]

Patients are deemed *highly* sensitized when they have pre-formed antibodies in their blood that react against a large fraction of the blood samples in a representative panel of potential donors. This degree of sensitization is reflected in a score known as the cPRA—that is, the calculated panel reactive antibody score. There are complex issues in how PRA scores are defined, including debates over the extent to which the panel of blood samples used in the test actually reflects the pool of potential donors in a given area.[115]

Throughout the 1990s, there was debate about the extent to which highly sensitized patients should be favored (if at all) in allocation. An "allocative preference for presensitized candidates . . . has the perverse effect of rewarding candidates who often already had the opportunity for transplantation."[116]

On the eve of the debate over the Kidney Allocation System, the system assigned four points (the equivalent of credit for four years of waiting time) to patients whose overall level of sensitization was greater than 80 percent— that is, those whose blood was calculated to be likely to react against 80 percent or more of the samples in the panel.

The Geography Battle

In the mid-1990s, at President Bill Clinton's urging, the Department of Health and Human Services sought to remake the geography of organ allocation. Rules that favored giving locally gathered organs to relatively nearby patients were, at the time, part of the system for all organs.

Geography can make a practical and medically significant difference: each type of organ can tolerate only so much cold ischemic time, and even when that period is kept within maximum limits, longer cold ischemic times may be associated with worse transplant outcomes. Moreover, the cost and logistical complexity of using charter flights to rush organs across the country are formidable, and sometimes even a special flight may not be fast enough to get the organ from its place of donation to a nationally distant recipient in a satisfactory time.

What was harder to defend, and more politically ticklish, was the practice of using arbitrary geographic boundaries—Donation Service Areas (DSAs) and groups of such areas—to distribute organs. As we explored above, the service areas had grown up around pioneering transplant centers before national sharing had developed and had effectively become catchment areas for organs. And each DSA had its own separate nonprofit responsible for collecting the donated organs—a group called the Organ Procurement Organization, or OPO. There were fifty-eight of them nationally, each with its own CEO. And they did not want to lose control over the organs in their territories.

In 2003, after a long debate replete with litigation and congressional intervention, a rule took effect that was known to all in transplant as the "Final Rule." It requires the OPTN to develop "policies for the equitable allocation of cadaveric organs among potential recipients."[117] Such policies must be "expressed, to the extent possible, through objective and measurable medical criteria."[118] They must also satisfy four substantive constraints, including that they are not "based on a candidate's place of residence or place of listing, except to the extent required" to achieve the rule's other stated goals.[119]

Introductory remarks that were included with the Final Rule shed further light on this last point:

> While present OPTN policies give weight to medical need, the "local first" practice thwarts organ allocation over a broad area and thus prevents medical need from being the dominant factor in allocation decisions. Under the provisions of this rule, it is intended that the area where a person lives or the transplant center where he or she is listed will not be primary factors in how quickly he or she receives a transplant. Instead, organs will be allocated according to objective standards of medical status and need. In this way, suitable organs will reach patients with the greatest medical need, both when they are procured locally and when they are procured outside the listed patients' areas. This objective reflects the views of many commenters on the proposed regulations, as well as the finding of the American Medical Association in its Code of Medical Ethics: "Organs should be considered a

national, rather than a local or regional resource. Geographical priorities in the allocation of organs should be prohibited except when transportation of organs would threaten their suitability for transplantation."[120]

The Final Rule also codified procedural requirements, directing the OPTN board to "provide opportunity for the OPTN membership and other interested parties to comment on proposed policies" and to "take into account the comments received."[121]

The Final Rule required the OPTN to "conduct an initial review of existing allocation policies" and, within a year of the rule's effective date, to transmit to HHS a revised allocation policy for each organ that would meet the newly established allocation requirements of the Final Rule.[122]

But by 2004 the OPTN was four years late in updating its kidney allocation policy to comply with the Final Rule. That was the immediate stimulus for the rewrite described in the next chapter.

Chapter 4 | An Algorithm in Focus: The Kidney Allocation System

By 2004, THE national kidney allocation algorithm had "become a collage of priorities."[1] It had also acquired the intricacy of a Rube Goldberg machine. Figure 4.1, for instance, shows one-quarter of the algorithm as it existed in 2014. This part, known as "Sequence A," was just for matching people to donors who were age thirty-five or younger.

The system operated nationwide, and it was triggered every time an "undirected" kidney donation became available, typically from a deceased donor. It would conduct a "match run" to make a prioritized list of potential recipients. The first step was to classify the donated kidney itself into one of four mutually exclusive categories called "sequences." Each sequence, in turn, consisted of a long series of patient selection rules, called "classifications" (represented by the boxes at the bottom of figure 4.1). The algorithm worked its way down the list of classifications.[2] The search continued until the algorithm found a classification that included at least one candidate. Then the system either listed that candidate first or, if there were multiple candidates within the same classification, used a system of points (based largely on waiting time) to prioritize candidates within the classification. The process was then repeated to find a second-ranked candidate, and so on, until a list of matching candidates had been assembled. Then, UNOS's operations center would reach out to the potential recipients' surgical teams until, ideally, someone accepted the organ and the dance of transplant could begin.

To what extent should patients who will benefit more from a transplant be favored over those who will benefit less? That was to become a central question in the decade-long redesign of this system. As this debate unfolded, "benefit" usually meant time added to someone's life span. "Utility" became shorthand for the total life-years gained from the pool of organs, and "equity" meant giving an equal chance to all in need. Many

Figure 4.1. OPTN's Allocation Algorithm for Kidney Transplants for Standard Criteria Donors Age Thirty-Five or Younger (Sequence A), c. 2014

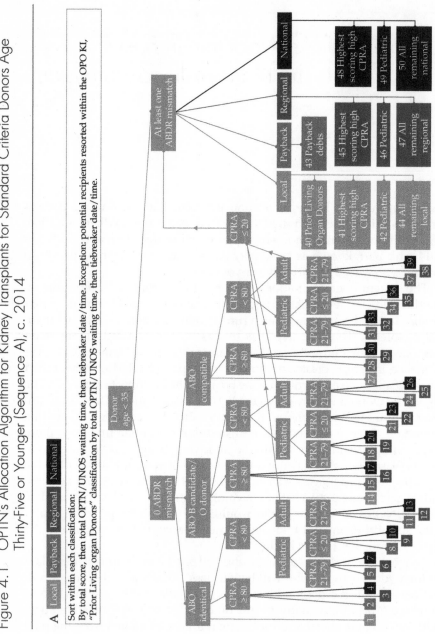

Sort within each classification:
By total score, then total OPTN/UNOS waiting time, then tiebreaker date/time. Exception: potential recipients resorted within the OPO KI, "Prior Living organ Donors" classification by total OPTN/UNOS waiting time, then tiebreaker date/time.

other questions were also explored, including racial equity and access for patients with highly sensitized immune systems. One of the most important moral challenges in the allocation of transplantable kidneys, the question of how geographic boundaries influence allocation, received scarcely any attention.

The review began in 2004, when the OPTN launched the Kidney Allocation Review Subcommittee (KARS), a subgroup of the existing OPTN committee on kidney transplantation.[3] Over the course of 2004 and 2005, this group conducted a "360°" review of kidney allocation policy.[4] The review included a series of twelve public hearings—some on patient perspectives generally, some on minority concerns in particular—as well as specific medical and operational issues.[5] Through those hearings, the working group found "that the current system may not be consistent with the Final Rule," in part because it "does not seek to achieve the best use of donated organs . . . and does not minimize organ wastage."[6]

TO SAVE THE MOST LIFE, 2004–2009

As it worked through these hearings, the subcommittee began to focus on the idea of moving away from waiting time by incorporating into the system a "net-benefit" model,[7] which would seek to rank transplant candidates based largely on how many years of life each candidate was forecast to gain from receiving a transplant.[8] This would do more to "achieve the best use of donated organs," as required by the Final Rule, than did the then-established system that focused largely on waiting time.

The subcommittee debated how to describe and justify this approach, and the members "wrestled with acronyms" that could be used to describe it, considering options that were "either too long (such as quality adjusted net lifetime survival benefit [QENSLB]), or too vague and value laden (such as transplant benefit)." Finally, the committee settled on the felicitous term Life Years From Transplant (LYFT).[9]

The subcommittee worked with the Scientific Registry of Transplant Recipients (SRTR) to quantify LYFT and then to "[create] a model to simulate what impact using LYFT would have on the allocation system."[10] In 2006, following two years of debate and development, the OPTN board provisionally endorsed the LYFT approach, charging the subcommittee to consider "net survival benefit with modifiers to balance justice and utility."[11]

A Rocky Rollout in Dallas, 2007

On February 8, 2007, the Kidney Allocation Review Subcommittee held a public forum in Dallas, Texas, to describe the allocation approach it was considering and to gather "initial public feedback including . . . public testimony and participant interaction with the committee."[12] More than four hundred people attended.[13] The full-day agenda included an overview of the allocation review to that point; a summary of findings from the earlier hearings; a detailed presentation from SRTR about how LYFT was defined and calculated; a second presentation describing simulations the SRTR had made of the impact of the new policy, and what it had found; testimony from seven public commenters; and table-by-table discussion and feedback from the assembled in-person participants.[14]

As of the Dallas Forum, the committee was planning to propose that LYFT be used as an important ingredient in the overall algorithm for allocating kidneys. But the subcommittee had not yet issued a full proposal for a complete, operational version of a new allocation algorithm. In other words, LYFT was effectively designed to become an algorithm-within-an-algorithm: a calculated measure of a patient's potential to benefit from a particular kidney if transplanted, which would in turn be used as an input to the matching procedure that allocates kidneys.

In a presentation explaining how LYFT was defined and calculated, an SRTR scientist explained that the formula considered more than a dozen factors about the candidate and the particular kidney available for transplant, including: the candidate's age, body mass index, time living with kidney failure, and diabetic status; the donor's age, cause of death, and weight; and the number of HLA mismatches between the donor's kidney and the prospective recipient.[15] These metrics (though not others that might have been useful for such an estimate) were available both for the patient-donor pairing whose LYFT score was being calculated and for a panel of more than 100,000 earlier patients who had spent time on dialysis and some of whom had received transplants. This earlier SRTR data included whether each of those earlier patients was still living at the end of 2006 or, if not, when they had died.[16] Using these data as training data and the duration of survival as its primary outcome of interest, SRTR could model the patient's likely survival on the waiting list and the likely number of years of post-transplant survival for any given patient-kidney pairing if the patient were to receive that kidney (including survival after the possible transplant's eventual failure).

These component models of survival-with-this-kidney and survival-on-dialysis were effectively three layers down: they were algorithmic estimates of survival that would be used as inputs in order to estimate LYFT, and then the LYFT estimate would itself be used as an input into the algorithm that would match organs with patients. Yet even these models were far from straightforward measurements. For instance, some younger and healthier transplant candidates also had a good prognosis on dialysis, so that their expected life-years *gained* by receiving a transplant only arrived long after transplantation, in the period fifteen to twenty-five years after their possible transplant.[17] (Other candidates are unlikely to live long on dialysis, and so they gain life-years in the period immediately following transplant.) In addition, different factors predicted graft failures that happen in the first few years after transplant, versus failures taking place in later years. SRTR scientists, in consultation with the Kidney Allocation Review Subcommittee, considered several modeling strategies and ultimately chose to use separate models to predict the first few years of post-transplant survival and survival during later years.[18]

Besides these models, LYFT held another important moral trade-off that could easily be left out of a casual summary of the metric: the subcommittee had "quality-adjusted" the years of life involved, so that living for 0.8 years (just under ten months) with the freedom of a working kidney held the same value as a full year of life on dialysis.[19] The subcommittee had reached this number "based on a synthesis of assessments in the published literature" about quality-adjusting life-years.[20] This meant that the formula for LYFT was

$$
LYFT = \left(\begin{array}{c} \textit{expected years of} \\ \textit{survival if transplanted} \end{array} + 0.8 * \begin{array}{c} \textit{expected survival} \\ \textit{on dialysis after} \\ \textit{transplant fails} \end{array} \right) - \left(0.8 * \begin{array}{c} \textit{expected years} \\ \textit{survival on dialysis} \\ \textit{without a transplant} \end{array} \right)
$$

In practice, the quality adjustment made transplants more likely for those patients who were expected to live a relatively long time on dialysis if not transplanted and thus mitigated the overall formula's focus on utility (that is, on maximizing actual years of life saved). Without the quality adjustment, each year of predicted survival on dialysis would remove a full point from a candidate's LYFT score. But with the adjustment, each year of predicted survival on dialysis removed only 0.8 years from the candidate's LYFT score. In effect, the formula credited candidates with 0.2 "life-years from transplant" for each year in which they were predicted to survive regardless of whether they were transplanted. By the same token, the adjustment was adverse to the interests of patients with a worse prognosis on dialysis, because it reduced the extent to which their scores would exceed those of other candidates.[21]

An SRTR scientist told those gathered in Dallas that its simulation had found LYFT would "have little effect on the racial and blood type distribution of recipients," but that it would shift transplants away from diabetics and highly sensitized candidates and toward "younger recipients."[22]

SRTR projected that incorporating LYFT into the allocation regime would increase the annual nationwide total benefit of kidney transplantation by more than ten thousand life-years.[23]

A passing remark in a summary of this presentation notes that, "additionally, wider geographic sharing would increase life years gained from transplantation (though this concept is not currently under consideration)."[24] Similarly, a summary of feedback provided by attendees noted that "even though geography is not being considered during the development of this policy, some [attendees] recommended that [Donation Service Area] boundaries should be reviewed to determine if there are opportunities to reduce disparities in transplant access due to geography."[25] That unresolved question would eventually come to haunt the entire process.

Clive Grawe, as we saw in the interlude before chapter 2, pointed out that age-based criteria could have counterproductive effects, especially if they came with potentially arbitrary bright lines.[26] As he explained in slides during a five-minute presentation, "getting a transplant is something I prepared for by taking care of my health for 50+ years[.] To not get one now is demoralizing and seems unfair."[27] Even though LYFT itself did not incorporate any bright lines based on age, it *did* risk disfavoring patients who, through careful management of lifelong kidney illness, had managed to stave off their need for a transplant until their remaining years of life were relatively few.

A Need to Protect the Old

Doug Penrod, a transplant nurse with thirty years' experience, is currently a transplant coordinator at Northwestern University's medical center in Chicago. He donated one his own kidneys—it was first going to go to a friend and then, when that plan fell through, he became one of the handful of people each year who give a living, undirected donation. He has also long been involved in transplant policy discussions both as a professional and as a living donor. He was present at the Dallas Forum and described the scene to me:

> Well, everybody went, "Yay, hooray, oh God, that's unbelievable" . . . then [SRTR] also showed the unintended consequences of if this system was adopted, and that's what nailed them to the cross. But give them props for actually showing all of this, you know. They did the whole presentation in the morning, and then we broke up into work groups to look at and then make comments in the afternoon. And I was the spokesman for our table. . . . The first thing we came out with was how discriminatory it was towards seniors.[28]

This concern about possible ageism in any LYFT-based allocation approach was ultimately central to the allocation debate. But most sources from the period appear to reflect an upbeat expectation that a new kidney allocation algorithm would soon be proposed and would soon thereafter be adopted. As the *American Journal of Transplantation* reported in January 2008 — eleven months after the Dallas Forum — "as the lengthy, consensus-driven approach continues, there's hope that the [OPTN] board will announce a new policy in June."[29]

After Dallas, the full Kidney Transplantation Committee (KTC) had months of further debates about the fairness of LYFT, and ultimately, in December 2007, it submitted a query to the HHS Office for Civil Rights, asking "whether or not the use of age in the LYFT calculation was discriminatory."[30]

Months passed, and by September 2008, the committee had waited nearly a year for a reply as it continued to develop the proposal. Members were "eager to release [their] proposal for public comment [and] concerned about the lack of communication with the transplant community. . . . Thus, the KTC decided to issue a Request for Information (RFI) to the public" about LYFT, even though it had not yet received a response about whether LYFT would be legal.[31]

LYFT Proposed and Rejected, 2008

Nineteen months after the Dallas Forum, on September 24, 2008, the Kidney Transplantation Committee published its first proposal.[32] Within the local geographic area where each organ was gathered, the committee proposed using a combination of LYFT and accumulated waiting time as the main factors in allocating kidneys.[33]

The proposal also introduced a new metric, the Donor Profile Index (DPI), which was a "continuous measure of organ quality."[34] The DPI was a number between zero and one, where "the [kidneys] with the longest survival potential are assigned a DPI score of zero," and those "with the shortest survival potential are assigned a DPI score of one."[35] In other words, the DPI was a numeric expression of the fraction of kidneys that were *higher*-quality than the one being scored — a low score meant a high-quality kidney. As a later paper from SRTR elaborated:

> The committee offered a mathematical formula for how these factors could be combined into a single Kidney Allocation Score, which could be used to prioritize among eligible candidates in the relevant geography:[36]

$$KAS = \underbrace{\left(LYFT * 0.8 * \left(1 - DPI\right)\right)}_{\substack{\text{Points for LYFT increase} \\ \text{when matching high quality} \\ \text{kidneys} \left(DPI \text{ near zero}\right).}} + \underbrace{\left(DT * \left(0.2 + \left(0.8 * DPI\right)\right)\right)}_{\substack{\text{Points for dialysis time increase} \\ \text{when matching low quality} \\ \text{kidneys} \left(DPI \text{ near one}\right).}} + \underbrace{\left(\dfrac{CPRA * 4}{100}\right)}_{\substack{\text{This term adds points for} \\ \text{highly sensitized patients.}}}$$

Under this proposed formula, LYFT would matter more when the kidneys being matched were of higher quality. By contrast, waiting time, while always making some contribution to the score, would add more points when the kidney being matched was of relatively lower quality.[37]

By more heavily prioritizing patients who were forecasted to gain the most years of life from a transplant, this approach promised to offer thousands of years of added life. Proposed in September 2008 following a three-year review, the request for information (RFI) proved immediately controversial. On January 26, 2009, just after the comment period had closed on the LYFT proposal, OPTN's Kidney Transplantation Committee held a second large public meeting—this one in St. Louis—focused on the controversy over LYFT.[38] Like the earlier Dallas gathering, this one brought more than two hundred people together for a day of discussions.

Both the written comments filed in reply to the RFI and the feedback received at the St. Louis meeting were strongly critical of the LYFT proposal. In June 2009—six months after collecting both types of feedback—the Kidney Transplantation Committee reported its frustratingly limited progress to the UNOS board.[39]

The Health Resources and Services Administration (HRSA), the federal agency supervising the OPTN, had not yet answered the committee's question, first posed eighteen months earlier, about whether a LYFT-based allocation algorithm would be allowable under the Age Discrimination Act. The committee reported that it had been told by an HRSA official that the HHS Office for Civil Rights "will not be able to deliver a pronouncement on the use of age in an allocation system" and "would not put itself into the position of approving a policy."[40] The office did provide some advice—namely, that it would be best to avoid the use of age if possible. At the same time, the HRSA official indicated that it *might* use a federal register notice in which "age would be declared as an appropriate factor" to use in allocation under the Final Rule.[41] This was a confusing situation for the committee—the propriety of LYFT, and of its age-reliant substitutes, remained in doubt.[42]

Commenters, including doctors, medical experts, patients, and advocates, were also concerned that both "professionals and patients were not able to understand the LYFT calculation,"[43] LYFT relied on subsidiary models of longevity that were difficult even for professionals in the transplant field, let alone patients, to evaluate.

For instance, experts vehemently disagreed about whether the predictive performance of LYFT's component models was satisfactory. The component models were judged partly by their c-statistic, which measured how often, between a pair of randomly chosen transplant candidates, the model gave a better score to the patient who would actually experience a better outcome. The model for post-transplant survival had a c-statistic of 0.68, meaning that the model would errantly predict a shorter survival time for the longer-lived patient about 30 percent of the time.[44] One critic, writing in the *American Journal of Transplantation*, argued that "the transplant community [was] being asked to invest substantial moral confidence" in a metric whose "predictive accuracy . . . [was only] slightly better than chance."[45] However, the designers of the model pointed out that most of the model's mistakes involved pairs of patients who were very similar. The models were "progressively more successful at predicting which of the two patients will live longer as their medical characteristics diverge."[46] Thus, the designers implied, LYFT could safely be used to avoid extreme mismatches, such as when a very short-lived kidney was given to a very long-lived patient, or vice versa.

Dr. John Friedewald, a member of the Kidney Transplantation Committee at that time, explained:

> Public feedback told us that the predictive equations were too complicated and [the public] didn't understand them. And they wanted simple equations. Well, simple equations don't work as well as complex equations in some cases, and so we weren't able to predict longevity as well, and so therefore, we couldn't justify allocating all the organs based on longevity because we weren't using a good predictive model because we were told we couldn't . . . and that gets to the point I think you're looking at . . . that public opinion mattered here, and UNOS has clear marching orders about public comment and how we have to be responsive to public comment. . . . I told everybody, "I don't know how my satellite radio works exactly, but I really like my satellite radio and I'm not going to throw it out just because I don't understand it," but patients very clearly said that it is too complicated, too confusing, "I don't, I don't trust it." Okay, we'll go back to, you know, the Flintstones car with no air conditioning and no satellite radio, but it's simple.[47]

Dr. Mark Stegall, a transplant surgeon and by then a former chairman of the Kidney Allocation Review subcommittee, described latent enthusiasm for the too-complex proposal: "A lot of people came up to me later, and still do today, saying, 'I kind of like LYFT, it was much better than this post-transplant survival thing' [which ultimately replaced it]. But the reason we abandoned it is because there was too much pushback because of its complexity."[48]

HRSA, however, "made arrangements for an independent consultant to assess stakeholder views on kidney allocation."[49] The consultant spoke with forty-five people, including committee members, stakeholder groups such as patient advocates, and UNOS and HRSA staff. Her findings paralleled the personal observations of Dr. Peter Stock, who was then leading the review: although LYFT was controversial, the two other components of the initial proposal—rating all kidneys based on quality for allocation purposes and using the start of dialysis as the initiation date for accumulated waiting time—were relatively widely accepted.[50]

In place of LYFT, some stakeholders had proposed simple heuristics using age. For instance, some suggested an approach "that would allocate organs from donors younger than 35 to candidates younger than 35," with the remainder of organs allocated to all eligible patients based on dialysis time.[51] Others proposed that the system "require that the donor and recipient be within 10 years of age of one another."[52]

The committee told the board that it was responding to the criticism and was planning to replace LYFT with "post-transplant survival," a much simpler calculation that would not try to account for performance on dialysis. The committee's overall goal would be preventing "the shortest lived 20% of kidneys . . . from going to the longest-lived 20% of candidates,"[53] an approach that also reflected an understanding of the statistical models by using them at their relatively more robust extremes, rather than in comparing very similar candidates or organs.

At the same time as they pressed ahead, key actors in the kidney allocation review also publicly shared their frustration and acknowledged the need for further efforts beyond what they could achieve. For instance, Dr. Peter Stock, who chaired the KTC between 2007 and 2009, wrote in a journal article that, while the contemplated allocation changes would not directly address geographic disparities in transplant access, the planned elimination of most local variances as part of the new system would make geographic disparities easier to diagnose and measure. "Any solutions that address the extreme geographic variations in kidney transplant rates will require a single national system."[54] He also wrote, with palpable frustration, of the need for "important strategies unrelated to a new allocation algorithm," such as changing Medicare's payment policy of cutting off reimbursements for immunosuppressive drugs three years after a transplant. "It makes little sense to discontinue payment for immunosuppression. . . . Many patients [have] stopped immunosuppression as a result of lack of funds." Such an outcome loses viable kidneys, puts patients back on costlier dialysis, and ultimately increases the size of "already bloated" waiting lists.[55]

LYFT by Another Name?

Modifying the allocation algorithm is the most obvious policy lever for reallocating kidneys. But it is not the only lever. Another route is to change the *scope* of the algorithm and allocate some organs using a different rule.

Among the patients who would have benefited the most from the LYFT proposal were young type I diabetics. These patients tend to have little accumulated waiting time, and they generally fare worse than other kidney patients do on dialysis, so that they gain more longevity from a transplant than other patients might. Diabetic patients usually need a pancreas transplant as well as a new kidney. Pancreas transplants are relatively rare: 837 were performed nationally in 2008, compared with more than 16,500 kidney-alone transplants that year.[56] There is no shortage of cadaver donors for the pancreas, and treating diabetes is the only reason for a pancreas transplant. For technical reasons, deceased donors who provide a pancreas usually also provide two excellent kidneys.[57]

As of the Dallas Forum, the tentative plan for the new algorithm was to allocate kidneys for kidney-alone transplants and for joint kidney-pancreas transplants from a single combined list—in other words, kidney-pancreas transplants would be possible when a kidney became available through the LYFT formula.[58]

But by the time the LYFT proposal was released in 2008, kidney-pancreas allocation had been split off into a separate policy project, and the decision had been tentatively made that when a pancreas was obtained from a deceased donor, one of that donor's kidneys would automatically "follow" the pancreas—that is, be offered along with the pancreas—to a waiting diabetic patient.[59] Thus, eligible kidney-pancreas candidates might be transplanted very rapidly, even more quickly than they would under the LYFT proposal. With this approach, a substantial part of the benefit from a LYFT-based kidney allocation system would be achieved through kidney-pancreas allocation, even if LYFT were ultimately rejected for kidneys (as in fact it was). Once proposed, that approach survived subsequent debate and became a part of the new allocation system.[60]

Mark Stegall, who chaired the Kidney Allocation Review Subcommittee during the debate over the LYFT proposal, explained:

STEGALL: [In] certain patients, transplant really increased people's longevity. It turned out most of those patients were diabetic, young, type 1 diabetics. And most of those patients actually are listed for kidney and a pancreas transplant, so the simplest way [to] work around this—and this became a lot of how ... the ethical things get put into policy—[is] we find other almost work-arounds... that fit into an algorithm that achieves pretty much the same thing, but it seems to be simpler for people to understand. And so those patients were given high allocation priority for the combined kidney and pancreas transplant, and most of those patients therefore got a significant allocation priority and were transplanted faster. Because their wait-list mortality was high.

AUTHOR: And so, because it was split up in this way, you were able to achieve a lot of the benefit that would have happened if the original LYFT proposal had been implemented?

STEGALL: Right.... It's about a thousand patients a year [who] get that type of transplant.... We were really trying to do something for these folks.... They have a wait-list mortality—their five-year survival on dialysis is about 20 percent. [Compared with an overall five-year survival rate of 35 percent, nearly twice as high.] They get such a differential benefit from transplant. So the deal now is . . . the kidney follows the pancreas. It's a little bit confusing, but the way the math works out is that if you are on the kidney-pancreas list, you get transplanted sooner.

Dr. John Friedewald, who presided over later stages of the development of the Kidney Allocation System, concurred in this assessment, telling me: "diabetic patients do very poorly on dialysis, and so they get a larger net benefit from a transplant, and so they were going to be prioritized.... There were tens of thousands of diabetic patients waiting for a transplant."[61]

FINDING COMPROMISE, 2009–2014

The 20/80 Proposal

Two more years of debate and simulation brought the process up to February 2011 and led the OPTN Kidney Transplantation Committee to its second major idea, which became known as the 20/80 proposal. Like the 2008 LYFT proposal, the 2011 document was a conceptual outline of a new allocation regime, which broadly described an approach without completely specifying the algorithm.

This new one was much simpler. In the 2008 proposal, a single allocation logic—the Kidney Allocation Score—would have set priority among eligible candidates for all undirected kidneys. But that score depended on extensive, complex calculations about each organ and each recipient.

Now the committee changed tack and proposed dividing kidneys into two groups, using a different allocation logic for each group. The new proposal referred to these two logics as "survival matching" and "age matching."

Each kidney would first be classified based on its predicted longevity, with a 10-factor model of how long that kidney would survive inside an average transplant recipient.[62] This was an updated version of the original Donor Profile Index, now called KDPI and given as a score out of 100.[63] As before, lower scores were better, because the number reflected the percentage of all kidneys that were forecast to last *longer* than the one being scored.

Patients, meanwhile, would be assigned an estimated post-transplant survival (EPTS) score. EPTS was similar to LYFT in that it addressed candidates' longevity, but it used only four factors—candidate age, time on dialysis, whether the person had received a prior transplant, and diabetes status—in its formula.[64] Unlike LYFT, EPTS was not specific to a given organ-patient pairing. Instead, it simply described the health of the patient, and it made no effort to differentiate candidates based on how well they might tolerate dialysis if *not* transplanted.

The best available 20 percent of kidneys—that is, those with KDPI 20 or less—would be prioritized by what the proposal called "survival matching."[65] That is, they would "first be offered to local candidates who have at least the 20% longest estimated post-transplant survival before being offered to all other candidates."[66] This matched the predicted longevity of kidney and recipient.

The remaining 80 percent of available kidneys would instead be age-matched. That is, the kidney would be offered first to "candidates who are between 15 years older and 15 years younger than the donor[,] before being offered to all other candidates."[67]

The committee had worked through detailed simulations of this policy and various alternatives—a total of more than forty scenarios—and described several of these in detail in its proposal.[68] It also described some judgments that it had needed to make but that were not directly compelled by medical facts. For instance, the committee wrote, it had chosen to set the breakpoint between the two allocation rules at the twentieth percentile of patients and kidneys (rather than, say, the tenth or thirtieth percentile) because the top 20 percent of candidates had survival rates that were "most discernible from [those of] other candidates."[69] Similarly, the committee decided to age-match using a range of plus or minus fifteen years, rather than, say, ten or twenty years, because it felt that this range best "smoothed out" the distribution of organs available to candidates of all ages.[70]

The committee also explained that its proposed system would cause no "major shifts in race/ethnicity, blood group and degree of mismatch" through the introduction of survival and age matching—given that the baseline model already incorporated important equity-enhancing changes, such as credit for dialysis time.[71]

As with the LYFT proposal, the 20/80 proposal would have made its largest difference to the age distribution of recipients: "Candidates in the top 20% in terms of post-transplant survival tend to be younger" and are also more likely to age-match with deceased kidney donors, many of whom have died young.[72] The system also preserved existing priority for pediatric patients (under the age of eighteen) to receive kidneys from donors under thirty-five, apart from other rules.

Thus, the net effect of the 20/80 proposal would have been to shift some kidneys—and their associated medical benefits—away from recipients over the age of fifty and toward recipients between the ages of eighteen and forty-nine.[73] In the aggregate, the committee forecast that survival matching and age matching together would increase the annual total number of years gained through transplant by about five thousand—or approximately half as much as the original LYFT proposal,[74] while reducing the annual number of transplants to patients over fifty by about 20 percent.[75] After opening up feedback on its new proposal through April 2011, the committee braced for a public response.

As with LYFT before it, the 20/80 proposal would have elevated "utility" over "equity," in the sense that it would have shifted kidneys toward younger and healthier candidates. This remained a source of controversy.

Dr. Lainie Feldman Ross, a pediatrician and medical ethicist, was a prominent critic of the proposal. A report in the *New York Times* noted that the new proposal did "nothing to fix geographic disparities that cause patients in New York and Chicago to wait years longer than those in Florida," a drawback shared with its predecessor, and quoted Dr. Ross's view that "the biggest problem is geography, and they're doing nothing to fix that."[76] She also opined that the proposal amounted to "age discrimination."[77] Other ethics authorities disagreed and "strongly endorse[d]" the new proposal.[78]

Protecting the Old

Now, Jim Bowman, the medical director of HRSA's Division of Transplantation (and formerly an Air Force transplant surgeon himself), told the KTC that his office had "concerns" about the use of age matching.[79]

The Age Discrimination Act (ADA) directs that "no person in the United States shall, on the basis of age, be excluded from participation in, be denied the benefits of, or be subjected to discrimination under, any program or activity receiving Federal financial assistance."[80] However, a careful study of the statute's applicability to organ allocation points out that the statute has seldom been invoked since it was enacted.[81] Its applicability to kidney allocation was unclear. Parsing the statute, the 20/80 proposal's age matching would appear to comport with the ADA if, but only if, it "'takes into account age as a factor necessary' either to the 'normal operation' of the organ transplantation program or to 'the achievement of any [of its] statutory objective[s].'"[82] Implementing regulations for the ADA permit age to be used as a "measure or approximation" of some other trait that is "impractical to measure directly on an individual basis."[83] Although the law is ambiguous, Benjamin Eidelson argues, the Final Rule's mandate that OPTN pursue the "best use" of donated organs gives it a colorable defense against age discrimination, given that age is an arguably reasonable proxy for longevity.[84]

Dr. Bowman explained that his office had no objection to using age as a factor in estimating post-transplant survival, since in that context age is a scientifically validated proxy for health factors that are not recorded in OPTN data and thus cannot be directly incorporated into the allocation algorithm (such as, for instance, cardiovascular disease). On the other hand, the use of the age matching within fifteen years "appeared arbitrary in that candidates who are sixteen years older or younger than a donor are not substantially clinically different than those who have 14 years age difference."[85]

This view, while reasonable enough on its face, was far from obvious. After all, the 20/80 proposal relied on a conceptually similar threshold to separate candidates who were just barely inside the top fifth of forecasted post-transplant survival from candidates who were just barely outside that top fifth. At the margin, a birthday could in principle push someone out of the top 20 percent. The use of age in EPTS is mediated by the EPTS formula. But even without the age matching component to which Dr. Bowman was objecting, it would remain true under the 20/80 regime that a tiny difference in age between two patients—under the right circumstances—could be the reason why one was allowed, and the other denied, preferential access to a certain kidney.

Moreover, as the scientists at SRTR had pointed out in the context of LYFT, statistical modeling provides low accuracy when comparing two very similar candidates. According to one report, when comparing a randomly chosen patient who scored in the top quintile of EPTS to one who scored in the next-to-top quintile, the top-quintile patient actually had longer post-transplant survival only 62 percent of the time.[86] Meanwhile, the fifteen-year age matching had first been embraced by the committee "because it allowed *greater* access for older candidates than other concepts considered," and because it was simpler than other approaches.[87]

The committee's report may be guilty of some understatement when it records that Dr. John Friedewald, who was chairing the allocation review at this time, "thanked Dr. Bowman for sharing" a clear if debatable federal view about the permissible role of age in allocation.[88] In fact, the committee had waited years for such a clear signal and could not confidently endorse any allocation scheme as long as this question remained unanswered.

Dr. Mark Stegall, a former chair of the allocation review and an OPTN board member at the time of the new algorithm's eventual approval, believes that this moment—which might at first have seemed just another roadblock—was in fact the key turning point in resolving the decade-long debate. He explained:

> The question [that] comes up is, can we use age as any part of an allocation system? That was the crux of the matter for many years. We forced the federal government to weigh in and take some of the responsibility, which is what I thought was pretty, always a pretty big deal also. And I think that it was good that they finally did. . . . [For a long time] they would not give us direction. They would not say yes or no. So you can probably hear the tone of my voice. I was pretty adamant that we should just stop having committee meetings if we are not going to get this ruling [on the age question].

The kidney committee went back and forth, he noted, considering alternative formulas without knowing which would be deemed acceptable. "They were like children trying to please their parents."[89]

Fortified with this information, the committee was free to propose a system that it could confidently predict would seem acceptable to its federal overseers. At the same time, years of earlier debate and simulation had clarified a number of areas of agreement among the stakeholders.

The committee saw a path forward that would avoid age matching yet would preserve the priority for those with high estimated post-transplant survival. It would also make the other changes (such as crediting patients for waiting time that they had spent on dialysis before being listed) that enjoyed broad support. And that is the path they took.

The Final Proposal, 2011–2014

"Even without age matching" for the bottom 80 percent of kidneys, the Kidney Transplantation Committee now believed, "it had a solid foundation for a new allocation system."[90] Without basing any decisions directly on the patients' ages, it would direct the top 20 percent of kidneys to the

20 percent of *recipients* with the highest expected survival. This approach was remarkably close to the suggestion Clive Grawe had made in Dallas in 2007, when he had urged the committee to "correct the problem of younger prime organs going to older people" by creating a special category for the youngest and healthiest kidneys (composed of 10 to 15 percent of available kidneys) that would preferentially be allocated to the younger recipients.

Nine years of debate had also established broad support for a suite of other subtle but significant ways to enhance equity with respect to the remaining 80 percent of available kidneys.

The committee spent just under a year developing its new proposal and published it in September 2012.[91] Unlike its predecessors, this document—which I will refer to as the Final Proposal—provided a complete specification for a new algorithm and was thus actionable for implementation.

One subtle but notable difference in the Final Proposal was rhetorical: Although the Final Proposal preserved the 20/80 matching, it referred to this process not as "survival matching" but as "longevity matching." Dr. John Friedewald, who spearheaded the development and adoption of the Final Proposal, told me:

> I remember coining the term "longevity matching" because people were using terms like "survival matching" and that seems too extreme. I mean, a lot of this, as you will see, is Madison Avenue, right? I mean, you have to sell this idea to people. In fact, longevity is quite accurate, but it sounds a lot better than survival matching. . . .
>
> I think I was successful because I recognized that a lot of people don't have a calculated scientific response to this—this is a very emotional response, so you have to deal with people's emotions. . . . That's where having patients on our committee and donor families on our committee that could provide that kind of insight was really valuable. I mean, talking about this for ten years until it finally got done really taught us a lot of important lessons.

In addition to providing priority access to the top 20 percent of kidneys for the 20 percent of patients forecasted to live the longest after transplant, the Final Proposal also simplified the allocation regime by eliminating a patchwork of regional variances and by making KDPI scoring the first step in allocating all cadaver kidneys.[92] It calculated each patient's wait-list priority from the start of dialysis (rather than from the sometimes later date at which patients with limited health access were added to the transplant list), a change that the committee hoped would "increase the transplant rate for underserved (often minority) populations who may not receive adequate information" when they start dialysis "and thus may be added to the wait list long after their . . . diagnosis."[93] The new system changed the blood type eligibility rules so that blood type A2 kidneys could be allocated to the majority-minority blood type B group, increasing access for minorities.[94] And it introduced a sliding scale of priority for sensitized patients so that those with the highest degree of sensitization would enjoy national priority for any kidney that matched them.[95] Meanwhile, as described above, patients in the mostly young population that needed combined kidney-pancreas transplants were already enjoying better access to kidneys thanks to the now-separate kidney-pancreas allocation regime.

Notwithstanding all these changes, the Final Proposal continued to rely heavily on waiting time for the bottom 80 percent of kidneys and thus was much less of a departure from existing practice than the earlier LYFT or 20/80 proposals would have been. Committee members argued that the new system's design would make it easy to adjust the relative importance of utility and equity by changing the location of the 20/80 split. "If longevity matching proves to be a successful approach for kidney allocation," they observed, "future policy iterations could expand the number of kidneys and candidates which participate" in the prioritized longevity matching process.[96] (Such an adjustment could have only a limited overall effect, however, since it would place all of the favored candidates in a single higher-priority bucket rather than further prioritizing *among* such candidates.)

The Final Proposal was open for comment from September to December 2012.[97] A total of 253 written comments were received, including feedback not only from several hundred individuals or other outside parties, but also from each of the OPTN's eleven geographic regions and from seventeen of its committees.[98] All but one of the regions supported the proposal and only one of the committees objected to it. Outside commenters were more evenly divided, with 121 in favor and 96 opposed.[99] A compendium of these comments and of the committee's responses to them, which runs to 237 pages, was provided to the OPTN board before its vote on the new kidney policy.

The most commonly cited concern among opponents of the new policy was reduced access for older candidates (forty-three comments), and in particular reduced access for polycystic kidney disease patients like Clive Grawe, who know from early in life that they are likely to experience kidney failure in their forties or fifties.[100] Commenters also raised detailed technical concerns about how sensitization among candidates would be measured and judged, and how broader sharing of organs for the highly sensitized would be implemented. A group of bioethicists objected that the KTC had used detailed metrics for efficiency but had kept its equity goals vague, leading to policies that were "arbitrary, flawed and incomplete."[101] They also objected that the process for "assigning candidates at top 20%

or not" was effectively arbitrary, since it led to mistaken classifications about 25 percent of the time.[102] They objected more broadly to the system's embrace of the geographic status quo, writing that the proposal "is unjust because it persists in primarily allocating kidneys procured in one area to candidates in that area."[103]

The committee considered these comments in detail but ultimately declined to revise this last proposal in any significant way. In response to complaints about age matching, the committee requested additional analysis, which showed that factors other than age play a major role in the EPTS longevity scoring, and that a fifty-year-old without diabetes or a prior transplant would score inside the top 20 percent group—and thus receive preferred access to the best-rated kidneys—while a twenty-five-year-old with diabetes would fall outside it.[104] The committee made a number of minor technical adjustments, but left the proposal essentially unchanged as it had been offered in September of 2012.[105]

At its June 2013 meeting, the OPTN board voted to approve the Final Proposal, with the minor adjustments that the KTC had made in response to comments.[106] An eighteen-month period of planning, software updates, and patient and practitioner education ensued.

What had happened, as these long debates unfolded, to Clive Grawe, whom we met at the start of this book? Grawe received a transplant in Seattle, in July 2009, at the age of fifty-seven. As of this writing, both Clive himself and that organ are still going strong.

Like many people in their fifties, at the moment of his transplant Clive was at the pinnacle of his career. As a project engineer for the City of Los Angeles, he was responsible for the design and implementation of millions of dollars' worth of traffic circles, median islands, and other traffic-calming measures.

In the years since his transplant, Clive has seen his daughter earn her PhD and become a tenured professor at an elite university. He has also welcomed two grandchildren into life. He is now about to turn seventy and may yet outlive the national life expectancy for men of seventy-eight years.

One intangible that the early LYFT proposals had failed to include is that patients who manage a slowly declining kidney for decades, as Clive did, may be likely to take good care of their newly transplanted kidney, for instance, by adhering with great care to the immunosuppression protocol.

GOING LIVE

The new system went into effect on December 4, 2014.

In the period since its implementation, observers both inside and outside the OPTN governance structure have conducted detailed analyses of

changes to the waiting list and of patterns of organ offering, transplantation, and waste. One important and tragic change is that the overall supply of
kidneys has grown because of the opioid epidemic: the number of donors
who died from drug overdoses has roughly tripled since 2014. As a result,
roughly two thousand additional deceased-donor kidneys become available each year. Those additional organs alone represent nearly 20 percent
of the pre-2014 total number of available kidneys.[107]

One of the most closely watched questions is how the change affects
rates of transplantation among candidates of different ages. The Final
Proposal had forecast that patients ages sixty-five or older would receive
about 20 percent fewer transplants under the new system; in other words,
their share would diminish from about 18 percent to 15 percent of all
transplants.[108] But a direct search of OPTN data suggests that the models
may have overestimated the extent of this disadvantage: the fraction of
deceased-donor transplants received by the sixty-five-or-older group
dipped by about 17 percent in the first full year after KAS implementation, but it has since grown, reaching more than 22 percent of all deceased-
donor transplants in 2018. That is, the share of all transplants going to
people in this group moved from 22.1 to 18.3 percent of all deceased-donor
transplants.[109] Meanwhile, the fraction of deceased-donor transplants taking
place in the younger and generally healthier eighteen-to-thirty-four age
bracket increased by 38 percent when KAS was implemented, from 8.9
to 12.3 percent of all deceased-donor transplants.[110] (These changes were
enabled by a slight reduction in the fifty-to-sixty-four age group, from 40.9
to 38.4 percent of all transplants.) In short, KAS did shift some transplants
away from older patients, but on the whole it placed older patients at *less*
of a disadvantage than its authors had expected.[111]

Meanwhile, there were notable gains in race equity. An independent
analysis published in 2017 compared the average monthly percentage of
wait-listed patients who received a deceased-donor transplant by race.[112]
They found that the new allocation algorithm had "led to a substantial
increase in the kidney transplantation rate for blacks and Hispanics in the
months following the policy change, and a decrease in the rate of kidney
transplantation for whites." These researchers concluded that KAS had "at
least temporarily eliminated racial/ethnic disparities in access to kidney
transplants for black and Hispanic patients on the waiting list, compared
to whites."[113] The Scientific Registry of Transplant Recipients publishes
an annual data report on kidney transplantation in the United States (as
it also does for other organs). The 2015 report observed that "deceased-
donor transplants among black and Hispanic patients increased notably
post-KAS and approached rates for white patients."[114] The SRTR report
also included an encouraging chart (figure 4.2).

Figure 4.2   Deceased-Donor Kidney Transplant Rates among Adult
Wait-Listed Candidates, by Race, 2006–2017

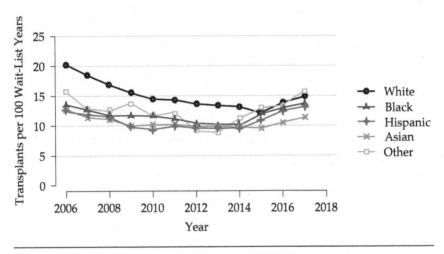

Source: Scientific Registry of Transplant Recipients (SRTR) 2022.

However, these positive developments come with important caveats.
First, the elimination of this racial gap might be partly due to a onetime
effect: many black and Hispanic patients received an overnight boost in
priority in 2014 because of the new policy of crediting all time on dialysis.[115] Moreover, moving from the list to a transplant is just one of the decision points along the path to a transplant; these studies do not track racial
disparities in getting listed for a transplant in the first place.[116] "Members
of minority groups are . . . less likely than whites to complete the medical
evaluation [or] be placed on the waiting list."[117]

One area where the algorithm apparently overshot was in its efforts
to boost access for highly sensitized candidates. Among the most highly
sensitized candidates—those considered 98 to 100 percent sensitized—the
formerly very low rates of transplants have soared, so much so that some
observers believe that too much priority was given to this group.[118] Some
of this increase brought rates of transplant for the highly sensitized into
equivalence with the rates for other groups; for instance, candidates who
were 98 percent sensitized experienced a near-doubling of their transplant
access under the new algorithm, yet were still slightly less likely to receive
a transplant than nonsensitized patients were.[119] But in an even more sensitized group, those between 99.5 and 99.9 percent sensitized, the rate of

transplant increased by a startling factor of 24, and their rate under the new algorithm rose to three and a half times the transplant rate for nonsensitized candidates.[120]

Amid the ongoing debates over equity, UNOS staff in 2017 developed the Access to Transplant Score (ATS), a standard metric of equity in access to transplant.[121] The ATS measures "differences in the expected time to deceased donor transplant among candidates on the waiting list," expressed as a standard deviation relative to the average waiting time across all candidates; by definition, the average ATS score is zero.[122] Better than expected access receives a more positive score, and negative scores reflect undesirable barriers to access. The authors controlled for the differences between candidates that are *supposed* to make a difference in how long each patient should expect to wait, such as "medical urgency, pediatric status [and already] accumulated waiting time." They then separately modeled the disparities in waiting time associated with factors that ideally should *not* change a person's waiting time, such as "ethnicity; age (among adults) . . . blood type; degree of immune sensitization; gender [and] socioeconomic factors such as income level, education and insurance type."[123]

The work was later published in a leading peer-reviewed academic journal, where the authors explained their methods in detail.[124] They chose the implementation of KAS as a case study, using five years prior to the implementation date and two years post.[125]

This analysis found that one factor stood apart, making more of a difference than age, blood type, sensitization, gender, race, or social factors: geography.[126] Among the nation's fifty-eight localized Donation Service Areas, the authors found "a 22-fold risk-adjusted difference in transplant rates," meaning that if all else were equal, being listed in the right DSA could make the same candidate roughly twenty-two times more (or less) likely to receive a kidney in the near future than they would be if located elsewhere.[127]

My interviewees were, in all but a few cases, directly involved in developing the new policy, and most of them expressed a qualified positive view of how the process had gone.

The ten-year course of the kidney allocation debate was evidently longer than anyone expected. Dr. Stegall, who led the process for several years, sees this as a problem: "You know, there is a time frame that you want to accomplish something in. This took ten years . . . to get implemented. And ten years is not acceptable, let's be real, for these kinds of things." At the same time, he said, "the Supreme Court is a good example of, social change has to precede legal change many times," and with any controversial issue, "there's always going to be people against it." "What we did, we probably kind of mimicked somewhat of that kind of hybrid process"—that is, the debate both reflected and shaped the community's beliefs about what an acceptable algorithm would look like. The competing ideals of utility and equity are ultimately "irreconcilable . . . at the end, we make some sort of sausage."[128] Other interviewees similarly told me that the process was long but that the resulting consensus was valuable.

MIRIAM'S STORY

Just as the new Kidney Allocation System was going into effect, a different story was beginning that would ultimately upend the new allocation system. Miriam Holman, a twenty-one-year-old Orthodox Jewish woman from Long Island, was one month into an intended yearlong visit to a seminary in Israel when she suddenly fell ill, with what turned out to be a rare and serious lung disease.[129]

Miriam and her family had long known about grief. For six years of her childhood, starting when she was two and her elder sister Nechama Liba was five, Nechama Liba had been gravely ill, ultimately passing away at the age of eleven, when Miriam was eight. The Holmans had created an annual weekend event—the Holman Bereavement Retreat—to support the siblings and families of other children who had passed away like Nechama. Miriam had long been a volunteer there.

For three years after returning to New York, Miriam fought for her life. But by September 2017, her condition had deteriorated, and she entered Columbia University Irving Medical Center. "Over the next four months, Miriam battled in a way that the staff at Columbia's MICU had never seen. According to hospital records, there were over one thousand visitors for Miriam. . . . She had a full schedule from 10 AM until 8:30 PM every day."[130]

Miriam needed a double lung transplant, but in the fall of 2017, her odds were grim. The existing algorithm for lungs prioritized any patient in the donor's DSA (that is, the same local zone in which the organ was gathered) over recipients elsewhere, including in adjacent service areas, regardless of urgency. Miriam was in Columbia University Irving Medical Center in Manhattan, but lungs gathered just a few miles away in New Jersey might go to a patient less urgently in need than she was, and who might also be farther from the donor hospital, just because they were over the line in a different zone.[131] There is no equivalent of dialysis for lung patients, and the lung allocation algorithm prioritizes medical urgency. The patients who need lungs are dying, and their needs are urgent.

On November 16, Miriam and her family took legal action. She was represented by Motty Shulman, a partner at Boies Schiller who, like the Holman family, was active in the New York–area Orthodox Jewish community.[132] "Miriam's attorneys sent a letter to HHS on her behalf requesting an end" to the DSA-first prioritization rule for lungs, and three days later they sued HHS in the Southern District of New York, writing in their complaint that the agency "has refused to act on [Holman's] request even though each day without a transplant may be [her] last."[133]

The complaint sought a temporary restraining order to "require the Acting Secretary of the U.S. Department of Health and Human Services to allocate lungs based on medical priority instead of the current antiquated and arbitrary system that gives priority based on a candidate's place of residence."[134] The complaint urged him to take this step by exercising his "authority and control" over the OPTN, whose activities take place under a contract administered by the HHS.

The arbitrary nature of DSA boundaries is undeniable and had been a topic of bitter debate since at least the 1990s.[135] Each DSA is defined as an exclusive territory within which a particular Organ Procurement Organization may gather organs for transplant. The number of people and the amount of land area they encompass varies widely among DSAs, and they do not consistently reflect state boundaries or any other organizing principle. DSA boundaries evolved when transplant was new, and some of them are even disjoint, covering multiple pockets of territory. In other words, DSA boundaries were first drawn by historical accident, but keeping them in place is something many in the transplant community have long regarded as a political necessity.

As the patient advocate Harvey Mysel told me, "There's no reason for it other than each [organization] is its own fiefdom. They have their own president and fifty or a hundred employees. . . . We don't need fifty-eight presidents. . . . Everyone agrees that changes need to be made, [but the] political willpower to do it isn't there. It was just set up too long ago, and it's just the way it is."[136]

Or at least, that's the way it *was*. The Holman complaint quoted the Final Rule's explicit statement that local-first allocation rules were generally inconsistent with the rule's conception of equitable allocation. The DSA-first policy to which the Holmans objected was vulnerable for being more arbitrary than a more uniform local-first policy might have been, and for sometimes allocating organs to patients who were both farther away and less urgently in need than other potential recipients. The legal complaint included a crash course on organ policy—the filing and its exhibits came to 260 pages—that took advantage of the extensive data published by the OPTN. It quoted a peer-reviewed study's finding that in more than 80 percent of lung transplant cases there were candidates in more urgent need in the same region as a lung's eventual recipient.[137] If DSA-first priority were eliminated from lung allocation, the complaint argued, then the remainder of the existing allocation policy would make Miriam a first-tier candidate for lungs recovered from thirteen additional transplant centers that were within a five-hundred-mile radius of her hospital because she would be within "Zone A" for those organs; likewise, she would have secondary priority for lungs gathered from seventeen additional centers for which she would fall inside Zone B but outside of Zone A.[138]

Such a change would have made distribution choices both less local and less arbitrary. It would have made a particularly stark difference in New York, where the track record on *local* recovery of organs is so poor that UNOS has threatened to shut down the local organ procurement organization.[139] In 2016, a total of just 67 lungs had been recovered for transplant in New York, compared with 1,121 lungs within Zone A range of Columbia University Irving Medical Center in upper Manhattan and 2,457 within Zone B (an area covering most of the eastern United States).[140]

The day after receiving the Holman complaint, Judge Laura Swain ordered HHS to "initiate an emergency review of the current [lung] allocation policy and file a written report" within a week "as to whether and to what extent the policy will be changed, and a timetable for implementation of any changes."[141] Holman's attorneys lodged an interlocutory appeal to the Second Circuit on the grounds that even this timetable was too slow. In the end, UNOS changed its nationwide lung allocation policy on "Friday, November 24, 2017 at approximately 7:15 p.m."[142] Earlier that day, the OPTN's executive committee had "voted unanimously to change the Lung Allocation Policy by eliminating the Donation Service Area ('DSA') as the first-level geographical designation used to allocate lungs, and replacing it with a radius of 250 nautical miles from the donor hospital."[143] Without explicitly conceding that the former policy had violated the Final Rule, the OPTN president wrote to HHS that the former policy had "contain[ed] an over-reliance on DSA as a unit of allocation," and that the new 250-mile policy "may make OPTN policy more consistent with" the Final Rule.[144] (These emergency changes remained in place for six months, and in June 2018, the OPTN board approved permanent changes to lung allocation.)

In total, this lung allocation rules had been substantially overhauled in five days. The litigation victory was ultimately hollow for Miriam, who received a lung transplant under the new rules but passed away a few weeks later.[145]

When these emergency changes to lung allocation policy were implemented, the OPTN was also on the cusp of resolving "an ugly, prolonged debate" about the geographic allocation of *livers*, which had been the central topic of controversy in the original debate over the Final Rule twenty years earlier.[146] The OPTN board was poised to approve a major overhaul of liver distribution at its December 2017 meeting. Under the new plan, livers would be offered first within a 150-nautical-mile circle of the donor hospital before being offered more broadly within DSA and regional boundaries.

However, on Friday, December 1, 2017—just a week after the emergency changes to lung allocation came into effect—the Holmans' lawyer Motty Shulman wrote again to HHS, this time to inform the agency that he now represented a different patient, a twenty-five-year-old woman named Tamiany de la Rosa who was in need of a liver transplant.[147] "As soon as we had some success on the lung side, my phone started ringing on the liver side," Shulman later told the *Los Angeles Times*. "Nobody should be getting a preference based on where they live."[148]

As with livers, so too with lungs: the prioritization process was within-DSA-first, and this led not only to cases in which a more urgent need slightly further away went unmet but also to cases in which a *nearer* and more urgent patient was denied an organ because they were on the wrong side of a DSA boundary. However, Shulman's letter in this case indicated objection not only to the DSA-first system but also to the then-pending 150-nm circle policy, warning that any policy should be based on "medical priority—not arbitrary geographical boundaries."[149]

The following Monday, the OPTN board did approve the liver proposal. A newspaper report of that outcome mentioned that the days-old demand for change was "hanging over the vote."[150] The policy was to be implemented at the end of 2018.

Later in December, the OPTN established a new ad hoc group to review the role of geography across all kinds of organs.

On March 1, with the approval of the new liver policy just three months old, Shulman received a reply from George Sigounas, the administrator of the Health Resources and Services Administration (the office within HHS that oversees the OPTN). Sigounas pointed out that "development of the [newly approved] liver allocation and distribution policy began in 2012 when the OPTN Board determined that geographic disparities in liver distribution were unacceptably high," and that "modelling predicts that the new liver allocation policy will decrease the variation across the country" in how sick a patient had to be in order to receive a liver transplant.[151]

But this mild defense of the newly approved policy did not resolve the concerns of Shulman's clients, and a flurry of letters and OPTN regulatory activity ensued. Shulman's client ultimately sued the HHS in mid-July, reproducing much of the strategy that had succeeded in the Holman lawsuit over lung allocation.

The complaint in the liver case had a section titled "Process, Process, and More Process" in which the plaintiffs recounted the earlier exchange of letters and flurry of administrative activity that had ultimately left them unsatisfied. In late May, Shulman wrote to the HHS secretary, on behalf of a broader group of New Yorkers in need of livers, to object that the newly approved liver policy, whose implementation was still pending, "does not solve" the problem of legally impermissible geographic arbitrariness because it "still includes region and DSA criteria."[152] The letter quoted extensively from academic work describing the arbitrary impact of DSA-based liver distribution on patients. On June 8, HHS advised Shulman that it had asked the OPTN to explain or change its reliance on DSAs in liver allocation.[153] On June 12, the OPTN board officially accepted a recommendation from its ad hoc geography committee that organs be recognized as a national resource and that DSA and region-based rules for all organs should be abandoned in favor of either fixed-distance zones (as for lungs), mathematically optimized distribution that would consider distance without fixed boundaries, or no geographic factoring at all.[154] However, as the plaintiffs told the court in their mid-July filing, "instead of taking action to abolish an illegal and inequitable policy, the OPTN took the position that, after decades of apparently futile deliberation, yet more review, discussion and public comment was necessary and took no meaningful action."[155]

As in the lung case, the court in the liver litigation was immediately receptive to the plaintiffs' concerns and requested swift justification from HHS and the OPTN as to why broader geographic sharing had not yet been implemented. The plot thickened a few days after the suit was filed when a group of hospitals led by the University of Kansas hospital system and Georgia-based Piedmont Health moved to intervene as defendants in the case, to argue the other side of the geography question, and to oppose the prospect of rerouting organs from the South (where organs were gathered in abundance) to New York (where they were not).[156] Calling the total elimination of DSAs from distribution policy a "drastic measure," they argued that the revised policies "comply with the spirit and language" of the National Organ Transplant Act.[157] They wrote that a broader distribution system would "funnel livers from communities with higher prevalence of social and economic disparities and inferior access to healthcare" to relatively affluent patients in areas like New York City. They further argued that patients in New York were less likely to die while on the waiting list, and that the medical urgency scores of New York liver patients were being routinely exaggerated in order to strengthen their access to scarce livers.[158]

Whatever the merits in these arguments about geography, the suits over lungs and livers had cast a clear shadow over the geographic distribution of other organs, including kidneys. A July 31, 2018, letter from HHS to UNOS contained this bombshell: "Because the problems associated with

DSAs and Regions are not limited to liver allocation, HRSA has considered their use in other allocation policies. . . . HRSA finds that the use of DSAs and Regions in all other (non-liver) organ allocation policies has not been and cannot be justified under the OPTN final rule."[159]

UNOS then rewrote the rules of kidney allocation so that, instead of using DSAs and regions, the system would operate with fixed concentric circles. These initially worked as smaller and larger areas that could be directly substituted for DSAs and regions within the newly approved kidney algorithm.

On March 15, 2021—after years of further policy development—a more developed policy took effect, in which preference is to be given first to recipients within 250 nautical miles of the donor hospital, and then to more distant candidates. Donation Service Areas are no longer used at all in allocation.

A FUTURE THAT'S EASIER TO UNDERSTAND?

As of this writing, kidneys continue to be allocated according to a zone system: patients have priority access to organs that are gathered at hospitals within a fixed radius of the transplant center where their surgery will take place. But UNOS is now planning to move away from these fixed circles to a more complex and flexible "continuous distribution" algorithm for allocating kidneys.

This new system will operate without any fixed circles or zones. Instead, the distance between each donor hospital and each potential recipient will be a matter of points. In fact, *everything* will be measured in points, and on the same scale. There will be no more complex decision trees, with their varied criteria. Candidates will be ranked in descending order, with the first offer going to whoever in the country has the most points.

The SRTR has released an interactive simulator that shows how this all might work in practice (figure 4.3).

Candidates who are nearest to an organ still get a large advantage. As the middle graph on the bottom row of figure 4.3 shows, you get many more points for being right near the organ (at the same hospital, or one down the street) than for being even a short distance away. Other factors are a simple binary—for instance, the lower-left graph shows that all pediatric candidates get a categorical hundred-point boost.

James Alcorn, the former UNOS policy director, described to me a sentiment that is echoed in the ongoing flood of UNOS policy documents: this system should be easier for everyone to understand. It should also be easier to adjust without causing unpredictable side effects.

Time will tell if they are right.

Figure 4.3 Interactive Tool to Visualize the Decisions Regarding the Continuous Distribution of Lungs

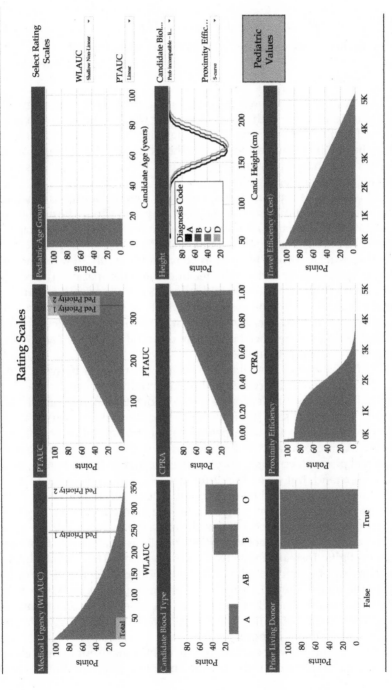

Source: OPTN 2020.

VALUES HIDING IN DECIMAL PLACES

What first appears most dull may conceal wonderful secrets.

—Porter, *Trust in Numbers* (2020)

In late May 2021, as I was working on this book, I received an email from Darren Stewart, one of the data scientists at UNOS who works on its allocation algorithms. Stewart has a long-standing interest in equity issues—in fact, he led the team that developed the Access to Transplant Score (ATS), which had shown how badly geography was distorting access to transplant among similar candidates.[160]

Now, Stewart explained, staff members were debating a tricky question and wanted my input: How many decimal places should be used when calculating each patient's allocation score? At first I did a double take: What could be interesting about decimal places?

The issue, as I soon learned in conversation with Stewart and his colleagues, was ethical rather than technical, and fascinating. The computers at UNOS *could* calculate each patient's allocation score out to sixteen decimal places. And in some cases, for patients in very similar situations, the system would need to carry things out to the umpteenth decimal place in order to find a difference between two candidates and offer an available organ to one rather than the other.

At first, the staff described the issue as a trade-off between precision and transparency: more decimal places might be more precise, but lots of digits might be harder for people to understand. On talking with them more, however, I saw the issue slightly differently. It wasn't a tradeoff between precision (or its appearance) and transparency or understandability. Using constants in their formulas that have more, or have fewer, decimal places doesn't necessarily make the system much harder, or easier, to understand. But when the difference between taking something out to five decimal places and taking it out to fifteen decimal places is that a different person will receive a particular organ, the issue—I suggested and they immediately agreed—is that the extra digits don't reflect a meaningful clinical difference between the candidates relative to a formula with fewer digits. Instead, they create *false* precision. The added digits don't tell us that one candidate has a better expected outcome, if transplanted, than the other. They just provide a technical pretext on which to award the organ to one candidate rather than the other, a reason that outwardly appears neutral. As all three on the call attested, not all digits of precision reflect clinically meaningful signals.

At one point, Stewart explained, "We want to make our decisions as much as possible based on clinical criteria and not flipping a coin." But this problem was similar to the one debated decades ago, described in chapter 3, about whether to use clinically marginal differences in antigen matching to justify giving a kidney to one patient rather than another. If two candidates are, as far as we can tell, clinically equivalent, then it may be wrong *not* to flip a coin between them.

I don't know how many decimal places the new continuous distribution framework for kidneys will ultimately end up using. That's a question for the policy committee to decide. But I found it remarkable that the data scientists at UNOS were in essence raising their hands to say that a seemingly technical question was actually a moral one, and that they were not the people to resolve it.

Chapter 5 | Conclusion: Ideas for Our Future

I BEGAN WRITING this book as a search for practical knowledge about better ways of making the hard moral choices that live inside of algorithms. I hoped for insights that could be transplanted out of the medical domain, clues about how to open up these trade-offs to a wider community, beyond the technical experts.

I felt instinctively that it must be possible—and would probably be good—to get non-engineers more involved in deciding the moral substance of high-stakes algorithms. That belief grew in part from personal frustration. As a technology adviser to civil rights groups, I had often encountered algorithms that seemed to wield power unwisely. Too often they had been designed without the kind of care that I would have hoped to see, based on how significant their impacts were. These were a mix of public sector applications and regulated commercial systems. I'd seen that many systems were poorly designed or misunderstood, and that the values choices within them were often made in unaccountable ways.

We can do better.

Facing the hard moral choices inside of algorithms—sharing those burdens more widely—is possible and sometimes worthwhile. But doing so can also be expensive and complicated and isn't always worth it. Putting it all together, I've gathered my conclusions into six key ideas.

1. Algorithms direct our moral attention. The architecture of a proposed algorithm often depends on practical factors, such as the available data. And that architecture in turn influences the terms of ethical debate.

2. Participation can shape opinions, albeit gradually. Creating buy-in and changing minds are at least as important as discovering people's initial beliefs.

3. Shared understanding benefits from shared infrastructure—investments that go beyond the effort entailed by building an algorithm itself.

4. Participation in deliberative processes can be costly, and its details matter. Deliberation can be a powerful tool to surface insights and build consensus. At the same time, it might or might not turn out to amplify the voices of the vulnerable. If the process makes unrealistic assumptions about who can or will participate, it can lead to unintended results, including an increase in power for the already well connected.

5. Quantification can act as a moral anesthetic. It can make morally challenging questions seem more technical and neutral than they really are. That's often, but not always, a bad thing.

6. Knowledge and participation don't always mean power. Even when dedicated processes are carefully established to govern a high-stakes algorithm, legislatures and courts can still be pressed into service as venues of final appeal for anyone displeased by an outcome.

In the pages that follow, we'll consider each of these ideas in turn. Then I'll offer a few closing thoughts about what these lessons might mean for you. But first, we should pause and consider: *Where* can this book's lessons best be applied?

WHERE IS THIS STORY USEFUL?

This book is about transplants in more than one sense.

We've seen how experts, patients, and advocates balanced hard trade-offs to remake the kidney allocation algorithm, leading to better health for more people and a fairer allocation of organs. Participation, transparency, forecasting, and auditing all played a role. People raised their voices. People were heard.

Our broader project is to learn how to share the moral burden of high-stakes software. Not just in medicine, but in criminal law, or hiring, or social services, or public education. In other words, part of my hope is to transplant some lessons from medicine itself into these other domains.

There will be no perfect matches, because the context of kidney transplantation is unique in some respects. Organs are classified both by law and by strong social convention as a nonmarket resource, a "gift."[1] That means the public needs to trust the system enough to donate their organs. Indeed, the system feels like a rare island of trust in an age of plummeting confidence in most expert institutions.[2] Deceased donors, just by the nature of their situation, haven't made plans for exactly who will get their organs, and the decision about each organ needs to be made quickly. In kidneys, in particular, dialysis sustains a large population of potential recipients. And people generally agree that kidney failure is not the patient's fault (an attitude that does not extend, for instance, to liver failure, where alcoholism and infections spread through injection drug use are two important drivers of the medical need for livers).[3]

And yet, each of the four strategies highlighted in this book—participation, transparency, forecasting, and auditing—is under discussion because scholars and policymakers have already decided that it may be useful across a range of high-stakes algorithms. Anyone with an interest in *any* of these four strategies has something to learn from the transplant story.

I hope you'll judge for yourself where the lessons of this book are most useful. But let me share three telltale signs that, when I see them, make me think that the experiences of the transplant community may be useful to others:

- *A strong need for public confidence in a system's competence and fairness.* Trust is hard to gain, easy to lose, and very useful. It matters not only for government but also for high-stakes private-sector systems, including the software used in hiring, insurance, and lending. Proving correctness to regulators and building confidence among customers and the public are perennial challenges. Transparency and auditing in particular—including independent audits like what SRTR does for transplant medicine—may be indicated when public confidence seems to be at stake.

- *A rationing problem involving a public resource.* Just as there are only so many kidneys available for transplant, there are only so many seats in each public school in New York City. When a resource is public, there is a strong presumption that a broad polity should help decide how it is shared. In some cases there may be a question about whether or not to regard the supply of the resource as fixed, as with the supply of shelter beds for homeless people. But wherever one does believe that a public resource needs to be rationed, that framing tends to concentrate discussion and clarify the moral stakes in ways that parallel the challenge of allocating kidneys.

- *Disappointment with existing governance strategies.* "If it ain't broke," as the saying goes, "don't fix it." In some places, traditional institutions seem to be capable of governing high-stakes algorithms effectively. For instance, in the financial domain, U.S. federal regulators have an elaborate regime of stress-testing for financial algorithms, known as "model risk management," which while not perfect could plausibly be said to vindicate the existing institutions that produced it.[4] And in the case of insurance pricing (described in chapter 1), legislators and others did succeed in opening up the moral workings of a high-stakes algorithm, partly by relying on a long-standing infrastructure of insurance regulation. In stories like the other five from chapter 1, the results suggest the need for a new approach.

These are "tells" that the experience of the kidney transplant algorithm might be relevant. But what are its lessons?

1. ALGORITHMS SHIFT OUR MORAL ATTENTION

One lesson of the transplant story, which reappears in the other stories of this book, is that the process of designing and governing an algorithm will open only a subset of the moral choices with which that algorithm is connected. Making an algorithm collaboratively takes time and attention. Whichever ethical questions can be answered by tuning the algorithm's dials, those questions will naturally find themselves taking center stage in policy debate. At the same time, other ethical trade-offs that are equally or more important may be "offstage" and less open to question, precisely because they cannot be dealt with by tweaking the algorithm. Engineering decisions thus control which moral questions are likely to be opened for broader input, and how those questions are likely to be understood.

The life-and-death outcomes people really care about—questions such as "How can I heighten my chance of getting a kidney?"—have answers that depend on *more* than just an algorithm. As scholars of science and technology studies often point out, human and cultural factors play important roles in these outcomes. And so, it is often more useful to conceive of a whole "socio-technical" system, including both the algorithms and the people who surround them, as being the one that is powerful, or that needs to be understood. Indeed, it might be more precise to say not that algorithms shift our moral attention but rather that we tend to *respond* to algorithms by shifting our attention ourselves, to focus on whatever features of a situation the algorithm makes easiest to understand and modify.

Several moral controversies during the development of KAS could be mapped directly onto features of the algorithm itself, making them relatively easy for the people involved—especially the laypeople—to observe, debate, and change. For instance, the debate over "utility" versus "equity" was a question of how to allocate the already available organs to the already listed patients within the already established geographic framework. That debate was resolved through "longevity matching," which changed allocations so that the youngest and healthiest recipients received the longest-expected-survival kidneys. And racial equity gaps were narrowed by changing how waiting time was calculated and embracing cross-ABO transplants for blood type B recipients. Highly sensitized patients, who earlier had very limited access to transplant, got better access through national sharing of zero-mismatched kidneys.

On the other hand, the arbitrary geographic barriers between donor service areas were something that the kidney allocation algorithm—and the people governing and debating it—took for granted. Those barriers can represent large differences in transplant access, but because they were understood as fixed constraints for the allocation algorithm, they were not considered for modification. And the ability of wealthy patients to "multi-list" across several transplant centers, which is etched into federal law, is a serious advantage that amplifies socioeconomic disparities but is beyond the reach of stakeholder governance to modify.

Why didn't geography come up more in the original debate over the kidney allocation system? At first I thought that the answer is simply that the issue was a political third rail, and the committee rewriting the algorithm had not been invited to consider it. But I now wonder if something else was also in play. I wonder if, particularly once the debate got going, people tacitly assumed that whatever was morally important about the situation must be reflected in the algorithm. I wonder if, perhaps unconsciously, they let the new technology drift into the center of their moral map of the situation. I wonder if they came to imagine, to some extent, that the moral problems they were dealing with had more technological causes, and also more technological solutions, than might really have been the case.

A similar problem may be happening today (early 2022) in the ongoing debate about social media and its role in democratic polarization and populism. After the Brexit referendum in the United Kingdom and the election of Donald Trump to the U.S. presidency in 2016, it became common for U.S. and European public figures and establishment commentators to assert that social media has had a profound and harmful effect on civics around the world. In this telling, people are isolated from contrary opinion and receive information, much of it inaccurate, that conforms to their preexisting worldview and undermines the possibility of a constructive exchange with those who hold different beliefs.[5] Algorithms that constantly give each of us the content we want (or alternatively, the content that most engages us by enraging us) are said to be at the root of those patterns.

I'll confess that such arguments sounded plausible to me, and still do. But a growing body of careful empirical work suggests they are not true. As one review article puts it, scholars have found that "even if most political exchanges on social media take place among people with similar ideas, cross-cutting interactions are more frequent than commonly believed, exposure to diverse news is higher than through other types of media, and ranking algorithms do not have a large impact on the ideological balance of news consumption on Facebook or Google."[6]

A different risk, apart from how the collective imagination shifts when an algorithm gets tweaked, is the possibility that moral challenges might drift offstage and get treated as technical details rather than moral decisions. This may have happened with the midstream decision to carve out kidney-pancreas transplants from the general kidney allocation algorithm (see the section "LYFT by Another Name" in chapter 4). As Dr. Stegall put it to me, "This became a lot of how . . . the ethical things get put into policy[:] we find other almost work-arounds . . . that fit into an algorithm that achieves pretty much the same thing, but it seems to be simpler for people to understand."[7]

Longevity matching was the most significant change in the new Kidney Allocation System, affecting about one in five of all organ allocation decisions, and it was a topic of broad debate. By contrast, the carve-out for kidney-pancreas transplants affected almost half as many kidneys as longevity matching did—approximately one in ten organ matches—yet was scarcely debated. Perhaps this just means it was a wise choice that no one had reason to question. Still, I find it surprising that the change did not get more attention.

A wide range of other questions matter to the challenge of allocating kidneys but played little or no part in the long debate. First, who is on the list in the first place? African Americans and other minorities are less likely to seek a transplant, even when they could benefit from one. How can their progress through the "referral funnel" be significantly improved? Second, what about the distorting effect of Medicare's reimbursement rules, which offer only three years for immunosuppressive coverage after a transplant even while they offer to fund dialysis in perpetuity? As Dr. Peter Stock pointed out during the debate, this policy makes immunosuppression financially inaccessible for some transplant recipients.[8] As a result, transplants fail and waiting lists grow even longer. Third, how can living donation be increased to reduce the demand for cadaver kidneys? Some important efforts are underway to increase paired and chained donation. Can the allocation of cadaver kidneys be altered to better support chains and paired donations?

Fourth, what about efforts to replace failing kidneys that do not rely on donated human organs at all? Just a few miles from where I live, a team at the University of California, San Francisco, is working on "a compact, surgically implanted, free-standing device to treat kidney failure [that] performs the vast majority of the biological functions of the natural kidney"—an artificial, some might say robotic, organ.[9] Another program of active research involves genetically engineering pigs so that their kidneys can be transplanted into human patients. While I was finalizing the text of this book, a major breakthrough was announced: surgeons in New York "successfully attached a kidney grown in a genetically altered pig to a human patient and found that the organ worked normally."[10] Some clinicians now think that these transplants from animals to humans, known as "xenografts," may be ready for clinical trials within the next two years.[11] In fact, just as this book was going to press, a new era of transplanting pig organs into human patients appeared to be dawning. In October 2021, surgeons in New York transplanted a pig's kidney into a human patient and documented that the kidney functioned normally for several days.[12] And in January 2022, a surgical team in Maryland transplanted a pig's heart into a man who lived for two months in the hospital.[13] There are significant barriers to be overcome before larger-scale human trials, let alone routine treatment, can begin. But the technology may ultimately transform the landscape of transplant medicine. I'm glad to know that these research programs are moving ahead. But I also wonder whether some of the effort that was devoted to tweaking the transplant algorithm might instead have been channeled into accelerating efforts like these.

If we think back to the stories we encountered in chapter 1, we can see this same dynamic of selective moral focus at work in several of them.

Take the New York City school screening algorithm: at first glance, it might seem like the system allows significant flexibility, since each school can establish its own selection criteria—and the system naturally invites debate about which criteria are fairest. Thanks to a recent policy change, those criteria are now public, which means that parents and others can potentially work together to verify that the system works as advertised. But if we take a step back and consider the problem of educational opportunity more holistically, it becomes apparent that the screening algorithm's whole premise, the way it frames the problem, reflects certain assumptions that could be opened to debate. It treats students as though they were on a relatively equal footing with each other at the time of application, and thus as though better performance on the test were an ethically sound reason to favor some with greater opportunity over others. More fundamentally, it approaches the whole question of fair criteria one student at a time.

Those who object to the current system are trying to move the moral spotlight from individual students to social groups. They don't simply want to change the criteria in the algorithms that are used to admit students, one by one, into the city's best public schools. They want to change the *kind* of algorithm that determines who gets those seats, so that placement decisions can be made with reference to entire school cohorts rather than just individual students. In other words, rather than tweak the dials of the current algorithm, they want to replace it. One idea that these critics have proposed is to return to a system called "ed-opt," in which each school aims for a student body with a representative distribution of standardized test scores. As the student activists wrote in their discrimination complaint, "Although standardized test scores often reflect and can compound racial inequality, structuring public high school admissions on a bell curve would mitigate the worst effects of using standardized test scores in public school admissions, while providing a positive first step towards integrating New York City's public high schools."[14]

The same kind of effort to challenge an algorithm's framing rather than tune its dials can be seen in the courtroom context. A debate about how a pretrial "risk assessment" algorithm ought to be designed implicitly assumes that the most useful thing to measure is risk and asks the best way to measure it. A different model might predict responsiveness to services and then, instead of asking, "Who is risky?" might ask, "Which services will best ensure that this particular person reappears at court?"[15] Under that model, someone is more likely to be sent home with text message reminders, rather than confined to a jail cell. More fundamentally, while courts may naturally think of risk as living inside a person, other algorithms might imagine risk as a property that places have, or situations, and predict those instead.

Similarly with the welfare fraud-detection system used in Australia, it's possible to have any number of discussions about how best to minimize fraud, but that process is different from a conversation about how to minimize errant denial of benefits. And as Virginia Eubanks explained in chapter 2, in the context of homelessness, an algorithm to ration the few available beds may distract from the need for more housing.[16] Even if the scarce resource must be rationed, elaborate scoring systems may create comforting fictions: perhaps that we can ethically distinguish the very *most* deserving fraction of the homeless from the rest and somehow place those people at the front of the line, or more fundamentally that if we were to rank the homeless by moral desert, it would become acceptable to leave many of them out in the cold. It may be nearer the truth to say that many of the homeless ought to be housed and otherwise supported by public services, and that a random lottery among these people would more fairly reflect the ethical structure of the situation.

2. PARTICIPATION CAN SHAPE OPINIONS, GRADUALLY

Before starting this project, I used to think about sharing the moral burden of algorithms in terms of a need for "stakeholder input." Such language is common in the literature: many scholars and policymakers have suggested that we should build high-stakes algorithms with input from the people who have reason to care about the system, particularly for algorithms that wield public authority.[17] Such conversations are borrowing the word "input" from a technological context, where it suggests something industrial, a raw material extracted in order to be fed to a machine. If we could only obtain enough of it, one might be tempted to imagine, we could find the most ethical answer and strike the best balance of competing interests inside a piece of software.

But in the transplant story, something much more interesting and complicated happened. In hearing one another out, the people involved gradually developed a shared belief in the legitimacy of the long and costly deliberations in which they were all engaged. After a ten-year period of learning and debate, a community of people changed its mind and gradually converged on what it wanted a morally impactful piece of software to do. That's why words like "participation" and "deliberation" ultimately seem to be a better fit.

It makes me think of the way that rocks can be polished in a tumbler, jostling together until their sharp edges are worn away. Creating that kind of interaction is resource-intensive, not only for the organization running the process but also for the participants. And one of the most important resources that it takes is time.

After the initial LYFT proposal, community feedback decisively rejected a pure focus on maximizing the total benefit from transplant. With this polar extreme ruled out, the window of acceptable policies narrowed, and the debate focused on how to improve utility without radically reducing access for any group of patients. The opinions people held through the middle and at the end of the process were partly products of the analyses, arguments, and ideas that they had encountered and put forward, and in some cases had rejected, during that period. People changed their minds or softened their stances.

Consensus was not achieved, so much as a kind of earned mutual acquiescence to a particular set of imperfect but tolerable values compromises. Partly, people wore each other down, until participants were even more eager to *end* certain arguments about how the system ought to work (and deploy something as a dividend for all their effort) than they were to *win* those arguments.

Something similar happened with the insurance-pricing algorithms that we saw in chapter 1. As Barbara Kiviat has explained, state legislators pulled back the curtain on the insurance underwriting process, looking for factors that might measure up as the same *amount* of risk but were of different kinds—for example, the risk from a morally blameless choice such as caring for a loved one or serving in the military.[18] Although individual states reached different policy decisions about which factors to exclude, a consensus did gradually emerge that *some* predictive factors should be excluded from counting against the policyholder. Such restrictions now exist in all fifty states.

In our current polarized political climate, debates over policy can often feel like futile, scorched-earth exercises: participants belong to well-defined camps, each focused on serving its own partisans. There's an ambient presumption of bad faith outside one's in-group, and few if any minds are changed. An alternative, liberal vision of political life, in which public discourse partly constitutes an earnest search for agreement and compromise, can seem naive today. But the transplant story at the heart of this book, and several of the other examples we've considered, show us that there are real-world circumstances under which participating in a debate really can serve to create buy-in from a broader public and can confer legitimacy on public authority for the making of difficult choices.

On the other hand, we've also seen that a lack of informed public debate can leave room for spectacular failures of algorithm-governing. Think about the Australian welfare algorithm that spewed false accusations of fraud at program recipients, or the courtroom algorithms that rely on outdated data to make "zombie" predictions of bad behavior. Those systems make decisions about people at the margins of society, whose lives are often treated as less valuable than others'. And a lack of public discussion can allow even terrible problems to persist uncorrected.

This picture of the benefits of participation emerges from our study of the kidney allocation algorithm. But the broader insight is really about deliberation, not about technology as such. Under the right conditions, preferences can shift and soften over time. People can end up with a policy decision (algorithmic or otherwise) that may be both objectively better on various dimensions and easier for a greater number of participants to accept, or perhaps even to celebrate.

The question of why and how this happens is deservedly the focus of a field of its own, the empirical study of participation as a political phenomenon. If you are curious about that work, you can look back to the "Participation" subsection in chapter 2 for a brief introduction.

3. SHARED UNDERSTANDING BENEFITS FROM SHARED INFRASTRUCTURE

To speak about what ought to be done, people first must be able to understand the possibilities. Shared governance over the moral logic of an algorithm presupposes shared understanding of how the system works. And the stories in this book show us that such understanding depends on more than mere disclosure. It depends, equally, on infrastructure.

Here we find an important parallel between participatory approaches to making high-stakes algorithms and participatory approaches to making important laws. Advocates for participatory democracy have developed a varied family of techniques for bringing laypeople to the table, such as citizens' juries, deliberative polling, and various forms of participatory budgeting (described in the "Participation" subsection in chapter 2). One of the most important common elements across these techniques is their focus on creating the conditions for a good discussion, including shared understanding. Citizens' juries are briefed about the controversial issue that they will be debating. Participants in a participatory budgeting exercise get a plain-language summary of the existing budget. And in many of these participatory settings, people meet repeatedly over time so that they can get to know each other.

The making of the new Kidney Allocation System followed this pattern. It was not only a matter of publishing the information already available to specialists, such as the mathematical formula for calculating a Kidney Allocation Score. On their own, disclosures of this kind are frequently incomprehensible to outsiders. As Guido Calabresi and Philip Bobbitt wrote in a different context, the official documents used by the people who run complex algorithms "are likely to be expressed in language accessible only to critics who are specially trained. This makes pleas for honesty or openness sound ironical or even pointless."[19]

Transparency matters when, as Tiago Peixoto has put it, "disclosed information actually reaches and resonates with its intended audiences," and when those audiences actually have political agency to influence the process that the disclosures are about.[20]

True understanding requires access not only to the numbers but also to the context that surrounds them. It can be created through an affirmative effort and dedicated resources. Specifically, true understanding requires access to three things—and these are what I mean by "infrastructure": clear public analyses of the available data, forecasts of how proposed algorithms might be expected to perform, and audits or other reporting that describe how any existing system actually *has* performed. These are things that few if any stakeholders, outside the powerful organization that creates a high-stakes algorithm, will have the resources to replicate.

This pattern plays out both in the transplant story and in the other examples mentioned throughout this book: where there is a relatively robust public debate over the moral substance of an algorithm, there is infrastructure to support that debate. And wherever such infrastructure is missing, an inclusive and informed conversation tends not to be feasible.

The kidney allocation algorithm is public. It doesn't rely on thousands of factors, nor does it include more data than a human can understand.

Both the reasons for a particular allocation decision and the reasons for the algorithm's overall match-making procedure are thoroughly documented. But take it from me: if you just sit down and read all of this documentation, you won't end up with a solid sense of what's actually happening in the system, where the organs are going, and who can benefit from them. Such insight requires some familiarity with the practice of transplant medicine. It was only after interviewing experts as well as patients who had gone through the system that I began to feel confident in my ability to understand what the documents *meant*. And there are probably many parts of the system I still don't understand.

The resources I found most helpful weren't the official policies and technical reports that the system's architects rely on. Instead, I learned most from a second tier of reports, explanatory slide decks, and other resources that had been created specifically in order to explain the process to laypeople. Clearly, this had also been the case for many people not involved in running the system: I heard from patients who attended webinars, and I listened to podcasts about the rival proposals. When the allocation committee requested comment on its policies and reports, it did an admirable job of clearly explaining the ideas that it wanted people to comment *on*. Much of this material was produced by UNOS itself, especially the Kidney Transplantation Committee. But interest groups representing various categories of patients, doctors, surgeons, and other professionals also did a significant amount of work to analyze and summarize what was happening.

All of this debate was built on a sense of shared reality about how the existing transplant algorithm worked and how the proposed new versions would be likely to work. By not only disclosing information about system performance but also sharing replicable analyses of that information, the independent analysts at the Scientific Registry of Transplant Recipients significantly reduce the barriers faced by patients, advocates, and others who may wish to enter the debate over how an allocation algorithm might work. Annual reports known as the U.S. Renal Data System, published by SRTR, track the fates of patients and of transplanted organs in a consistent way each year. Crucially, the SRTR has access to data about each patient and each transplant, directly from the hospitals where transplants take place. Hospital participation in the system is mandatory, and the SRTR analysts have both the practical ability and the legal mandate to analyze these sensitive data and report what they find, while protecting patient privacy. The system is not perfect—as the surgeon Göran Klintmalm pointed out to me, the reporting metrics emphasize transplant success at one year out from surgery and may therefore miss the chance to specifically acknowledge and reward the longest-lasting (decade-plus) transplants differently from shorter-term success.

Analysts at OPTN have used SRTR data to produce streamlined metrics that speak to public concerns, such as the Access to Transplant Score, which describes factors associated with undesired differences in transplant outcomes. A starting point such as the ATS can be very useful for discussions of racial, geographic, and other inequities.

It's not just what has already happened but what might happen in the future that people need a shared way to understand. I asked Dr. Stegall whether simulation had been important to the deliberations. He replied:

> Oh baby, oh my God, yes. We had more simulations than you could ever—seriously. And it was a little bit of the slowness of the process, was it took a while to run the simulations, right? And simulations would [show that] just tweaking a piece of [the algorithm] would get you a very different distribution of organs. And some people would say, "Oh yeah, I really like this one," and some people would—so it was, it was kind of like Netflix. There were almost too many options to go through.

The producer of such analyses and simulations is in a powerful position to shape how participants will understand an algorithm and their interests in it.[21] There is a significant risk that any analyst may, consciously or otherwise, shape analyses or simulations in ways that lend support to personal normative commitments.

The political scientist Bruce Cain has described "an unavoidable tradeoff in expertise," because providing it centrally can both enable informed debate and "[increase] the chances of manipulation through framing bias.... Citizens relying too heavily on expertise may be sacrificing independent judgment and unintentionally reflecting the status quo orientation or political biases of the experts."[22] This is one reason why analysis *without* disclosure of the underlying data would be insufficient. Analysis of performance data by outside scholars, and the SRTR's practical and formal independence from the UNOS office that actually operates the allocation algorithm, both act as safeguards on the accuracy of the information thus generated.

The flip side of this risk may be a crucial benefit: with the help of shared analysis, it is possible to establish a shared set of beliefs about what the problem is, and which feasible solution is most appropriate.

If people are to participate in making something complicated, in other words—whether it's an algorithm, a law, or a municipal budget—centralized infrastructure may be useful on two different levels. First, centralization can save people the need to reinvent the analytical wheel, thus broadening access to participation. And second, shared, trustworthy, and actually trusted analyses of the options can bring shared focus to a conversation and allow progress and understanding to be reached.

Even with all this infrastructure, there were still some questions it remained hard for me to answer without having personally toiled in the vineyards of transplant medicine. For instance, what would a heat map of the allocation tree look like? That is, visually speaking, which of the several hundred allocation sequences for kidneys are actually used most often? (I've now ended up with a clear grasp of the broad outlines, but not the level of clarity I would have liked to develop.) The feel for the system's operation that practitioners develop by watching candidates progress through it over time — and that candidates develop by being candidates and watching people they know go through the system — is not easily conjured through text or conveyed to a new participant, such as a newly diagnosed patient. To fully understand the system's functioning requires a hybrid of medical and organizational knowledge that, realistically speaking, most people cannot plausibly find the time to develop. People in the real world, including the real world of transplant, operate with tacit knowledge, and there is always "practical drift" between the official policies and actual practice. The deepest understanding of a system requires more than official disclosure: it requires meaningful conversations between people who already deeply understand a system and people who do not. The question is not just who has access to information, but who has access to firsthand knowledge and expertise.

Something similar happened — admittedly in a more haphazard way — with the state-by-state ethical regulation of insurance scoring: with a constellation of preexisting infrastructure, the discussion became "a rare case of extended public debate about a particular type of algorithmic prediction."[23] Insurance regulation officials in many states had expertise in how the industry worked, and they coordinated and shared knowledge through a national association. So too did the state lawmakers who were active on insurance issues. The same handful of insurance industry lobbyists appeared repeatedly at legislative hearings in different states, where the issues were hashed out in public and in plain language. Important algorithms might be kept secret in other areas of commerce, but because the insurance industry is heavily regulated, insurers shared a significant amount of information in public (and they may have been required to disclose even more in private). Auditing insurers' activities and approving their contemplated plans were central to the mission of these long-established regulatory bodies.

Likewise with the long, careful public debate over child abuse risk scoring in Allegheny County, described in chapter 2: a years-long pattern of substantial investment in community outreach, public debate, and outcome monitoring was not just coincidental but catalytic for the public debate that has taken place there. The half-dozen impact evaluations, ethical analyses, and other reports that have made their way into my files—and that have also informed the work of many other scholars interested in these questions—are part of why this example has become a widely discussed bellwether for scholars and policymakers, in Allegheny County and beyond.

By the same token, thinking about some of the other examples of ethically dubious algorithms we've encountered in this book, the *lack* of infrastructure is a recurring theme. In New York City's school screening process, even after the admissions rubrics were made public, it remained difficult to draw precise links between particular admissions criteria and the resulting impact on racial balance, school academic climate, or the post–high school plans of graduating seniors. The problem is that nobody with access to the per-student data has the mandate and incentive to produce public reporting about what's happening, in terms of either school admissions or subsequent learning outcomes. One partial remedy would be to create an independent statistics and analysis office (analogous to SRTR in the transplant case) that would provide ongoing analysis of admissions and education outcomes—a function that would be useful not only in the admissions context but also for other debates over schools and school policy.

In the criminal justice area, the availability of meaningful data to public observers is generally quite limited. One reason is that some vital data are never even collected. Most criminal law and law enforcement play out at the local or municipal level, where reformers have struggled recently to increase citizen control over police and courtroom algorithms.[24] In those cases, the community over which decision and deliberation costs are spread is much smaller than in a national context like transplant, and the impacts of new surveillance technologies are concentrated on vulnerable groups that are particularly unlikely to have necessary resources. A few cities have begun to host consultations with community groups, but rigorous public analysis of deployed systems remains vanishingly rare.[25]

The data that *are* available concerning crime are often manipulated for public consumption—police are wont to "juke the stats," as the rough language common to law enforcement has it. Such behaviors may have been made nationally famous by the fictional world of the HBO television series *The Wire*, but they've also been extensively documented in real-world cases, including in Baltimore, Chicago, and New York City.[26] Sometimes arrests are taken as the yardstick of police "productivity," which leads to more arrests. This can increase the risk that a person will be arrested (the typical focus of courtroom risk scores) without actually signaling any increase in danger to the community.[27] Conversely, while arrests go up, reports of serious crimes may be artificially pushed down, since law enforcement authorities (and mayors and other responsible authorities) spotlight the rate of such crimes and claim credit whenever it decreases.[28] For instance, residents who try to report thefts may find that the officer at the precinct insists on recording the crime as "lost property," a less serious offense, unless the thief was actually spotted in the act.

It's not just that crime numbers are unreliable. A related and deeper problem is that other relevant numbers, such as the secondary costs of coercive police enforcement techniques, unjustified arrests, or detentions of the innocent, typically are not measured at all.[29] And even when data about one place or time period are available and excellent, it's often hard to know how well the data will predict what happens in a different time and place. The independence and incentives of those analyzing system performance are likely to be a perennial concern.

The general solution to this need for shared and trustworthy data is independent auditing or reporting. I did find one place where criminal justice authorities make a serious effort to insulate the metrics from the performers, much as SRTR does for transplant: New South Wales, the most populous state in Australia, "has an independent Bureau of Crime Statistics to assess police crime reports. The Bureau's findings contradicted and corrected official New South Wales police crime statistics and prompted a Deputy Commissioner's resignation."[30]

Although crime numbers might be particularly unreliable, the general pattern of numbers becoming less meaningful once algorithms start to use them is so widespread that it has its own name: Campbell's Law. "The more any quantitative social indicator is used for social decision-making," wrote Donald Campbell in 1979, "the more subject it will be to corruption pressures and the more apt it will be to distort and corrupt the social processes it is intended to monitor."[31] It's the same problem whether we consider teachers and standardized test scores, surgeons and transplant success rates, or police and reported crime.

This observation aligns with the conclusion in the last section: it would be a mistake to think of stakeholder opinions about a system's design as static "inputs" that need to be measured and reflected during system design. It would be better, instead, to think of these as dynamic beliefs that need to be *created*, partly through the intentional coproduction of a shared understanding about problems and possible solutions. In fact, one of the core elements of "shared infrastructure" that has made the kidney deliberations possible is something so basic it might be tempting to overlook: the stakeholders often get together in person for their meetings. Even though they are governing a nationwide computer system, vital meetings take place in person, face-to-face, where people can more easily come to trust and appreciate each other.

4. PARTICIPATION IS COSTLY, AND ITS DETAILS MATTER

Seen in a certain light, the story of the moral debate over transplant algo-rithms is beautiful. It had all or most of the things reformers tend to want: There was participation and transparency. There were published forecasts. Once the system finally did roll out, there were audits. Complex technical matters were rewritten in plain English so that patients and journalists could decipher what was going on.

Not only that, but these procedures weren't just frills: they made a prac-tical difference. At first the idea was to give each organ to whoever would benefit the most, but when the relevant committee pitched the idea pub-licly, people pointed out that this would starkly disadvantage old people and would also disadvantage the poor and other folks who had had bad medical luck. So the community ended up compromising on a more mod-erate a system that still valued waiting time and also made it easier for people to join the list.

People working together to open the black box and take control over the ethical choices that matter most, rather than leaving them up to technical experts or machines? I could end this book in celebration, with the claim that although it was far from perfect, this process was basically good. I might claim that we should initiate similar processes in criminal justice and other areas. (Advocates have sought things like this for a while: in 2018 I worked with a group of more than one hundred advocacy organizations urging that criminal justice algorithms be constrained by "community advisory boards.") I might say, let's have more transparency, and more meetings.

I do think that there are many places where this kind of participatory approach is worthwhile in governing an algorithm—and the transplant story told in this book is one of them.

But there is also another side to the story: the new transplant algorithm took ten years to get done. Endless hours of salaried time and volunteer time, travel and analysis and writing and reading—millions of dollars' worth. I'm not saying this wasn't worth the cost. But, *was* it? How would we know? We can't deliberate this heavily over everything.

By the time the new kidney algorithm went live, my informants had developed complicated and mixed feelings about whether the process had been worth it. Let me reproduce here one paragraph from the section "Going Live" in chapter 4:

The ten-year course of the kidney allocation debate was evidently longer than anyone expected. Dr. Stegall, who led the process for several years, sees this as a problem: "You know, there is a time frame that you want to accomplish something in. This took ten years . . . to get implemented. And ten years is not acceptable, let's be real, for these kinds of things." At the same time, he said, "the Supreme Court is a good example of, social change has to precede legal change many times," and with any controversial issue, "there's always going to be people against it." "What we did, we probably kind of mimicked somewhat of that kind of hybrid process," that is, the debate both reflected and shaped the community's beliefs about what an acceptable algorithm would look like. The competing ideals of utility and equity are ultimately "irreconcilable . . . at the end, we make some sort of sausage." Other interviewees similarly told me that the process was long but that the resulting consensus was valuable.

Concerns like these turn out to be very common when people try to address a moral burden embedded inside a lot of technical complexity. Interestingly, although there is a widespread intuition that decentralized processes tend to be more democratic than centralized ones, the reverse may be true when an algorithm (or something else intricate) is being governed: a single centralized process may have the resources to go deep or to build shared understanding, whereas a process that tries to reinvent the wheel in a series of local communities might not have enough resources (or where the stakes might not justify enough resources) for inclusive governance to get off the ground.

Oscar Wilde is reputed to have said that "socialism will never work because there aren't enough evenings in the week." The quote turns out to be apocryphal, but it still rings true. In 1968 it inspired the philosopher Michael Walzer to write a zany essay in the journal *Dissent*. As Walzer put it:

> Self-government is a very demanding and time-consuming business . . . and when the organs of government are decentralized so as to maximize participation . . . it may well require almost continuous activity, and life will become a succession of meetings.
>
> We can assume that a great many citizens, in the best of societies, will do all they can to avoid [all this]. While the necessary meetings go on and on, they will take long walks, play with their children, paint pictures, make love, and watch television. They will attend sometimes, when their interests are directly at stake or when they feel like it. But they will not make the full-scale commitment necessary for socialism or participatory democracy. How are these people to be represented at the meetings? What are their rights?[32]

In the real world, participation is costly. It's a matter not just of money but of time: people are busy. The whole thing can sometimes go sideways and be "captured" by interests with the most money at stake. For instance, in the 1970s and 1980s new land use laws were introduced in the United States, requiring additional approvals before construction of new real estate projects could begin. These laws, which empowered members of the local community by giving them new tools for delaying, modifying, or preventing suggested projects, aimed to protect the environment and prevent developers from riding roughshod over poor neighborhoods. But in practice they have also become tools for wealthy homeowners to resist the new housing and mass transit that the country urgently needs.[33] For instance, the California Environmental Quality Act (CEQA) of 1970 was meant to stop environmentally harmful development practices, but a study of all CEQA lawsuits brought between 2010 and 2012 found that "too often enforcement . . . is aimed at promoting the economic agendas of competitors and labor union leaders, or the discriminatory 'Not In My Backyard' (NIMBY) agendas of those seeking to exclude housing, park, and school projects that would diversify communities by serving members of other races and economic classes."[34]

Bruce Cain argues that these kinds of direct, participatory mechanisms— all the new committees and meetings—reflect a "populist distrust [of] representative government" that reaches back to the American founding. It's the same impulse that gave us the separation of powers, a drive to keep our representatives honest. But now reformers are pushing for "greater citizen control over public officials by maximizing opportunities for transparency, participation, observation, and control." The fly in the ointment is that most people just don't have time and interest to do that stuff: "Populism's hold on the modern political reform community," Cain asserts, "rests on denying cognitive reality and promising unmediated citizen empowerment." Cain argues instead for what he calls "pluralism," which is when the system depends on expert advocates from different groups to pull the levers of power on behalf of various competing interests. If we plan for too much *direct* input, Cain contends, we're kidding ourselves.[35] As Walzer said, it's reasonable to fear that "participatory democracy means the sharing of power among the activists. Socialism means the rule of the men with the most evenings to spare."[36]

Objections like these are not new. Advocates and theorists of participatory governance—who are mostly focused on laws and policies rather than algorithms—have much to say about how common such problems are and what can be done to address them.[37] As one recent review summarized, "Ordinary people are capable of high-quality deliberation, especially when deliberative processes are well-arranged: when they include the provision of balanced information, expert testimony, and oversight by a facilitator."[38]

Steps like these can indeed be costly: "Many positive effects are demonstrated most easily in face-to-face assemblies and gatherings, which can be expensive and logistically challenging at scale. Careful institutional design—involving participant diversity, facilitation, and civility norms—enables well-known problematic psychological biases and dynamics to attenuate or disappear."[39] A report about citywide participatory governance in midsized American cities where hard choices needed to be made about balancing budgets and balancing growth with environmental preservation found that such dialogues were "neither cheap, fast, nor easy."[40]

In fairness to participatory approaches, it is important to note that traditional, expert techniques of rule-making, law-making, and algorithm-making are also susceptible to elite capture, gridlock, and many other forms of unloveliness.

At their best, deliberative and participatory processes can (as the author claims those exercises in American cities actually did) "[enable] local governments to take effective action on previously intractable issues."[41] That's the biggest claim at the root of such work: attractive political outcomes can be reached through these methods that would not happen otherwise.

Another illustration comes from Finland, where researchers put together like-minded and diverse-minded groups for conversations about their attitudes on immigration. Given a structured, moderated conversation with shared facts provided at the beginning, the authors found that "people with anti-immigrant attitudes become more tolerant even when they deliberate in like-minded groups."[42] And in two real-world Australian planning exercises, deliberation "correct[ed] preexisting distortions" in how people saw the issues, partly by "shaping a shared understanding of the issue."[43] Research into when and why such efforts succeed—and about what exactly it should even *mean* to say that they have or have not succeeded—is ongoing.[44]

One common technique for increasing the responsiveness and legitimacy of participation mechanisms is called "sortition," or alternatively, "lottocratic selection" (an idea we first encountered in chapter 2). It means choosing people at random from the broader community that the participatory process aspires to reflect. There are endless variations on this because the random selection process can itself be adjusted or controlled to make sure that the people chosen end up "looking like" the broader public whose interests they are meant to represent.[45] For example, it might be important in some context to have gender balance; in another, the aim may be to choose a group reflecting a representative distribution of different wealth levels, or religious opinions, or political party memberships. In a constitutional referendum process that took place in Iceland, for instance, "for each of the 1,000 seats . . . there were four backup candidates in the same age/gender/geographic bracket to ensure that, should the first, second, or third candidate decline to participate, there was someone relatively similar to replace that individual."[46] That might be an approach worth trying in transplant, as opposed to giving influence to whoever happens to have the resources, motivation, and confidence to volunteer themselves as a participant.

Even if the invitations to participate are randomized, actual participation will still depend on the resources available to participants—both what they already have and what the participatory process may provide them. For example, unsurprisingly, a study of more than a thousand town meetings in New England found that women participate more actively when the meeting organizers provide childcare.[47] Similarly, in the context of participatory budgeting, "providing childcare decreases the costs of participation for families who would otherwise struggle to take time out or to pay for childcare. Serving food provides an extra incentive to participate, especially for low-income people."[48]

5. QUANTIFICATION CAN BE A MORAL ANESTHETIC

Beneath the practicalities, there is also a deeper argument against asking lots of people to weigh in on "tragic choices," such as picking which dying person to save with a transplant. It might be an excruciating experience that drains our scarce supply of moral attention without providing much of a practical dividend.

Quantification—the recourse to numbers—acts as a kind of moral anesthesia. As the technology critic L. M. Sacasas has put it:

> A lot of the systems that are in place now can be seen as machines for the evasion of responsibility.... Algorithmically structured processes might [make it] hard to then hold anyone responsible for their outcomes.... Bureaucratic structures did this even prior to the age of algorithms. You distribute human agency into the operations of a system in such a way that someone can plausibly, if not ultimately legitimately, say, this wasn't my fault, or I had no power over this process.[49]

A computed score "seems dispassionate, impartial and objective."[50] The ideals here are complex: if "objective" means lacking any normative consequence, then quantification applied to human fates is not objective. But numbers can indeed be dispassionate.

The most obvious thing to say about this effect is that it's bad, because it could make us indifferent to suffering or injustice. When it comes to justified moral emotions, we might at first want to say that more is always better.

But we couldn't reopen all the hard choices all at once, all the time—even if we wanted to. Some people focus their limited supply of attention and energy on factory farming, or on what's happening in Afghanistan, or on child and maternal health. Yet none of us have the personal capacity, either emotionally or cognitively, to consider all the world's woes.

In the context of organ transplantation, we'd like to value every life equally—but in some sense we can't, because ultimately only one patient can receive each organ. In their 1978 book *Tragic Choices*, Calabresi and Bobbitt explore situations like this, where every possible way forward requires us to violate our society's most basic principles. Looking at such a choice head-on can be a painful experience for everyone, and so (given that the trade-off is, in a case like transplant, tragically unavoidable), we have developed ways of making such choices *seem* more decent or tolerable, rather than accept them as horrifying and violent daily travesties. If we stare a choice like that straight in the face, Calabresi and Bobbitt seem to fear, we'll either go mad or pay "a price in ideals" by being forced to acknowledge that our system doesn't really work. To make the situation tolerable, they suggest, we need to find a way through the moral conflict. And numbers and algorithms often help us do that.

Take an algorithm's decision that Alice and not Bob will get a heart transplant that each one urgently needs:

> By making the result seem necessary, unavoidable, rather than discretionary, [the algorithm] attempts to convert what is tragically chosen into what is merely a fatal misfortune. But usually this will be no more than a subterfuge, for, although scarcity is a fact, a particular . . . decision [for instance, about who gets an urgently needed organ] is seldom necessary in any strict sense.[51]

The transplant system's willingness to carry allocation scores out to many decimal places—past the point at which the numbers reflect meaningful medical differences between the patients—can be seen as a means of dodging the reality that such choices are, at some level, arbitrary.

We can see a similar subterfuge in—and derive a similar sense of comfort from—private-sector algorithms that purport to give each job candidate a precise score on a rank-order list. As my colleagues at Upturn wrote in a civil rights analysis of hiring algorithms, "Hiring tools that assess, score, and rank jobseekers can overstate marginal or unimportant distinctions between similarly qualified candidates."[52]

Their picture is: The moral anesthesia that comes with quantifying ethical choices, and putting them through software, is sometimes a mercy. We learn to explain these impossible choices in neutral quantitative terms, rather than directly confronting the element of arbitrariness that inevitably infects the design of our quantification scheme, so that we can make it through the day. The terrible moral trade-offs will happen whether we attend to them or not.

In a world of scarce moral attention and effectively endless suffering, each of us is in fact insensitive to most moral claims, most of the time. When does it make sense to pry the lid off a seemingly neutral algorithm and peer inside? When should this "subterfuge" of neutrality be dropped, and the impossible and horrifying problem honestly confronted?

Calabresi and Bobbitt argue that whether such a process is worth it "depends on whether, now that we are aware of what we are doing, we can do sufficiently better [than before the process started] to make up for the costs of clearly choosing. But whether we can or not, we cannot turn back: we now know that either way, we are choosing to take some people's lives."[53]

I'm not persuaded by the *Tragic Choices* argument that it's important to tiptoe around the inevitable contradictions in our society's core ideals. But Calabresi and Bobbitt's idea about when to bother having an ethical debate does make sense to me.

In the transplant case, it was worth trying to collaboratively and publicly rewrite the kidney algorithm not only because the algorithm was ethically significant but also because it was feasible to improve the system. The redesign not only let everyone fight for their preferences but also brought about a situation that was both fairer and more efficient than its precursor. We should bother with an ethical debate about an algorithm when, by doing so, we can actually make things better.

6. KNOWLEDGE AND PARTICIPATION DON'T ALWAYS MEAN POWER

The transplant story shows that with the right tools, the ethics inside of complex algorithms can be subjected to a broadly inclusive, well-informed governance process. At the same time, the story also shows that processes like these—even when they do happen—will not always get the last word on contentious ethical questions.

The consensus-seeking, committee-based, publicly engaged approach that brought about the Kidney Allocation System created space for impacted groups, including not only physicians and other professionals but also patients and living donors, to understand and reflect on the inevitable trade-offs in allocating kidneys. And by airing out different stakeholder perspectives, the process appears to have helped generate buy-in and give a sense of legitimacy to the final result.

However, stakeholder input mechanisms are vulnerable to reversal on the most important moral questions that they consider. Those questions can always be reopened by higher authorities. When those who are disadvantaged by a particular policy are sufficiently motivated, they do have recourse to the executive branch, the courts, and the legislature. The debates over organ allocation policy, for instance, have included appeals to all three of branches of government. For example, the veto of age matching by executive branch officials was arguably the key turning point in the decade-long effort to get a kidney allocation rule approved. Until that intervention, the participatory process run by UNOS was basically stuck. Recall Dr. Mark Stegall's remark that "they would not give us direction. They would not say yes or no" (see chapter 4). The committee was "like children trying to please their parents."[54]

And resistance to the wider geographic sharing of organs has included legislative intervention. During the debate over the Final Rule several states enacted legislation to bar the export of organs across state lines, and in the more recent debates over the geography of allocation U.S. senators have written public letters to indicate potential interest in limiting the geographic sharing of organs, which Congress could do by revising NOTA.

The recent series of courtroom battles over the geography of organ allocation—first for lungs, then for livers—show that stakeholders who are unsatisfied with the UNOS algorithm-governing process can, by filing a lawsuit and seeking injunctive relief, rapidly introduce a previously uninvolved federal judge as a forcing factor in organ allocation policy.

PASSING THE TORCH TO YOU

No matter how complicated an algorithm gets, the moral choices inside it can still belong to a wider community beyond just the technical experts. Few if any human activities are more intricate or more technologically demanding than transplanting organs. Yet even in that arena, we can create a clear picture of what is at stake and what is (or is not) possible. That picture can be shared, criticized, and changed.

It's a lesson that can travel. Whether an algorithm is at work in a courtroom, a hospital, or a college admissions office, the values at its core can be made clear and held open to scrutiny. Making one's voice heard need not require any technical expertise. An inclusive discussion, where many voices are reflected in the code, is within our grasp.

The algorithm that matches people to kidneys in the United States is full of compromises. The process of making it was messy and slow. The debates and waves of modifications never really end. Those traits may not be virtues, exactly, but signs that things are going well. Democracy itself is similarly messy.

Sharing moral burdens in a complex technical domain won't happen by accident, or by default. It takes careful planning, and infrastructure, and resources. It also takes political will. At both a cultural and a personal level, we need to recognize that technical expertise is no special source of moral authority. Participation in the design of a complex algorithm is a realistic possibility, if the right kind of careful and well-resourced setting can be put together—and if we learn, as citizens and as publics, to expect an inclusive approach to high-stakes code.

The future depends on you. Whether you work to change software, to change laws, or simply to live the best life you can in our increasingly automated world, I hope this story has inspired you. I hope you are moved to imagine a world where our most important algorithms reflect many voices, including your own. Our future may depend on it.

Notes |

CHAPTER 1: THE HUMAN VALUES THAT HIDE IN ALGORITHMS

1. Porter 1995, 8.
2. Turing 1948.
3. The *theoretical* Turing machine has no limits on its storage or running time. Real physical computers do have such limits. But apart from that, they are equivalent.
4. Citron 2008a.
5. Citron 2008b; Koepke and Robinson 2018.
6. Mulligan and Bamberger 2018, 740.
7. Krafft et al. 2020.
8. For instance, see Stark, Greene, and Hoffmann 2021; Cath 2018. It's also worth noting that while the term "AI" is often used quite broadly, the category's boundaries can also *shrink* when a formerly remarkable software function comes to seem mundane. The scholar Pamela McCorduck, in her 1979 book *Machines Who Think*, coined the term "AI effect" for technologies ceasing to be considered AI once they become sufficiently familiar. For instance, once a computer is able to play a game or solve a math problem, people are likely to reason that these activities do not actually constitute "thinking"; the prevalence of algorithms—of what one might call AI—in our daily lives is thus obscured (McCorduck 1979).
9. Mondragon, Aichholzer, and Leutner 2019.
10. Harwell 2019.
11. Zuloaga 2021.
12. Ibid. The blog post, dated January 11, 2021, asserted that the relevant research had been "conducted early this year," that is, presumably within the eleven days preceding the announcement.
13. Venkatasubramanian (@geomblog) tweeted on January 12, 2021: "It's about time. I used to work with HireVue on their issues around bias

and eventually quit over their resistance to dropping video analysis" (Venkatasubramanian 2021).

14. This was true at the time of the report's original publication. Later, while working on this book, I tried to request a copy using the same process, but the relevant page on HireVue's website did not appear to be functional. I later located a copy of the report on a different public website and obtained that copy without agreeing to HireVue's distribution terms.
15. Engler 2021.
16. Rieke et al. 2021, 5.
17. Ibid., 5.
18. This discussion summarizes Kiviat 2019a.
19. Kiviat 2019b.
20. Kiviat 2019a, 1135.
21. Fourcade and Healy 2013, 565.
22. Kiviat 2019a, 1148.
23. National Conference of Insurance Legislators 2015.
24. Kiviat 2019a, 1148.
25. Huizinga et al. 2016. There are actually three NarxScores for each patient—one each for opiates, sedatives, and stimulants—as well as an overdose risk score. Here I refer specifically to the score that predicts opiate abuse.
26. Szalavitz 2021.
27. For example, Huizinga et al. 2016.
28. Appriss Health 2020.
29. Hu and Harris 2018.
30. This is similar to the process used to match medical students with residencies.
31. Hu and Harris 2018.
32. Fordham University School of Law 2019.
33. Varner and Lecher 2021a and 2021b.
34. Teens Take Charge 2020.
35. City of New York 2020.
36. Teens Take Charge 2020.
37. This approach, known as the "ed-opt" model, had been used before in New York City schools.
38. John Koepke and I (Koepke and Robinson 2018) explore these and other problems with pretrial risk assessment in much more detail.
39. For important references on this theme—all standouts in a growing literature—see Benjamin 2019; Buolamwini and Gebru 2018; Noble 2018; Obermeyer and Mullainathan 2019.
40. Koepke and Robinson 2018; Robinson, Sassaman, and Stevenson 2018; Rieke, Robinson, and Yu 2014.
41. Benjamin 2019.
42. Koepke and Robinson 2018.

43. Partnership on Artificial Intelligence 2019; Leadership Conference on Civil and Human Rights 2018.
44. Starr 2014.
45. Leadership Conference on Civil and Human Rights 2018.
46. Citron 2008b, 1256.
47. Terzis 2017.
48. Senate of Australia 2017.
49. Lecher 2018.
50. Jay Stanley (2017) describes a situation in which errant coding in an Excel spreadsheet, whose contents the state asserted were a trade secret, had mistakenly denied benefits to thousands of developmentally disabled Idaho residents.
51. Citron 2008b, 1288.

INTERLUDE: DALLAS, 2007

1. The primary alternative, peritoneal dialysis, is used by fewer than one in ten patients in the United States. This process involves daily exchanges of fluid in your abdomen and can be done at home.
2. University of California–San Francisco, "The Kidney Project: Statistics," https://pharm.ucsf.edu/kidney/need/statistics.
3. This was the number quoted to me by Douglas Penrod, who has worked for decades as a transplant nurse. Some studies peg the unemployment number even higher. For instance, one study found that over an eighteen-year period only one-quarter of patients starting dialysis were employed, and that among those who had been employed six months earlier, 38 percent had stopped working by the time they began dialysis (Erickson et al. 2018). The authors used a broad definition of employment, including part-time work and study.
4. Veatch and Ross 2015.
5. The description in this section is drawn from the agenda and other materials circulated at the February 8, 2007, public forum held in Dallas by the UNOS/OPTN (United Network for Organ Sharing/Organ Procurement and Transplantation Network)—including a slide deck of Mr. Grawe's presentation—all of which is held in the UNOS/OPTN archives, on file with the author (hereinafter "Dallas Forum").
6. The estimated glomerular filtration rate is itself an algorithm, an indirect measure of how well the kidneys filter toxins out of the blood. As I write (early 2022), this algorithm is in the process of being replaced throughout kidney medicine because it is racially biased: the eGFR assigns extra points to patients identified as black, resulting in scores that "suggest better kidney function" for them than it would give for an otherwise identical non-black

candidate, thus reducing their access to transplant and other care (Vyas, Eisenstein, and Jones 2020). The eGFR's creators "justified [the special scoring of black patients] with evidence . . . that black people release more creatinine into their blood at baseline, in part because they are reportedly more muscular. Analyses have cast doubt on this claim, but the 'race-corrected' eGFR remains the standard" (ibid.). In the wake of that study, spurred in part by petitions from medical students, the National Kidney Foundation and the American Society of Nephrology convened a joint task force to study the issue (Gaffney 2020). In late 2021, the committee recommended a revised approach that did away with the race correction factor (C. Delgado et al. 2021).

7. Dallas Forum, slide show.
8. Douglas Penrod, interview with the author, December 13, 2018.

CHAPTER 2: DEMOCRACY ON THE DRAWING BOARD

1. Calo and Citron 2021, 832.
2. We might be tempted to suppose that market discipline should obviate the need for any such demonstrations. But at least in the case of HireVue, this apparently did not happen: HireVue's customers were not sophisticated or demanding enough to prevent the company from selling a service that its own internal analyses later prompted it to retract. In fact, when the company finally did stop using facial analysis in 2021, a leading AI researcher who had formerly advised the company said, "It's about time. I used to work with HireVue on their issues around bias and eventually quit over their resistance to dropping video analysis" (Venkatasubramanian 2021).
3. Veatch 1973, 36.
4. Burrell and Fourcade 2021, n.p.
5. For a treatment of the literature on "bureaucratic morality"—and a rebuttal defending bureaucracy from its ethics-driven critics—see Gay 2000.
6. See, for instance, Avellan, Sharma, and Turunen 2020; Doshi-Velez et al. 2019; Kroll et al. 2017.
7. Binns et al. 2018; Logg, Minson, and Moore 2019; Martin and Waldman 2021; Zhang 2021.
8. Peter 2017.
9. Concerns like these animate the "Participation" subsection below.
10. Arnstein 1969; Sloane et al. 2020.
11. There is a vast literature on what it could mean to say or deny that a particular algorithm is "fair," some of which stretches the meaning of that word to cover important issues that might more reasonably be discussed in other terms. For a partial survey of how the term is defined in the computer science literature, see Narayanan 2018. Maximilian Kasy and Rediet Abebe (2021)

highlight algorithms' impact on inequality as a vital dimension of evaluation. For a discussion of the importance of welfare, see Birhane and van Dijk 2020.

12. Peter 2017.
13. Raz 1996.
14. Dryzek et al. 2019; Fishkin 2011.
15. Landemore 2020.
16. Organization for Economic Cooperation and Development 2020.
17. New York City Council 2018.
18. Budds 2019.
19. New York City Council 2018. Professor Rashida Richardson, a trenchant critic of the New York City process, led a series of workshops and devoted an article to this question of scope. She argues that "Automated Decision Systems" are "any systems, software, or process that use computation to aid or replace government decisions, judgments, and/or policy implementation that impact opportunities, access, liberties, rights, and/or safety. Automated Decisions Systems can involve predicting, classifying, optimizing, identifying, and/or recommending" (Richardson 2021). Each part of this definition gives some flavor of how hard it is to say precisely which technologies should be covered, or to apply the definition to reach a specific verdict about whether a given system is covered or not.
20. The definition covers any software that is developed with a "logic-based" approach—as any software not otherwise captured by the definition arguably is—and that "can, for a given set of human-defined objectives, generate outputs." The additional examples given in the text of the proposal do not constrain the operative meaning of "AI." See European Commission 2021, article 3 ("Definitions") and annex I ("Artificial Intelligence Techniques and Approaches").
21. Some systems, like the software that controls railroads or elevators, are included as "high-risk" because they are covered by other, existing EU law. I am not describing that portion of the text here. These preexisting regulatory regimes are listed in annex II of the proposal (European Commission 2021).
22. Johnson 2021.
23. Each of these eight categories is described in further detail in annex III of the proposal (European Commission 2021).
24. To reach this conclusion I assume that pain relief in medicine is a "public benefit" and that insurance pricing is a form of "creditworthiness." Apparently, not everyone agrees with such a reading: "The Standing Committee of European Doctors asks that AI for determining an insurance premium or assessing medical treatments should be considered high risk." The implication here is that European health care providers believe that these categories are not already covered (Johnson 2021).
25. European Commission 2021.
26. Ibid.

27. Johnson 2021.
28. Kaminski 2019.
29. Citron 2008b is the leading example of the first strand of thought about algorithmic accountability (Kaminski 2019).
30. For instance, Danielle Citron and Frank Pasquale (2014, 1) argue that "the American due process tradition should inform basic safeguards" for the private-sector scoring algorithms that shape employment opportunities and are not covered by existing statutory or regulatory regimes. Kate Crawford and Jason Schultz (2014) propose "data due process rights" that job applicants could enjoy against a hypothetical employer who "used Big Data to predict how honest" they were.
31. Kaminski 2019; Mulligan and Bamberger 2018.
32. For instance, though Citron (2008b, 1310–1312, note 11) centers her discussion on due process rights, she equally argues that "automated systems must be designed with transparency and accountability as their primary objectives." To achieve this she proposes a range of systemic measures, including source code disclosure; mandatory testing by public agencies of software on which they plan to rely; exploration of "new ways to allow the public to participate in the building of automated decision systems"; and deliberate avoidance of automation under some circumstances. See also her argument that vendors should be required to open-source the software code used for voting machines and certain other high-stakes systems (Citron 2008b).
33. Kroll et al. 2017. See also Desai and Kroll 2017; Edwards and Veale 2017.
34. For an overall discussion of such requirements, see Coglianese and Lehr 2016.
35. Robert Brauneis and Ellen Goodman (2018) provide an inspiring example; see also Bloch-Wehba 2020. For background on the use of these and other statutes in litigation, see Richardson, Schultz, and Southerland 2019.
36. See Edwards and Veale 2017.
37. See the descriptions of the proposal for the European AI Act earlier in this chapter and the federal Algorithmic Accountability Act later in this chapter.
38. Dryzek et al. 2019.
39. Fishkin and Luskin 2005.
40. Ibid., 287.
41. Landemore 2020. It is important to remember that while willingness and ability may have been widely distributed, citizenship was not. For example, only men could be citizens and thus eligible for the council.
42. Farrell, Suiter, and Harris 2019.
43. Thorarensen 2011.
44. Weeks 2000, 361.
45. Zimmerman, Di Rosa, and Kim 2020.
46. Wong 2020, 14.
47. Citron 2008b, 1312.

48. McQuillan 2018a. These would be "horizontal structures in which everyone has an equal say about the matter decided," a deliberate institutional counterweight to the risk that the numerical judgments of people can seem "to reveal a hidden mathematical order in the world that is superior to our direct experience" (McQuillan 2018b, 253). While acknowledging that this proposal is "speculative," he writes that his aim is to "create structures where those affected can contest machine decisions" (McQuillan 2018a, 6, 8).
49. See, for example, the discussion of New York City's recent task force above.
50. Specifically, "a funded and staffed community advisory board, supported by data scientists" (Leadership Conference on Civil and Human Rights 2018).
51. Ibid.
52. Lee et al. 2019.
53. Wolf et al. 2018; Madras et al. 2020.
54. Costanza-Chock 2020.
55. Ibid., 72.
56. Himmelreich, n.d., 7.
57. Himmelreich, n.d.
58. Ubel, Baron, and Asch 1999.
59. Okidegbe, forthcoming.
60. Sloane et al. 2020.
61. Organ Procurement and Transplantation Network, "Bylaws," https://optn .transplant.hrsa.gov/policies-bylaws/bylaws/. See also Legal Information Institute, "42 CFR, § 121.3—The OPTN," https://www.law.cornell.edu/cfr /text/42/121.3 (accessed April 4, 2018).
62. Mulligan and Bamberger 2018.
63. Kroll 2018.
64. See, for example, the discussion in Kaminski 2019.
65. Kroll et al. 2017.
66. Ananny and Crawford 2016.
67. Levy and Johns 2016.
68. Gebru et al. 2018.
69. See, for instance, Mitchell et al. 2019; Yang et al. 2018.
70. See, for instance, Edwards and Veale 2017; Doshi-Velez et al. 2019.
71. Selbst and Barocas 2018.
72. Nicholas Diakopoulos and his colleagues (2016) have recommended that a "social impact statement" be created at the design stage for an unspecified class of high-stakes system and urge that "when the system is launched, the statement should be made public as a form of transparency so that the public has expectations for social impact of the system."
73. Reisman et al. 2018; Diakopoulos et al. 2016 (a group of researchers advocating a "Social Impact Statement for Algorithms," which would be developed first at the design stage).

74. Selbst 2018.
75. Katyal 2019; Mulligan and Bamberger 2018.
76. Moss, Watkins, Metcalf, et al. 2021, 1 (emphasis added).
77. Ibid.
78. Selbst 2021.
79. See the discussion in Metcalf et al. 2021.
80. Edwards and Veale 2017, 80.
81. Kaminski and Malgieri 2021.
82. Koene et al. 2019.
83. See Friedman and Nissenbaum 1996.
84. Brauneis and Goldman 2018, 104.
85. For instance, Cathy O'Neil (2016, 208) asserts the need to "measure [the] impact and conduct algorithmic audits" of high-stakes systems. See also Mayer-Schönberger and Cukier 2013, 179–280.
86. One of the strongest reviews of the concrete possibilities is Raji, Smart, et al. 2020.
87. Buolamwini and Gebru 2018; Raji, Gebru, et al. 2020. For a synthesis of this part of the field, see Sandvig et al. 2014.
88. Raji and Buolamwini 2019.
89. Citron 2008b, 1305.
90. Sandvig et al. 2014; Kim 2017.
91. Zhang and Zhou 2019.
92. Mayer-Schönberger and Cukier 2013, 179.
93. Wilson et al. 2020.
94. KPMG International 2019.
95. See Chowdhury and Mulani 2018.
96. For instance, Hart et al. 2019; Hart et al. 2018; Hart et al. 2017.
97. Chandraker et al. 2019.
98. See Keddell 2016; MetroLab Network 2017; Wald and Woolverton 1990.
99. Eubanks 2018.
100. Wald and Woolverton 1990.
101. Chouldechova et al. 2018.
102. Eubanks 2018; Hurley 2018.
103. Dare and Gambrill 2017.
104. Allegheny County Department of Human Services 2019.
105. Brown et al. 2019.
106. Abebe et al. 2019.
107. Robinson and Koepke 2019.
108. Leadership Conference on Civil and Human Rights 2018.
109. See, for instance, Washington 2018.
110. Okidegbe, forthcoming.
111. Eubanks and Adler-Bell 2018, n.p.

112. Ibid.
113. The Algorithmic Fairness and Opacity Group's (AFOG) "Refusal Conference" was held virtually on October 14–16, 2020. For more information, see the conference website at https://afog.berkeley.edu/programs/the-refusal-conference.
114. Cifor et al. 2019, n.p.
115. Knight 2021.
116. Scott 1998, 354–55.
117. Selbst et al. 2019.
118. See, for instance, Passi and Barocas 2019.
119. Raji and Yang 2019.
120. Here I follow and endorse Green and Viljoen 2020.
121. Ibid.
122. The Cornell Institutional Review Board reviewed the research plan for these interviews and found that the study was exempt from IRB review (notice of exemption dated November 5, 2018, on file with author, protocol ID 1811008382). The study was explained to each participant. Each participant explicitly consented to take part in the study and to have the interview recorded. In all but one instance, subjects agreed to be quoted by name in this book. Interviews were transcribed for analysis in accordance with the protocol.

CHAPTER 3: A FIELD OF LIFE AND DEATH

1. Inker and Perrone 2014.
2. Groth et al. 2000.
3. *New York Times* 1914.
4. David Hamilton (2012) provides an authoritative account of the development of transplantation. Hamilton, himself a transplant surgeon, worked on the book for fifteen years and benefited from extensive correspondence with pioneering transplant surgeons of the modern era, including Thomas Starzl. See "Dr. David Hamilton," The Official Dr. Thomas E. Starzl Website, n.d., https://www.starzl.pitt.edu/people/hamilton.html.
5. See Murray, n.d.
6. Merrill et al. 1956, 282.
7. Hemodialysis is now, and has always been, the primary method of dialysis, but there is also a second method that involves exchanging fluid in a patient's abdominal cavity rather than exchanging blood. That is known as peritoneal dialysis.
8. See Cameron 2002, 74–80. Dr. Willem Kolff, who built this first machine and is now remembered as the inventor of dialysis, went to heroic lengths to construct it: "All metal was commandeered for use in the Nazi war effort,

so the metal used came largely from a shot-down bomber. The rest of the apparatus was made from wood wherever possible. Between them, Kolff and [Richard] Berk falsified affidavits to obtain materials, which were then used for the artificial kidney; an offence for which either might have been shot" (ibid., 77). The practical artificial kidney was actually invented three different times, independently, in the 1940s: the other two inventors were a Canadian named Gordon Murray and a Swede named Nils Alwall (ibid., 75).

9. Satel and Hippen 2007, 164.
10. Blagg 2010.
11. Dr. Scribner and his colleagues, in their publication reporting the invention and first use of this new device, wrote that it "greatly simplifies the problem of repeated dialysis . . . and makes it possible to attempt long-term treatment of patients with chronic renal failure" (Quinton, Dillard, and Scribner 1960, 109). In a companion article, they described two cases in which "patients who were dying of chronic renal failure have been treated by means of repeated hemodialyses"(Scribner et al. 1960, 120).
12. Satel and Hippen 2007, 165.
13. Scribner et al. 1960, 120.
14. Initially the clinic could treat just four patients, though its capacity grew to ten by 1962 (Rettig 1982, 117).
15. Rettig 1982.
16. Sattel and Hippen 2007, 165.
17. Rettig 1982, 116.
18. Murray et al. 1962, 315.
19. Alexander 1962.
20. Ibid.
21. Rettig 1982, 115 (citing Alexander 1962).
22. Rettig 1982, 117.
23. Sanders and Dukeminier 1967, 378.
24. Rettig 1982, 117.
25. Satel and Hippen 2007, 171.
26. Ibid.
27. Lamas 2021.
28. Rettig 1982, 118–19.
29. Ibid.
30. Ibid., 119. "'We just parked it, as I recall,' said Charles Zwick, then assistant director of the bureau (and director soon thereafter): 'we had a little war going on in Southeast Asia'" (ibid., 116).
31. Glazer 1971.
32. Representative Donald G. Brotzman (R-CO), quoted in U.S. Congress, House Committee on Ways and Means, 1972, 1546.
33. Social Security Amendments, Pub. L. No. 92-603, 86 Stat. 1463 § 2991 (1972).

34. National Kidney Foundation, "FAQ about Medicare for Kidney Patients," https://www.kidney.org/atoz/content/faq-about-medicare-kidney-patients.
35. Ibid.
36. 42 U.S.C. 426-1: End Stage Renal Disease Program.
37. Satel and Hippen 2007. Some patients undergo hemodialysis at night while they sleep, and another 10 percent of patients use an alternative treatment approach called peritoneal dialysis, a typically home-based treatment in which toxins are removed through filtration fluid that is flushed into and out of the patient's abdomen.
38. U.S. Renal Data System 2019.
39. Sixty percent was the number quoted to me by Douglas Penrod, who has worked for decades as a transplant nurse. Some studies peg the number even lower. For instance, Kevin Erickson and his colleagues (2018) found that, over an eighteen-year period, only one-quarter of patients starting dialysis were employed, and that among those who had been employed six months earlier, 38 percent had stopped working by the time they began dialysis. These authors used a broad definition of "employment," one that included part-time work and study (ibid., 266).
40. Satel and Hippen 2007, 155.
41. Roberts and Klintmalm 2002, 296.
42. Starzl, Marchioro, and Waddell 1963.
43. Linden 2009, 168.
44. Roberts and Klintmalm 2002, 305.
45. Ibid. 297.
46. "The discovery of the immunomodulatory properties of cyclosporine by Swiss physician Jean Borel in 1977, its clinical investigational introduction in 1978, and its approval by the Food and Drug Administration as 'Sandimmune' in 1983 were the most important immunosuppressive developments in organ transplantation" (Linden 2009, 170).
47. Svarstad, Bugge, and Dhillion 2000.
48. Calne et al. 1978; Calne et al. 1979.
49. Roberts and Klintmalm 2002, 298.
50. Göran Klintmalm, phone interview with the author, November 28, 2018.
51. Linden 2009, 170.
52. U.S. Department of Health and Human Services, OPTN, "National Data," last visited 2019, https://optn.transplant.hrsa.gov/data/view-data-reports/national-data/.
53. The account in this section comes from my interviews with Dr. Klintmalm and Mr. Powell, as well as from Klintmalm's published account of events (Klintmalm 2004; Roberts 2001; Roberts and Klintmalm 2002).
54. Klintmalm 2004, 26.
55. For a snapshot of the national debate during this period, see Friedrich, Thompson, and Dolan 1984.

56. Satel and Hippen 2007, 186.
57. Kurtz and Schwartz 1984.
58. Iglehart 1984, 864.
59. Roberts and Klintmalm 2002, 301.
60. Iglehart 1984, 865.
61. Pub. L. No. 98-507, 98 Stat. 2339 (1984). Congress also hoped to increase the share of medically usable organs that were "procured" for transplantation from dying patients; to prevent the emergence of a commercial market in organs; and to provide some high-level ethical guidance on how the new national system should operate.
62. Ibid.
63. The Hippocratic Oath originated in ancient Greece and begins with an invocation of "Apollo the physician," committing the oath-taker, among other things, to "follow that system of regimen which, according to my ability and judgment, I consider for the benefit of my patients, and abstain from whatever is deleterious and mischievous [and to] give no deadly medicine to any one if asked, nor suggest any such counsel," in the words of one 1849 translation cited in the *Encyclopaedia Britannica* ("Hippocratic Oath: Definition, Summary, and Facts," https://www.britannica.com/topic/Hippocratic-oath).
64. Quoted in Jacobs 1983.
65. See Satel and Hippen 2007. The restriction on payment or in-kind exchange for an organ was prompted almost entirely by the activities of Dr. Jacobs. In the fall of 1983, Jacobs, whose medical license had been revoked five years earlier on a conviction for Medicare fraud, was making plans to establish an organ brokerage called the International Kidney Exchange. "For a markup of $2,000 to $5,000, he would sell the organ to a patient needing a transplant to escape the tyranny of dialysis," explained the *New York Times*, describing Jacobs's enterprise (Wade 1983). To say that his testimony was not well received is an understatement. When Jacobs soon became a lightning rod for a general outcry against the idea of paying for organs, Representative Gore promptly inserted a provision prohibiting payment for organs in his draft bill.
66. Satel and Hippen 2007.
67. Every person has human leukocyte antigen (HLA) proteins on the surface of their cells, and the body's immune system recognizes such proteins as either familiar or foreign. An HLA "mismatch" occurs when a particular organ has HLA proteins on it that are not already present in the recipient's body; such a mismatch thus might be predicted to provoke rejection of the organ.
68. Hamilton 2012, 325.
69. Linden 2009, 172.
70. As Ian Ayres, Laura Dooley, and Robert Gaston (1993, 816) explain: "Doctors hoped that by matching antigens between donor and recipient as closely as possible the results achievable in twins could be approximated with minimal

immunosuppression. In transplants from living relatives of the recipient this has proven true because genetic inheritance of all antigens makes pheno-typic status (antigen matching) a good proxy for the underlying genotypic status. However, with transplantation of cadaveric organs, which are obtained from persons of diverse genetic backgrounds, the use of antigen matching is a poorer proxy for the underlying MHC genes that more directly control the immune response."

71. Rettig 1989, 205.
72. Pub. L. 98-507, 98 Stat. 2339, § 2048 (1984).
73. U.S. Task Force on Organ Transplantation 1986, 86.
74. Ibid.
75. Ibid., 89.
76. Ibid., 69.
77. Weimer 2010, 104; U.S. Task Force on Organ Transplantation 1986, 92.
78. U.S. Task Force on Organ Transplantation 1986, 92.
79. Ibid.
80. Ibid., 89.
81. Rettig 1989, 206.
82. Stegall et al. 2017. For further discussion of the governance evolution described here, see Weimer 2010, 46–52.
83. Pub. L. 100–607, 102 Stat. 3057, § 403a (1988) (emphasis added).
84. Weimer 2010, 105; Starzl et al. 1987.
85. Weimer 2010.
86. Starzl, Shapiro, and Teperman 1989, page not available.
87. Ibid., page not available.
88. McCartney 1993, A9.
89. Gjertson et al. 1991, page not available.
90. U.S. Department of Health and Human Services, Office of Inspector General, 1991, ii.
91. Inker and Perrone 2014, n.p.
92. Gaston et al. 1993.
93. Inker and Perrone 2014, describing Su et al. (2004).
94. Ayres, Dooley, and Gaston 1993, 811.
95. Weimer 2010, 105–14.
96. Göran Klintmalm, phone interview with the author, November 28, 2018.
97. Klintmalm and Kaplan 2017, 2999; see also Williams et al. 2016.
98. Inker and Perrone 2014. Note that a zero-antigen mismatch is distinct from a six-antigen match because some patients have no antigens at a particular location and thus are neither a match nor a mismatch for the antigens on a particular organ.
99. Weimer and Wilk 2019, 145.
100. Ibid.

101. Code of Federal Regulation, "42 CFR, part 121—Organ Procurement and Transplantation Network," https://www.ecfr.gov/cgi-bin/text-idx?SID=bb 60e0a7222f4086a88c31211cac77d1&mc=true&node=pt42.1.121&rgn=div5 #se42.1.121_18 (accessed April 13, 2018).
102. James Alcorn, phone interview with the author, June 27, 2019.
103. Weimer 2010, 107–13.
104. Weimer and Wilk 2019, 148.
105. Brennan n.d.
106. Williams et al. 2015.
107. Brennan n.d.
108. Breimer et al. 2006.
109. Park et al. 2003.
110. Weimer 2010, 107–13.
111. Williams et al. 2015, 3135.
112. Institute of Medicine 1999, 63.
113. See, for example, Pondrom (2008, 264): "According to the OPTN/UNOS Kidney Transplantation Committee, the current system of waiting time considers neither the needs of patients with limited survival on dialysis nor the estimated graft life-years as paired with estimated patient survival. In other words, a kidney that could potentially last another 20 to 30 years may be transplanted into a patient whose life span is perhaps another five years. 'Everyone has been frustrated that one of the major reasons of graft loss was death with a functioning kidney,' says Timothy Pruett, MD, president of OPTN/UNOS."
114. U.S. Department of Health and Human Services, Organ Procurement and Transplantation Network, "About cPRA," https://optn.transplant.hrsa.gov /resources/allocation-calculators/about-cpra/.
115. Ibid.
116. Ayres, Dooley, and Gaston 1993, 840.
117. 42 CFR, § 121.8(a).
118. 42 CFR, § 121.8(b)(2).
119. 42 CFR, 121.8(a).
120. 63 FR 16297.
121. 42 CFR 121.4(b).
122. 42 CFR 121.8(e).

CHAPTER 4: AN ALGORITHM IN FOCUS: THE KIDNEY ALLOCATION SYSTEM

1. Stegall, quoted in Dallas Forum synopsis (OPTN/UNOS 2007).
2. It considered only patients whose blood type was compatible with the kidney being offered, except where otherwise noted, and excluded patients on

other policy grounds as well. For instance, kidneys from hepatitis-positive donors are generally not offered to hepatitis-negative patients.

3. Dallas Forum synopsis (OPTN/UNOS 2007, 5).
4. Stegall 2005. Dr. Stegall chaired this initial review and, as noted elsewhere, was one of my interview subjects.
5. Dallas Forum synopsis (OPTN/UNOS 2007, 5–6). There were eleven of these hearings over the course of 2005 (Weimer and Wilk 2019, 150).
6. Dallas Forum synopsis (OPTN/UNOS 2007, 10).
7. Ibid., 5–6.
8. Ibid., 6.
9. Ibid.
10. Ibid.
11. Dr. Mark Stegall, Dallas Forum presentation.
12. Dallas Forum synopsis (OPTN/UNOS 2007, 3).
13. Ibid.
14. Ibid., 29.
15. Ibid., 13.
16. Ibid.
17. See the section "Measuring Typical Lifetimes" in Wolfe et al. (2008) for more detail on the issues described here.
18. Ibid.
19. Dallas Forum synopsis (OPTN/UNOS 2007, 13).
20. Wolfe et al. 2008.
21. I did not encounter a clear description of these effects in any of the materials I read.
22. Dallas Forum synopsis, (OPTN/UNOS 2007, 17).
23. Ibid.
24. Ibid.
25. Ibid.
26. Clive Grawe, Dallas Forum presentation.
27. Ibid.
28. Douglas Penrod, phone interview with the author, December 13, 2018.
29. Pondrom 2008, 264.
30. Weimer and Wilk 2019, 154.
31. Ibid.
32. See LYFT proposal (OPTN/Kidney Transplantation Committee 2008). Hereinafter "LYFT proposal."
33. Ibid.
34. Ibid. 20.
35. Ibid., 21.
36. Ibid., 16.
37. The contribution of waiting time is reflected in the 0.2 number in the middle term of the equation. Dr. Mark Stegall, who chaired the KTC when it developed

the LYFT proposal, wrote that the committee included the 20 percent factor for waiting time because it feared that a purely LYFT-based approach could have a perverse result: if patients with the best LYFT scores "were transplanted immediately after listing," then those patients might "not choose living-donor kidney transplantation" and total transplants could be reduced. By its adjustment to the numbers, the committee hoped to "ensure that all candidates would be forced to wait at least a year or two before receiving a [deceased donor] transplant" (Stegall 2009, 1528, 1529). This concern may have been informed by the paradoxical consequences of an earlier proposal known as "Share 35," which had made it much easier for children to receive immediate or nearly immediate transplants from the waiting list and evidently deterred some of their parents from making live donations, perhaps because parents wished to preserve the option to provide another kidney if their child's first transplant failed (see Ross et al. 2012, 2115, 2119).

38. Bromberg and Gill 2009.
39. OPTN/UNOS 2009. Kidney Transplantation Committee, report to the board of directors, June 22–23, 2009.
40. Ibid, 16.
41. Ibid.
42. Dr. Mark Stegall, phone interview with the author, June 18, 2019.
43. OPTN/UNOS 2009. Kidney Transplantation Committee, report to the board of directors, June 22–23, 2009, 5. David Weimer and Laura Wilk (2019, 154) call this a "main reason" why the RFI was criticized.
44. Wolfe, McCullough, and Leichtman 2009, 1523, 1524.
45. Hippen 2009, 1507, 1508.
46. Wolfe et al. 2009, 1523.
47. Dr. John Friedewald, phone interview with the author, June 24, 2019.
48. Dr. Mark Stegall, interview with the author, June 18, 2019.
49. OPTN/UNOS 2009. Kidney Transplantation Committee, report to the board of directors, June 22–23, 2009, 6.
50. Stock 2009; see also OPTN/UNOS 2009. Kidney Transplantation Committee, report to the board of directors, June 22–23, 2009.
51. OPTN/UNOS 2009. Kidney Transplantation Committee, report to the board of directors, June 22–23, 2009, 4.
52. Ibid., 7.
53. Ibid., 19.
54. Stock 2009, 1522.
55. Ibid.
56. Health Resources and Services Administration, "Organ Donation Statistics," https://www.organdonor.gov/statistics-stories/statistics.html#glance.
57. Dr. Mark Stegall, phone interview with the author, June 18, 2019.
58. See Dallas Forum synopsis (OPTN/UNOS 2007, 6): "Although a final proposal has not yet been developed, the Committee is considering . . . allocating

kidneys to candidates waiting for simultaneous kidney-pancreas transplants and kidney-alone transplants from the same [kidney transplant candidate] list."

59. See LYFT proposal, 8: "The pancreas allocation algorithm would determine placement for SPK transplantation."

60. See, for example, OPTN/Kidney Transplantation Committee 2011, which describes the "baseline" for simulations had "allocated [kidneys for] simultaneous kidney-pancreas transplants according to the pancreas rules, not the kidney rules (i.e. 'kidney follows pancreas')" (20).

61. Dr. John Friedewald, phone interview with the author, June 24, 2019.

62. The factors were the recipient's age, the donor's age, the donor's race (as a binary for African American donors or others), hypertension, diabetes, creatinine, cerebrovascular cause of death, height, weight, whether the donor's heart was beating at the time of donation, and whether the donor tested positive for hepatitis (OPTN/Kidney Transplantation Committee 2011, 10).

63. Ibid.

64. Ibid., 13.

65. OPTN/Kidney Transplantation Committee 2011, 15.

66. Ibid., 10.

67. Ibid.

68. Ibid., 20.

69. Ibid., 16.

70. Ibid., 19.

71. Ibid., 22.

72. Ibid., 26.

73. Ibid., 27, table 4.

74. Ibid., 22. This average recipient was most likely a statistical composite of fifty-year-old transplant recipients who were not diabetic and were average in all other respects (see Rao et al. 2009, 231, 234, cited in OPTN/Kidney Transplantation Committee 2011, 10).

75. This number was predicted to decline from 5,817 transplants per year under baseline assumptions to 4,538 with the introduction of survival matching (Organ Procurement and Transplantation Network 2011, 27).

76. Harris 2011.

77. Stein 2011.

78. Ibid.

79. Ibid.

80. 42 U.S.C. § 6102 (2006).

81. Eidelson 2012.

82. Ibid., 1639, citing 42 U.S.C. § 6103(b)(1)(A) (brackets in Eidelson's original).

83. 45 CFR § 91.13 (2012).

84. Eidelson 2012.

85. Ibid.

86. That is, the c-statistic between these two quintiles specifically was 0.62 (Ross 2012).
87. Friedewald and Formica 2011, 3.
88. Ibid.
89. Dr. Mark Stegall, phone interview with the author, June 18, 2019.
90. Friedewald and Formica 2011.
91. OPTN Kidney Transplantation Committee, "Proposal to Substantially Revise the National Kidney Allocation System (UNOS)," September 21, 2012 (hereinafter "Final Proposal").
92. Ibid., 8.
93. Ibid., 18.
94. Ibid., 24.
95. Ibid., 11.
96. Ibid., 15.
97. Ibid., 5.
98. OPTN 2013, 99.
99. Ibid.
100. Ibid., 220.
101. Ibid., 164.
102. Ibid.
103. Ibid., 166.
104. Ibid., 225.
105. For example, it changed to updating candidates' EPTS scores daily rather than quarterly (ibid., 231). See OPTN 2013, board briefing paper, 219–37.
106. U.S. Department of Health and Human Services 2013.
107. U.S. Department of Health and Human Services, OPTN, "National Data," last visited 2019, https://optn.transplant.hrsa.gov/data/view-data-reports/national-data/.
108. See Final Proposal, 30, fig. 12.
109. Ibid.
110. Ibid.
111. Such an analysis might be misleading if beliefs about the new algorithm deterred transplant centers from listing older candidates in the first place. Harvey Mysel, a kidney transplant recipient who trains other patients in how to pursue living donation, told me that older patients are being discouraged from pursuing deceased-donor transplants:

   > They're being told in no uncertain terms, go find a living donor, you're not gonna get one from the waiting list. Especially someone that's sixty or sixty-five years old, the odds of them getting a deceased-donor kidney are significantly reduced since the KAS. . . . They're basically telling patients, "We're not putting you on the waiting list . . . because you're not going to get a transplant."

By keeping older candidates off the list, Mysel pointed out, a transplant center can improve its numbers: a higher fraction of those who are on its list will receive a transplant, and fewer patients while die while wait-listed (Harvey Mysel, phone interview with the author, December 6, 2018).

However, OPTN statistics on waiting list additions by age show that the annual number of new waiting list registrations for patients over sixty-five has held steady or gone up throughout the period since KAS was implemented, and that the fraction of all new registrations coming from this age group has increased steadily, from 17.1 percent in 2013 (the last full year under the old algorithm) to 19.9 percent in 2018.

112. Melanson et al. 2017.
113. Ibid., 1082, 1083.
114. Hart et al. 2017, 5.
115. Melanson et al. 2017, 1084.
116. As Hart and colleagues (2017, 3) note, diagnosing racial disparities in listing is difficult "given limited data on the proportions of patients in the United States with advanced chronic kidney disease."
117. Melanson et al. 2017, 1084.
118. John Friedewald and Nicole Turgeon (2017) report on such views without endorsing them.
119. Kyle Jackson and his colleagues (2019) report an adjusted incidence ratio of 1.77.
120. Ibid.
121. OPTN/UNOS 2017.
122. Ibid., 6.
123. Ibid.
124. Stewart et al. 2018.
125. Notably, the metric compares equity across *registrations*, not across candidates, because different registrations can have different start dates, geographies, and other factors (ibid., 1925). This makes the analyses inapplicable to the small group of highly mobilized patients who engage in multiple listing.
126. Ibid., 1928.
127. Ibid., 1929.
128. Dr. Mark Stegall, phone interview with the author, June 18, 2019.
129. The events recounted here are based on Bensousan (2021) and Schwamm (2018), as well as on *Miriam Holman Sheloshim* (2018).
130. Schwamm 2018.
131. *Iriam Holman v. United States Department of Health and Human Services*, Complaint, November 19, 2017, United States District Court for the Southern District of New York (hereinafter "Holman Complaint"), paragraph 6: "If a pair of lungs suitable for Miriam became available from a donor in Fort Lee, New Jersey (a three mile drive from [her hospital bed]), the lung would be

offered first to all suitable candidates in the DSA encompassing Northern and Central New Jersey, even if those candidates have lower [Lung Allocation Scores, reflecting less medical urgency]—even much lower—than Miriam's. Moreover, given the arbitrary nature of the DSA's geographic area, that candidate would likely be *geographically further away* from the donated lung than Miriam" (emphasis in original).

132. Shulman practices in Armonk, New York, holds a BA degree in Talmud, and is a leading patron of Yeshiva Aderes Hatorah, a Jewish religious school for boys (see "Aderes Hatorah—10th Anniversary Inaugural Dinner—Motty Shulman," posted on YouTube on April 6, 2017, https://www.youtube.com/watch?v=Ussx9pMfqxo). The Holman family held an Orthodox memorial service for Miriam after she passed.

133. Holman Complaint, paragraph 51.

134. Ibid., paragraph 1.

135. For further discussion of the origins of DSAs, see Glazier (2018, 141): "DSAs are geographic boundaries that were created for CMS administrative purposes to define which hospitals OPOs [organ procurement organizations] are responsible for working with to coordinate donation. At the time they were put in place, DSAs primarily reflected existing catchment areas OPOs were working within prior to the establishment of a national system formalized under federal law. As a result, there is wide variation in the size of DSAs and even patchwork patterns in which a single DSA is comprised of non-contiguous service areas. DSAs range in size from four thousand square miles—the OPO based in Washington DC—to eight hundred thousand square miles—the OPO based in Washington state."

136. Harvey Mysel, phone interview with the author, December 6, 2018.

137. Russo et al. 2013.

138. Holman Complaint, paragraph 32.

139. Bernstein and Kindy 2018.

140. Holman Complaint, paragraph 33.

141. Holman Complaint, 6.

142. Ibid., docket 10.

143. US Attorneys Office (USAO), counsel for HHS, to Circuit Judge Katzman, letter reproduced as Holman Complaint, docket 10-1.

144. Holman Complaint, report from Yolanda Becker, president of the OPTN/UNOS board of directors.

145. A moving sheloshim memorial service was held for her on March 2, 2018, thirty days after her death, as is traditional among Orthodox Jews (see *Miriam Holman Sheloshim* 2018).

146. Glazier 2018, 143.

147. Motty Shulman, letter to HHS, December 1, 2017. On file with author.

148. Zarembo 2018.

149. Shulman, letter to HHS, December 1, 2017.

150. Bernstein 2017.

151. George Sigounas to Motty Shulman, March 1, 2018, on file with author.

152. Motty Shulman to HHS Secretary, letter, May 30, 2018, 7, on file with author.

153. *Wilnelia Cruz, Susan Jackson, Deborah McNeill, Robert Nourse, Luis Torres, and Marilyn Walto v. U.S. Department of Health and Human Services*, filed July 13, 2018, in U.S. District Court, Southern District of New York, https://www .courthousenews.com/wp-content/uploads/2018/07/OrgansHHS.pdf (hereinafter "Cruz Complaint"), paragraph 112.

154. Ibid., paragraph 113.

155. Ibid., paragraph 116.

156. Ibid., docket 9.

157. Ibid., docket 5; Piedmont Health, letter, June 29, 2018, in Cruz Complaint, docket 9-3.

158. Cruz Complaint, docket 3-4.

159. George Sigounas to Sue Dunn, UNOS president, letter, July 31, 2018 (on file with author), https://unos.org/wp-content/uploads/unos/HRSA_to_OPTN _Organ_Allocation_20180731.pdf.

160. Stewart et al. 2018.

CHAPTER 5: CONCLUSION: IDEAS FOR OUR FUTURE

1. The social underpinnings for this way of thinking are fascinating. As Kieran Healy (2010, 113) has written, we should not accept "the image of the individual altruist who simply chooses, in the absence of organization-ally managed opportunities or culturally sustained exchange relations, to come forward and do good." Exchanges of organs for transplant, he points out, "are moral economies sustained by procurement organizations, [which] produce donations by providing opportunities to give and sustain them by generating accounts of what giving means. Doing so entails a great deal of logistical and cultural work."

2. There is a large debate about waning trust in institutions. Ethan Zuckerman (2017) provides a good roundup of the evidence that trust in all kinds of institutions has declined.

3. Ubel, Baron, and Asch 1999.

4. See, for example, Burt et al., n.d.; Crespo et al. 2017.

5. Barberá 2020.

6. Ibid.

7. There are several ways to understand this comment and the overall shift in policy. On the one hand, the shift to a joint kidney-pancreas list was a simpler approach to increasing total benefit, and the shift that it made toward

younger recipients may have seemed less like age discrimination because these young people were outliers, even when compared with other candidates their own age, in how much they would benefit from a transplant. On the other hand, this shift also received much less public attention and debate, and that too might have helped to make it possible.

8. Namely, those of limited means who have exhausted their three years of Medicare coverage.

9. Fissell, Roy, and Davenport 2013; Hojs, Fissell, and Roy 2020.

10. Rabin 2021.

11. Cooper et al. 2020.

12. Rabin 2021.

13. Rabin 2022.

14. Teens Take Charge 2020.

15. Robinson and Koepke 2019.

16. Virginia Eubanks makes this argument through her ethnography in *Automating Inequality* (2017) and in other writings.

17. For a discussion and critique of this model, see F. Delgado et al. 2021.

18. Kiviat 2019a.

19. Calabresi and Bobbitt 1978, 69.

20. Peixoto 2013, 204.

21. See Abebe et al. 2019.

22. Cain 2014, 84.

23. Kiviat 2019a, 1135.

24. See, for example, the ACLU's Community Control Over Police Surveillance (CCOPS) campaign (ACLU 2021).

25. For instance, criminal justice authorities in New York City and Philadelphia have established "research advisory committees" to provide input into the revision and use of risk assessment algorithms in criminal justice. Among the committee members are policy scholars who work on criminal justice reform and, in Philadelphia, community representatives from system-involved communities.

26. Bernstein and Isackson 2014; Eterno 2012; Eterno and Silverman 2012; Keller 2015.

27. Eterno and Silverman 2012.

28. Sparrow 2015.

29. Harmon 2015.

30. Eterno and Silverman 2012, page not available.

31. Campbell 1979.

32. Walzer 1968.

33. Quigley and Raphael 2005.

34. Hernandez 2018, 22.

35. Cain 2014.

36. Walzer 1970.
37. For a roundup of such evidence from an optimistic perspective, see Curato et al. 2017. See also Dryzek et al. 2019.
38. Dryzek et al. 2019, page not available.
39. Ibid., 1146.
40. Weeks 2000, 371.
41. Ibid., 360.
42. Grönlund, Herne, and Setälä 2015, 995.
43. Niemeyer 2011, 103.
44. One of the hard problems is determining how policymakers or scholars can or should judge the results of a participation exercise. Participants, policy-makers, and researchers may disagree as to whether the process was good, and whether its outcome was a wise one, and that disagreement itself is a subject of study. See, for instance, Rowe and Frewer 2000.
45. What it means for one group to be "representative" of another turns out to be fascinating as a matter of both math and philosophy (Chasalow and Levy 2021).
46. Landemore 2020.
47. Smith 2009, citing Bryan 2003.
48. Secondo and Lerner 2020, n.p.
49. Klein and Sacasas 2021, n.p.
50. Fourcade and Healy 2017, 17.
51. Calabresi and Bobbitt 1978, 21.
52. Bogen and Rieke 2018, 45.
53. Calabresi and Bobbitt 1978, 47.
54. Dr. Mark Stegall, phone interview with the author, June 18, 2019.

References |

Abebe, Rediet, Solon Barocas, Jon Kleinberg, Karen Levy, Manish Raghavan, and David G. Robinson. 2019. "Roles for Computing in Social Change." In *Proceedings of the 2020 Conference on Fairness, Accountability, and Transparency* (January), 252–60. DOI: https://doi.org/10.1145/3351095.3372871.

Alexander, Shana. 1962. "They Decide Who Lives, Who Dies." *Life*, November 9, 1962.

Allegheny County Department of Human Services. 2019. "Impact Evaluation Summary of the Allegheny Family Screening Tool." April. https://www.alleghenycountyanalytics.us/wp-content/uploads/2019/05/Impact-Evaluation Summary-from-16-ACDHS-26_PredictiveRisk_Package_050119_FINAL-5.pdf.

American Civil Liberties Union (ACLU). 2021. "Community Control Over Police Surveillance (CCOPS) Model Bill." April. https://www.aclu.org/legal-document /community-control-over-police-surveillance-ccops-model-bill.

Ananny, Mike, and Kate Crawford. 2016. "Seeing without Knowing: Limitations of the Transparency Ideal and Its Application to Algorithmic Accountability." *New Media and Society* 20(3): 973–89. DOI: https://doi.org/10.1177/1461444816676645.

Appriss Health. 2020. "How to Utilize NarxCare." Louisville, Ky.: Appriss, Inc. (May). https://pharmacy.ks.gov/docs/default-source/ktracs/user-guides/risk -indicator-score-explanation.pdf?sfvrsn=ebe8aa01_6.

Arnstein, Sherry R. 1969. "A Ladder of Citizen Participation." *Journal of the American Institute of Planners* 35(4): 216–24. DOI: https://doi.org/10.1080/01944366908977225.

Avellan, Tero, Sumita Sharma, and Markku Turunen. 2020. "AI for All: Defining the What, Why, and How of Inclusive AI." In *Proceedings of the 23rd International Conference on Academic Mindtrek* (January): 142–44. DOI: https://doi.org/10.1145 /3377290.3377317.

Ayres, Ian, Laura G. Dooley, and Robert S. Gaston. 1993. "Unequal Racial Access to Kidney Transplantation." *Vanderbilt Law Review* 46: 805–64.

Barberá, Pablo. 2020. "Social Media, Echo Chambers, and Political Polarization." In *Social Media and Democracy: The State of the Field and Prospects for Reform*, edited by Nathaniel Persily and Joshua A. Tucker. Cambridge: Cambridge University Press.

Benjamin, Ruha. 2019. *Race after Technology: Abolitionist Tools for the New Jim Code.* Medford, Mass.: Polity.

Bensousan, Barbara. 2021. "Sweetening the Bitter Waters." *Mishpacha Magazine* (blog). January 20. https://mishpacha.com/sweetening-the-bitter-waters/.

Bernstein, David, and Noah Isackson. 2014. "The Truth about Chicago's Crime Rates: Part 1." *Chicago Magazine*, April 7.

Bernstein, Lenny. 2017. "Liver Transplant Distribution Changed after Years of Debate." *Washington Post*, December 4. https://www.washingtonpost.com /national/health-science/liver-transplant-distribution-changed-after-years-of -debate/2017/12/04/fedefc0e-d92c-11e7-b859-fb0995360725_story.html.

Bernstein, Lenny, and Kimberly Kindy. 2018. "New York Organ Collection Agency, Nation's Second-Largest, Threatened with Closure." *Washington Post*, July 11. https://www.washingtonpost.com/national/health-science/new-york-organ -collection-agency-nations-second-largest-threatened-with-closure/2018/07/11 /09c52824-847b-11e8-8f6c-46cb43e3f306_story.html.

Binns, Reuben, Max Van Kleek, Michael Veale, Ulrik Lyngs, Jun Zhao, and Nigel Shadbolt. 2018. "'It's Reducing a Human Being to a Percentage': Perceptions of Justice in Algorithmic Decisions." In *Proceedings of the 2018 CHI Conference on Human Factors in Computing Systems*, paper 377 (April): 1–14. DOI: https://doi.org /10.1145/3173574.3173951.

Birhane, Abeba, and Jelle van Dijk. 2020. "Robot Rights? Let's Talk about Human Welfare Instead." In *Proceedings of the AAAI/ACM Conference on AI, Ethics, and Society* (February): 207–13. DOI: https://doi.org/10.1145/3375627.3375855.

Blagg, Christopher R. 2010. "Belding Hibbard Scribner—Better Known as Scrib." *Clinical Journal of the American Society of Nephrology* 5(12): 2146–49. DOI: https:// doi.org/10.2215/CJN.07640810.

Bloch-Wehba, Hannah. 2020. "Access to Algorithms." *Fordham Law Review* 88: 1265.

Bogen, Miranda, and Aaron Rieke. 2018. "Help Wanted: An Exploration of Hiring Algorithms, Equity and Bias." Washington, D.C.: Upturn (December). https:// apo.org.au/sites/default/files/resource-files/2018-12/apo-nid210071.pdf.

Brauneis, Robert, and Ellen P. Goodman. 2018. "Algorithmic Transparency for the Smart City." *Yale Journal of Law and Technology* 20: 103–76.

Breimer, Michael E., Johan Mölne, Gunnela Nordén, Lennart Rydberg, Gilbert Thiel, and Christian T. Svalander. 2006. "Blood Group A and B Antigen Expression in Human Kidneys Correlated to A1/A2/B, Lewis, and Secretor Status." *Transplantation* 82(4): 479–85.

Brennan, Daniel C. n.d. "Kidney Transplantation in Adults: ABO Incompatibility." UpToDate. Last updated January 13, 2020. Accessed April 26, 2022. https://www .uptodate.com/contents/kidney-transplantation-in-adults-abo-incompatibility /print.

Bromberg, J., and J. Gill. 2009. "Heavy LYFTing: KASting Pearls before Swine." *American Journal of Transplantation* 9(7): 1489–90. DOI: https://doi.org/10.1111 /j.1600-6143.2009.02688.x.

Brown, Anna, Alexandra Chouldechova, Emily Putnam-Hornstein, Andrew Tobin, and Rhema Vaithianathan. 2019. "Toward Algorithmic Accountability in Public Services: A Qualitative Study of Affected Community Perspectives on Algorithmic Decision-Making in Child Welfare Services." In *Proceedings of the 2019 CHI Conference on Human Factors in Computing Systems* (May), 1–12. DOI: https://doi.org/10.1145/3290605.3300271.

Bryan, Frank M. 2003. *Real Democracy: The New England Town Meeting and How It Works*. Chicago: University of Chicago Press.

Budds, Diana. 2019. "New York City's AI Task Force Stalls." *Curbed New York*, April 16, 2019. https://ny.curbed.com/2019/4/16/18335495/new-york-city-automated-decision-system-task-force-ai.

Buolamwini, Joy, and Timnit Gebru. 2018. "Gender Shades: Intersectional Accuracy Disparities in Commercial Gender Classification." *Proceedings of Machine Learning Research* 81: 1–15. Conference on Fairness, Accountability, and Transparency, New York, February 23–24. http://proceedings.mlr.press/v81/buolamwini18a/buolamwini18a.pdf.

Burrell, Jenna, and Marion Fourcade. 2021. "The Society of Algorithms." *Annual Review of Sociology* 47(1). DOI: https://doi.org/10.1146/annurev-soc-090820-020800.

Burt, Andrew, Brenda Leong, Stuart Shirrell, and Xiangnong (George) Wang. n.d. "Beyond Explainability: A Practical Guide to Managing Risk in Machine Learning Models." Future of Privacy Forum. https://www.immuta.com/wp-content/uploads/2018/06/Beyond_Explainability.pdf.

Cain, Bruce E. 2014. *Democracy More or Less: America's Political Reform Quandary*. New York: Cambridge University Press.

Calabresi, Guido, and Philip Bobbitt. 1978. *Tragic Choices: The Conflicts Society Confronts in the Allocation of Tragically Scarce Resources*. New York: W. W. Norton.

Calne, R. Y., K. Rolles, S. Thiru, P. McMaster, G. N. Craddock, S. Aziz, D.J.G. White, et al. 1979. "Cyclosporin A Initially as the Only Immunosuppressant in 34 Recipients of Cadaveric Organs: 32 Kidneys, 2 Pancreases, and 2 Livers." *Lancet* 314(8151): 1033–36. DOI: https://doi.org/10.1016/S0140-6736(79)92440-1.

Calne, R. Y., D. J. White, S. Thiru, D. B. Evans, P. McMaster, D. C. Dunn, G. N. Craddock, B. D. Pentlow, and K. Rolles. 1978. "Cyclosporin A in Patients Receiving Renal Allografts from Cadaver Donors." *Lancet* 2(8104/8105): 1323–27. DOI: https://doi.org/10.1016/s0140-6736(78)91970-0.

Calo, Ryan, and Danielle Keats Citron. 2021. "The Automated Administrative State: A Crisis of Legitimacy." *Emory Law Journal* 70: 50.

Cameron, John Stewart. 2002. *A History of the Treatment of Renal Failure by Dialysis*. Oxford: Oxford University Press.

Campbell, Donald T. 1979. "Assessing the Impact of Planned Social Change." *Evaluation and Program Planning* 2(1): 67–90. DOI: https://doi.org/10.1016/0149-7189(79)90048-X.

Cath, Corinne. 2018. "Governing Artificial Intelligence: Ethical, Legal, and Technical Opportunities and Challenges." *Philosophical Transactions of the Royal Society A: Mathematical, Physical, and Engineering Sciences* 376 (2133, October): 20180080. DOI: https://doi.org/10.1098/rsta.2018.0080.

Chandraker, Anil, Kenneth A. Andreoni, Robert S. Gaston, John Gill, Jayme E. Locke, Amit K. Mathur, Douglas J. Norman, et al. 2019. "Time for Reform in Transplant Program–Specific Reporting: ASTS Transplant Metrics Taskforce." *American Journal of Transplantation* 19(7): 1888–95. DOI: https://doi.org/10.1111/ajt.15394.

Chasalow, Kyla, and Karen Levy. 2021. "Representativeness in Statistics, Politics, and Machine Learning." arXiv:2101.03827v3 [cs. CY]. Submitted January 11, 2021; updated February 10, 2021. http://arxiv.org/abs/2101.03827.

Chouldechova, Alexandra, Emily Putnam-Hornstein, Diana Benavides-Prado, Oleksandr Fialko, and Rhema Vaithianathan. 2018. "A Case Study of Algorithm-Assisted Decision Making in Child Maltreatment Hotline Screening Decisions." In *Proceedings of Machine Learning Research* 81: 1–15. Conference on Fairness, Accountability, and Transparency, New York, February 23–24. http://proceedings.mlr.press/v81/chouldechova18a/chouldechova18a.pdf.

Chowdhury, Rumman, and Narendra Mulani. 2018. "Auditing Algorithms for Bias." *Harvard Business Review*, October 24. https://hbr.org/2018/10/auditing-algorithms-for-bias.

Cifor, Marika, Patricia Garcia, T. L. Cowan, Jasmine Rault, Tonia Sutherland, Anita Say Chan, Jennifer Rode, Anna Lauren Hoffmann, Niloufar Salehi, and Lisa Nakamura. 2019. "Feminist Data Manifest-No." https://www.manifestno.com/home.

Citron, Danielle Keats. 2008a. "Open Code Governance." *University of Chicago Legal Forum*, 355–87. https://ssrn.com/abstract=1081689.

———. 2008b. "Technological Due Process." *Washington University Law Review* 85: 1249–1314.

Citron, Danielle Keats, and Frank Pasquale. 2014. "The Scored Society: Due Process for Automated Predictions." *Washington Law Review* 89(1): 1–34.

City of New York. 2020. "Mayor de Blasio and Chancellor Carranza Announce 2021–22 School Year Admissions Process." New York: Office of the Mayor (December 18). http://www1.nyc.gov/office-of-the-mayor/news/874-20/mayor-de-blasio-chancellor-carranza-2021-22-school-year-admissions-process.

Coglianese, Cary, and David Lehr. 2016. "Regulating by Robot: Administrative Decision Making in the Machine-Learning Era." *Georgetown Law Journal* 105: 1147–1224.

Cooper, David K. C., Hidetaka Hara, Hayato Iwase, Takayuki Yamamoto, Abhijit Jagdale, Vineeta Kumar, Roslyn Bernstein Mannon, Michael J. Hanaway, Douglas J. Anderson, and Devin E. Eckhoff. 2020. "Clinical Pig Kidney Xenotransplantation: How Close Are We?" *Journal of the American Society of Nephrology* 31(1): 12–21. DOI: https://doi.org/10.1681/ASN.2019070651.

Costanza-Chock, Sasha. 2020. *Design Justice: Community-Led Practices to Build the Worlds We Need.* Cambridge, Mass.: MIT Press.

Crawford, Kate, and Jason Schultz. 2014. "Big Data and Due Process: Toward a Framework to Redress Predictive Privacy Harms." *Boston College Law Review* 55(1): 93, 109. https://lawdigitalcommons.bc.edu/bclr/vol55/iss1/4.

Crespo, Ignacio, Pankaj Kumar, Peter Noteboom, and Marc Taymans. 2017. "The Evolution of Model Risk Management." McKinsey & Company (February 10). https://www.mckinsey.com/business-functions/risk/our-insights/the-evolution -of-model-risk-management.

Curato, Nicole, John S. Dryzek, Selen A. Ercan, Carolyn M. Hendriks, and Simon Niemeyer. 2017. "Twelve Key Findings in Deliberative Democracy Research." *Daedalus* 146(3): 28–38. DOI: https://doi.org/10.1162/DAED_a_00444.

Dare, Tim, and Eileen Gambrill. 2017. "Ethical Analysis: Predictive Risk Models at Call Screening for Allegheny County." March. http://www.alleghenycounty.us /WorkArea/linkit.aspx?LinkIdentifier=id&ItemID=6442457402.

Delgado, Cynthia, Mukta Baweja, Deidra C. Crews, Nwamaka D. Eneanya, Crystal A. Gadegbeku, Lesley A. Inker, Mallika L. Mendu, et al. 2021. "A Unifying Approach for GFR Estimation: Recommendations of the NKF-ASN Task Force on Reassessing the Inclusion of Race in Diagnosing Kidney Disease." *Journal of the American Society of Nephrology* 32(12): 2994–3015. DOI: https://doi.org/10.1681/ASN.2021070988.

Delgado, Fernando, Stephen Yang, Michael Madaio, and Qian Yang. 2021. "Stakeholder Participation in AI: Beyond 'Add Diverse Stakeholders and Stir.'" arXiv:2111.01122 [Cs], November. http://arxiv.org/abs/2111.01122.

Desai, Deven R., and Joshua A. Kroll. 2017. "Trust but Verify: A Guide to Algorithms and the Law." *Harvard Journal of Law and Technology* 31(1): 64. https://jolt.law .harvard.edu/assets/articlePDFs/v31/31HarvJLTech1.pdf.

Diakopoulos, Nicholas, Sorelle Friedler, Marcelo Arenas, Solon Barocas, Michael Hay, Bill Howe, H. V. Jagadish, et al. 2016. "Principles for Accountable Algorithms and a Social Impact Statement for Algorithms." Accessed January 3, 2020. https:// www.fatml.org/resources/principles-for-accountable-algorithms.

Doshi-Velez, Finale, Mason Kortz, Ryan Budish, Chris Bavitz, Sam Gershman, David O'Brien, Kate Scott, et al. 2019. "Accountability of AI under the Law: The Role of Explanation." Cornell University, arXiv:1711.01134v3 [cs., AI]. Submitted November 3, 2017; last revised December 20, 2019. http://arxiv .org/abs/1711.01134.

Dryzek, John S., André Bächtiger, Simone Chambers, Joshua Cohen, James N. Druckman, Andrea Felicetti, James S. Fishkin, et al. 2019. "The Crisis of Democracy and the Science of Deliberation." *Science* 363(6432): 1144–46. DOI: https://doi.org/10.1126/science.aaw2694.

Edwards, Lilian, and Michael Veale. 2017. "Slave to the Algorithm? Why a 'Right to Explanation' Is Probably Not the Remedy You Are Looking For." *Duke Law and Technology Review* 16(1): 18.

Eidelson, Benjamin. 2012. "Kidney Allocation and the Limits of the Age Discrimination Act." *Yale Law Journal* 122: 1635–52.

Engler, Alex C. 2021. "Independent Auditors Are Struggling to Hold AI Companies Accountable." *Fast Company* (blog), January 26. https://www.fastcompany.com/90597594/ai-algorithm-auditing-hirevue.

Erickson, Kevin F., Bo Zhao, Vivian Ho, and Wolfgang C. Winkelmayer. 2018. "Employment among Patients Starting Dialysis in the United States." *Clinical Journal of the American Society of Nephrology* 13(2): 265–73. DOI: https://doi.org/10.2215/CJN.06470617.

Eterno, John A. 2012. "Policing by the Numbers." *New York Times*, June 17. http://www.nytimes.com/2012/06/18/opinion/the-nypds-obsession-with-numbers.html.

Eterno, John, and Eli B. Silverman. 2012. *The Crime Numbers Game: Management by Manipulation*. Boca Raton, Fla.: CRC Press.

Eubanks, Virginia. 2018. *Automating Inequality: How High-Tech Tools Profile, Police, and Punish the Poor*. New York: St. Martin's Press.

Eubanks, Virginia, and Sam Adler-Bell. 2018. "The High-Tech Poorhouse." *Jacobin* (January). https://jacobinmag.com/2018/01/virginia-eubanks-interview-automating-inequality-poverty.

European Commission. 2021. *Proposal for a Regulation of the European Parliament and of the Council Laying down Harmonised Rules on Artificial Intelligence (Artificial Intelligence Act) and Amending Certain Union Legislative Acts*. https://eur-lex.europa.eu/resource.html?uri=cellar:e0649735-a372-11eb-9585-01aa75ed71a1.0001.02/DOC_1&format=PDF.

Farrell, David M., Jane Suiter, and Clodagh Harris. 2019. "'Systematizing' Constitutional Deliberation: The 2016–18 Citizens' Assembly in Ireland." *Irish Political Studies* 34(1): 113–23. DOI: https://doi.org/10.1080/07907184.2018.1534832.

Fishkin, James. 2011. *When the People Speak: Deliberative Democracy and Public Consultation*. Oxford: Oxford University Press.

Fishkin, James S., and Robert C. Luskin. 2005. "Experimenting with a Democratic Ideal: Deliberative Polling and Public Opinion." *Acta Politica* 40(3): 284–98. DOI: https://doi.org/10.1057/palgrave.ap.5500121.

Fissell, William H., Shuvo Roy, and Andrew Davenport. 2013. "Achieving More Frequent and Longer Dialysis for the Majority: Wearable Dialysis and Implantable Artificial Kidney Devices." *Kidney International* 84(2): 256–64. DOI: https://doi.org/10.1038/ki.2012.466.

Fordham University School of Law. 2019. "Screened Out: The Lack of Access to NYC Screened Program Admissions Criteria." Policy brief. New York: Fordham University School of Law, Feerick Center for Social Justice. https://www.fordham.edu/download/downloads/id/13966/Fordham___Screened_Out_Rubrics_Report_2019_FINAL.

Fourcade, Marion, and Kieran Healy. 2013. "Classification Situations: Life-Chances in the Neoliberal Era." *Accounting, Organizations, and Society* 38(8): 559–72.

——. 2017. "Seeing Like a Market." *Socio-Economic Review* 15(1): 9–29. DOI: https://doi.org/10.1093/ser/mww033.

Friedewald, John J. n.d. "Slide Presentation: Proposal to Substantially Revise the National Kidney Allocation System." Unpublished material from the OPTN/UNOS archive. On file with the author.

Friedewald, John, and Richard Formica. 2011. "OPTN/UNOS Kidney Transplantation Committee Report." Report to the board of directors of UNOS for a meeting on November 14–15, 2011.

Friedewald, John J., and Nicole Turgeon. 2017. "Early Experience with the New Kidney Allocation System: A Perspective from a Transplant Center." *Clinical Journal of the American Society of Nephrology* 12(12): 2060–62. DOI: https://doi.org/10.2215/CJN.07520717.

Friedman, Batya, and Helen Nissenbaum. 1996. "Bias in Computer Systems." *ACM Transactions on Information Systems (TOIS)* 14(3): 330–47.

Friedrich, Otto, Dick Thompson, and Barbara B. Dolan. 1984. "One Miracle, Many Doubts." *Time*, December 10, 76.

Gaffney, Theresa. 2020. "A Yearslong Push to Remove Racist Bias from Kidney Testing Gains New Ground." *STAT* (blog), July 17. https://www.statnews.com/2020/07/17/egfr-race-kidney-test/.

Gaston, Robert S., Ian Ayres, Laura G. Dooley, and Arnold G. Diethelm. 1993. "Racial Equity in Renal Transplantation: The Disparate Impact of HLA-Based Allocation." *Journal of the American Medical Association* 270(11): 1352–56. DOI: https://doi.org/10.1001/jama.1993.03510110092038.

Gay, Paul du. 2000. *In Praise of Bureaucracy: Weber — Organization — Ethics*. Thousand Oaks, Calif.: Sage Publications.

Gebru, Timnit, Jamie Morgenstern, Briana Vecchione, Jennifer Wortman Vaughan, Hanna Wallach, Hal Daumeé III, and Kate Crawford. 2018. "Datasheets for Datasets." Cornell University, arXiv:1803.09010v8 [cs. DB]. Submitted March 23, 2018; last revised December 1, 2021. http://arxiv.org/abs/1803.09010.

Gjertson, David W., Paul I. Terasaki, Steve Takemoto, and M. Ray Mickey. 1991. "National Allocation of Cadaveric Kidneys by HLA Matching." *New England Journal of Medicine* 324(15): 1032–36. DOI: https://doi.org/10.1056/NEJM199104113241505.

Glazer, Shep. 1971. Testimony in hearings on national health insurance proposals before House Ways and Means Committee, 92nd Cong., 1st sess., November 4, 1971.

Glazier, Alexandra K. 2018. "The Lung Lawsuit: A Case Study in Organ Allocation Policy and Administrative Law." *Journal of Health and Biomedical Law* 14: 139–48.

Google Books. n.d. Popular technology terms, 1980–2019. Google Books Ngram Viewer. Accessed May 13, 2022. https://books.google.com/ngrams.

Green, Ben, and Salomé Viljoen. 2020. "Algorithmic Realism: Expanding the Boundaries of Algorithmic Thought." In *Proceedings of the 2020 Conference on Fairness, Accountability, and Transparency* (January), 19–31. DOI: https://doi.org/10.1145/3351095.3372840.

Grönlund, Kimmo, Kaisa Herne, and Maija Setälä. 2015. "Does Enclave Deliberation Polarize Opinions?" *Political Behavior* 37(4): 995–1020. DOI: https://doi.org/10.1007/s11109-015-9304-x.

Groth, Carl G., Leslie B. Brent, Roy Y. Calne, Jean B. Dausset, Robert A. Good, Joseph E. Murray, Norman E. Shumway, et al. 2000. "Historic Landmarks in Clinical Transplantation: Conclusions from the Consensus Conference at the University of California, Los Angeles." *World Journal of Surgery* 24(7): 834–43. DOI: https://doi.org/10.1007/s002680010134.

Hamilton, David. 2012. *A History of Organ Transplantation: Ancient Legends to Modern Practice.* Pittsburgh: University of Pittsburgh Press.

Harmon, Rachel. 2015. "Federal Programs and the Real Costs of Policing." *New York University Law Review* 90: 870.

Harris, Gardiner. 2011. "New Kidney Transplant Policy Would Favor Younger Patients." *New York Times*, February 24. https://www.nytimes.com/2011/02/25/health/policy/25organ.html.

Hart, A., S. K. Gustafson, M. A. Skeans, P. Stock, D. Stewart, B. L. Kasiske, and A. K. Israni. 2017. "OPTN/SRTR 2015 Annual Data Report: Early Effects of the New Kidney Allocation System." *American Journal of Transplantation* 17(S1): 543–64. DOI: https://doi.org/10.1111/ajt.14132.

Hart, A., J. M. Smith, M. A. Skeans, S. K. Gustafson, A. R. Wilk, S. Castro, A. Robinson, et al. 2019. "OPTN/SRTR 2017 Annual Data Report: Kidney." *American Journal of Transplantation* 19(S2): 19–123. DOI: https://doi.org/10.1111/ajt.15274.

Hart, A., J. M. Smith, M. A Skeans, S. K. Gustafson, A. R. Wilk, A. Robinson, J. L. Wainright, et al. 2018. "OPTN/SRTR 2016 Annual Data Report: Kidney." *American Journal of Transplantation*, 18(S1): 18–113. https://pubmed.ncbi.nlm.nih.gov/29292608/.

Harwell, Drew. 2019. "A Face-Scanning Algorithm Increasingly Decides Whether You Deserve the Job." *Washington Post*, November 6. https://www.washingtonpost.com/technology/2019/10/22/ai-hiring-face-scanning-algorithm-increasingly-decides-whether-you-deserve-job/.

Healy, Kieran. 2010. *Last Best Gifts: Altruism and the Market for Human Blood and Organs.* Chicago: University of Chicago Press.

Hernandez, Jennifer. 2018. "California Environmental Quality Act Lawsuits and California's Housing Crisis." *Hastings Environmental Law Journal* 24(1): 21–72.

Himmelreich, Johannes. n.d. "Against 'Democratizing AI.'" https://johanneshimmelreich.net/papers/against-democratizing-AI.pdf.

Hippen, B. 2009. "The Kidney Allocation Score: Methodological Problems, Moral Concerns, and Unintended Consequences." *American Journal of Transplantation* 9(7): 1507–12.

Hojs, Nina, William H. Fissell, and Shuvo Roy. 2020. "Ambulatory Hemodialysis-Technology Landscape and Potential for Patient-Centered Treatment." *Clinical Journal of the American Society of Nephrology* 15(1): 152–59. DOI: https://doi.org/10.2215/CJN.01970219.

Hu, Winnie, and Elizabeth A. Harris. 2018. "A Shadow System Feeds Segregation in New York City Schools." *New York Times*, June 17, 2018. https://www.nytimes.com/2018/06/17/nyregion/public-schools-screening-admission.html.

Huizinga, J. E., B. C. Breneman, V. R. Patel, A. Raz, and D. B. Speights. 2016. "NARxCHECK® Score as a Predictor of Unintentional Overdose Death." Louisville, Ky.: Appriss, Inc. (October). https://apprisshealth.com/wp-content/uploads/sites/2/2017/02/NARxCHECK-Score-as-a-Predictor.pdf.

Hurley, Dan. 2018. "Can an Algorithm Tell When Kids Are in Danger?" *New York Times Magazine*, January 2. https://www.nytimes.com/2018/01/02/magazine/can-an-algorithm-tell-when-kids-are-in-danger.html.

Iglehart, John K. 1984. "The Politics of Transplantation." *New England Journal of Medicine* 310(13): 864–68. DOI: http://dx.doi.org/10.1056/NEJM198403293101330.

Inker, Lesley A., and Ronald D. Perrone. 2014. "Assessment of Kidney Function." UpToDate. https://www.uptodate.com/contents/assessment-of-kidney-function#!.

Institute of Medicine. Committee on Organ Procurement and Transplantation Policy. 1999. *Organ Procurement and Transplantation: Assessing Current Policies and the Potential Impact of the DHHS Final Rule.* Washington, D.C.: National Academies Press. http://www.ncbi.nlm.nih.gov/books/NBK224647/.

Jackson, Kyle R., Karina Covarrubias, Courtenay M. Holscher, Xun Luo, Jennifer Chen, Allan B. Massie, Niraj Desai, Daniel C. Brennan, Dorry L. Segev, and Jacqueline Garonzik-Wang. 2019. "The National Landscape of Deceased Donor Kidney Transplantation for the Highly Sensitized: Transplant Rates, Waitlist Mortality, and Posttransplant Survival under KAS." *American Journal of Transplantation* 19(4): 1129–38. DOI: https://doi.org/10.1111/ajt.15149.

Jacobs, H. Barry. 1983. "Let Consenting Adults Sell Their Kidneys." *USA TODAY*, September 27, 1983.

Johnson, Khari. 2021. "The Fight to Define When AI Is 'High Risk.'" *Wired*, September 1. https://www.wired.com/story/fight-to-define-when-ai-is-high-risk/.

Kaminski, Margot E. 2019. "Binary Governance: Lessons from the GDPR's Approach to Algorithmic Accountability." *Southern California Law Review* 92(6): 1529. DOI: https://doi.org/10.2139/ssrn.3351404.

Kaminski, Margot E., and Gianclaudio Malgieri. 2021. "Algorithmic Impact Assessments under the GDPR: Producing Multi-Layered Explanations." *International Data Privacy Law* 11(2): 125–44. DOI: https://doi.org/10.1093/idpl/ipaa020.

Kasy, Maximilian, and Rediet Abebe. 2021. "Fairness, Equality, and Power in Algorithmic Decision-Making." In *Proceedings of the 2021 ACM Conference on Fairness, Accountability, and Transparency* (March): 576–86. DOI: https://doi.org/10.1145/3442188.3445919.

Katyal, Sonia K. 2019. "Private Accountability in the Age of Artificial Intelligence." *UCLA Law Review* 66: 54.

Keddell, Emily. 2016. "Substantiation, Decision-Making and Risk Prediction in Child Protection Systems." *Policy Quarterly* 12(2). DOI: https://doi.org/10.26686/pq.v12i2.4587.

Keller, Bill. 2015. "David Simon on Baltimore's Anguish." *The Marshall Project* (blog), April 29. https://www.themarshallproject.org/2015/04/29/david-simon -on-baltimore-s-anguish.

Kim, Anne. 2017. "The Dialysis Machine." *Washington Monthly* (December 2017).

Kiviat, Barbara. 2019a. "The Moral Limits of Predictive Practices: The Case of Credit-Based Insurance Scores." *American Sociological Review* 84(6): 1134–58. DOI: https://doi.org/10.1177/0003122419884917.

Kiviat, Barbara. 2019b. "The Moral Limits of Predictive Practices: The Case of Credit-Based Insurance Scores." Lecture, Cornell University, February 6.

Klein, Ezra, and L. M. Sacasas. 2021. "This Conversation Changed the Way I Interact with Technology." *New York Times*, August 3. https://www.nytimes .com/2021/08/03/opinion/ezra-klein-podcast-lm-sacasas.html.

Klintmalm, Göran B. 2004. "The History of Organ Transplantation in the Baylor Health Care System." *Baylor University Medical Center Proceedings* 17(1): 23–34.

Klintmalm, Göran B., and Bruce Kaplan. 2017. "The Kidney Allocation System Claims Equity: It Is Time to Review Utility and Fairness." *American Journal of Transplantation* 17(12): 2999–3000. DOI: https://doi.org/10.1111/ajt.14457.

Knight, Will. 2021. "Europe's Proposed Limits on AI Would Have Global Consequences." *Wired*, April 21. https://www.wired.com/story/europes -proposed-limits-ai-global-consequences/.

Koene, Ansgar, Chris Clifton, Yohko Hatada, Helena Webb, et al. 2019. *A Governance Framework for Algorithmic Accountability and Transparency*. Brussels: Directorate-General for the European Parliamentary Research Office (April). DOI: https://data .europa.eu/doi/10.2861/59990.

Koepke, John Logan, and David G. Robinson. 2018. "Danger Ahead: Risk Assessment and the Future of Bail Reform." *Washington Law Review* 93: 1725.

KPMG International. 2019. "KPMG Launches Framework to Help Businesses Gain Greater Confidence in Their AI Technologies." *Cission PR Newswire*, February 13. https://www.prnewswire.com/news-releases/kpmg-launches-framework-to-help -businesses-gain-greater-confidence-in-their-ai-technologies-300794410.html.

Krafft, P. M., Meg Young, Michael Katell, Karen Huang, and Ghislain Bugingo. 2020. "Defining AI in Policy versus Practice." In *Proceedings of the AAAI/ ACM Conference on AI, Ethics, and Society* (February): 72–78. DOI: https://doi.org /10.1145/3375627.3375835.

Kroll, Joshua A. 2018. "The Fallacy of Inscrutability." *Philosophical Transactions of the Royal Society A: Mathematical, Physical, and Engineering Sciences* 376(2133): 20180084. DOI: https://doi.org/10.1098/rsta.2018.0084.

Kroll, Joshua A., Joanna Huey, Solon Barocas, Edward W. Felten, Joel R. Reidenberg, David G. Robinson, and Harlan Yu. 2017. "Accountable Algorithms." *Pennsylvania Law Review* 165(3): 633. https://scholarship.law.upenn.edu/penn _law_review/vol165/iss3/3.

Kurtz, Howard, and James Schwartz. 1984. "Organ Transplants Turn into Form of Patronage." *Washington Post*, April 23. https://www.washingtonpost.com /archive/politics/1984/04/23/organ-transplants-turn-into-form-of-patronage /8d822f80-8561-45b4-89eb-528388f1a482/.

Lamas, Daniela J. 2021. "Who Deserves a Lifesaving Organ?" *New York Times*, November 24. https://www.nytimes.com/2021/11/24/opinion/organ-transplant .html.

Landemore, Hélène. 2020. *Open Democracy: Reinventing Popular Rule for the Twenty-First Century*. Princeton, N.J.: Princeton University Press. Kindle.

Leadership Conference on Civil and Human Rights. 2018. "The Use of Pretrial 'Risk Assessment' Instruments: A Shared Statement of Civil Rights Concerns." Accessed August 31, 2021. https://www.supremecourt.ohio.gov/sites/PJRSummit /materials/pretrialRiskAssessInstruments.pdf.

Lecher, Colin. 2018. "A Healthcare Algorithm Started Cutting Care, and No One Knew Why." *The Verge*, March 21. https://www.theverge.com/2018/3/21/17144260 /healthcare-medicaid-algorithm-arkansas-cerebral-palsy.

Lee, Min Kyung, Daniel Kusbit, Anson Kahng, Ji Tae Kim, Xinran Yuan, Allissa Chan, Daniel See, et al. 2019. "WeBuildAI: Participatory Framework for Algorithmic Governance." *Proceedings of the ACM on Human-Computer Interaction* 3(CSCW): 1–35. DOI: https://doi.org/10.1145/3359283.

Levy, Karen E. C., and David Merritt Johns. 2016. "When Open Data Is a Trojan Horse: The Weaponization of Transparency in Science and Governance." *Big Data and Society* 3(1): 2053951715621568. DOI: https://doi.org/10.1177/2053951715621568.

Linden, Peter K. 2009. "History of Solid Organ Transplantation and Organ Donation." *Critical Care Clinics* 25(1): 165–84. DOI: https://doi.org/10.1016 /j.ccc.2008.12.001.

Logg, Jennifer M., Julia A. Minson, and Don A. Moore. 2019. "Algorithm Appreciation: People Prefer Algorithmic to Human Judgment." *Organizational Behavior and Human Decision Processes* 151(March): 90–103. DOI: https://doi.org /10.1016/j.obhdp.2018.12.005.

Madras, David, Smitha Milli, Inioluwa Deborah Raji, Angela Zhou, and Richard Zemel. 2020. "Participatory Approaches to Machine Learning." Presented at International Conference on Machine Learning Workshop, July (virtual).

Martin, Kirsten E., and Ari Ezra Waldman. 2021. "When Are Algorithmic Decisions Perceived as Legitimate? The Effect of Process and Outcomes on Perceptions of Legitimacy of Algorithmic Decisions." SSRN Scholarly Paper ID 3964899. Rochester, NY: Social Science Research Network. https://papers.ssrn.com /abstract=3964899.

Martins, Paulo N., Margaux N. Mustian, Paul A. MacLennan, Jorge A. Ortiz, Mohamed Akoad, Juan Carlos Caicedo, Gabriel J. Echeverri, et al. 2018. "Impact of the New Kidney Allocation System A2/A2B → B Policy on Access to Transplantation among Minority Candidates." *American Journal of Transplantation* 18(8): 1947–53. DOI: https://doi.org/10.1111/ajt.14719.

Massie, Allan B., Xun Luo, Bonnie E. Lonze, Niraj M. Desai, Adam W. Bingaman, Matthew Cooper, and Dorry L. Segev. 2016. "Early Changes in Kidney Distribution under the New Allocation System." *Journal of the American Society of Nephrology : JASN* 27 (8): 2495–2501. DOI: https://doi.org/10.1681/ASN.2015080934.

Mayer-Schönberger, Viktor, and Kenneth Cukier. 2013. *Big Data: A Revolution That Will Transform How We Live, Work, and Think.* Boston: Houghton Mifflin Harcourt.

McCartney, Scott. 1993. "Tissue Typing in Kidney Transplants Is Said to Hurt Black Patients' Chances." *Wall Street Journal*, April 1.

McCorduck, Pamela. 1979. *Machines Who Think: A Personal Inquiry into the History and Prospects of Artificial Intelligence.* San Francisco: W. H. Freeman.

McQuillan, Dan. 2018a. "People's Councils for Ethical Machine Learning." *Social Media + Society* 4(2): 2056305118768303. DOI: https://doi.org/10.1177/2056305118768303.

———. 2018b. "Data Science as Machine Neoplatonism." *Philosophy and Technology* 31: 253–72.

Melanson, Taylor A., Jason M. Hockenberry, Laura Plantinga, Mohua Basu, Stephan Pastan, Sumit Mohan, David H. Howard, and Rachel E. Patzer. 2017. "New Kidney Allocation System Associated with Increased Rates of Transplants among Black and Hispanic Patients." *Health Affairs* 36(6): 1078–85.

Merrill, John P., Joseph E. Murray, J. Hartwell Harrison, and Warren R. Guild. 1956. "Successful Homotransplantation of the Human Kidney between Identical Twins." *Journal of the American Medical Association* 160(4): 277–82. DOI: https://doi.org/10.1001/jama.1956.02960390027008.

Metcalf, Jacob, Emanuel Moss, Elizabeth Anne Watkins, Ranjit Singh, and Madeleine Clare Elish. 2021. "Algorithmic Impact Assessments and Accountability: The Co-Construction of Impacts." In *Proceedings of the ACM Conference on Fairness, Accountability, and Transparency* (March), 735–46. DOI: https://dl.acm.org/doi/10.1145/3442188.3445935.

MetroLab Network. 2017. "First, Do No Harm: Ethical Guidelines for Applying Predictive Tools within Human Services." https://metrolabnetwork.org/wp-content/uploads/2017/09/Ethical-Guidelines-for-Applying-Predictive-Tools-within-Human-Services_Sept-2017.pdf.

Miriam Holman Sheloshim (video). 2018. Recorded March 3, 2018, at The White Shul, Far Rockaway, N.Y., by Steinberg Media. https://vimeo.com/259559412.

Mitchell, Margaret, Simone Wu, Andrew Zaldivar, Parker Barnes, Lucy Vasserman, Ben Hutchinson, Elena Spitzer, Inioluwa Deborah Raji, and Timnit Gebru. 2019. "Model Cards for Model Reporting." In *Proceedings of the Conference on Fairness, Accountability, and Transparency,* (January), 220–29. DOI: https://doi.org/10.1145/3287560.3287596.

Mondragon, Nathan, Clemens Aichholzer, and Kiki Leutner. 2019. "The Next Generation of Assessments." White Paper. HireVue (February). https://hrlens.org/wp-content/uploads/2019/11/The-Next-Generation-of-Assessments-HireVue-White-Paper.pdf.

Moss, Emanuel, Elizabeth Anne Watkins, Jacob Metcalf, and Madeleine Clare Elish. 2021. "Governing with Algorithmic Impact Assessments: Six Observations." In *Proceedings of the 2021 AAAI/ACM Conference on AI, Ethics, and Society* (July), 1010–22. DOI: https://dl.acm.org/doi/10.1145/3461702.3462580.

Mulligan, Deirdre K., and Kenneth A. Bamberger. 2018. "Saving Governance-by-Design." *California Law Review* 106: 697.

Murray, Joseph E. n.d. "The Fight for Life." *Harvard Medicine*. https://hms.harvard.edu/magazine/science-emotion/fight-life.

Murray, J. S., W. H. Tu, J. B. Albers, J. M. Burnell, and B. H. Scribner. 1962. "A Community Hemodialysis Center for the Treatment of Chronic Uremia." *ASAIO Journal* 8(1): 315–19.

Narayanan, Arvind. 2018. "Tutorial: 21 Fairness Definitions and Their Politics." Posted on YouTube March 1. https://www.youtube.com/watch?v=jIXIuYdnyyk.

National Conference of Insurance Legislators (NCOIL). 2015. "Model Act Regarding Use of Credit Information in Personal Insurance." Washington, D.C.: NCOIL (re-adopted November 15, 2015; originally adopted November 22, 2002). http://ncoil.org/wp-content/uploads/2016/04/11262015PropertyCasualtyModelAct.pdf.

"New Kidney Organ Allocation System - The Management of the Wait List in the New Allocation System." 2014. UCSF, May 30.

New York City Council. Committee on Technology. 2018. "Automated Decision Systems Used by Agencies." Law 2018/049. January 11. https://legistar.council.nyc.gov/LegislationDetail.aspx?ID=3137815&GUID=437A6A6D-62E1-47E2-9C42-461253F9C6D0.

New York Times. 1914. "World's Surgeons in Sessions Here; Dr. Depage, President of International Congress, Protests against Cruelties of War." *New York Times*, April 14. https://www.nytimes.com/1914/04/14/archives/worlds-surgeons-in-sessions-here-dr-depage-president-of.html.

Niemeyer, Simon. 2011. "The Emancipatory Effect of Deliberation: Empirical Lessons from Mini-Publics." *Politics and Society* 39(1): 103–40. DOI: https://doi.org/10.1177/0032329210395000.

Noble, Safiya Umoja. 2018. *Algorithms of Oppression: How Search Engines Reinforce Racism*. New York: New York University Press.

Obermeyer, Ziad, and Sendhil Mullainathan. 2019. "Dissecting Racial Bias in an Algorithm That Guides Health Decisions for 70 Million People." In *Proceedings of the Conference on Fairness, Accountability, and Transparency* (January), 89. DOI: https://doi.org/10.1145/3287560.3287593.

Okidegbe, Ngozi. Forthcoming. "The Democratizing Potential of Algorithms?" *Connecticut Law Review*. https://papers.ssrn.com/abstract=3835370.

O'Neil, Cathy. 2016. *Weapons of Math Destruction: How Big Data Increases Inequality and Threatens Democracy*. New York: Crown.

"Open Government Declaration." 2011. https://www.opengovpartnership.org/process/joining-ogp/open-government-declaration/.

Organ Procurement and Transplantation Network (OPTN). 2013. "Board Briefing Paper: Proposal to Substantially Revise the National Kidney Allocation System." June 24. On file with author.

———. 2020. "Interactive Tool to Visualize the Decisions Regarding the Continuous Distribution of Lungs." Tableau. Updated February 23, 2021. Accessed April 20, 2022. https://public.tableau.com/app/profile/optn.committees/viz/ContinuousDistributionofLungs/Home.

Organ Procurement and Transplantation Network (OPTN). Kidney Transplantation Committee. 2008. "Kidney Allocation Concepts: Request for Information." OPTN (September 24).

———. 2011. "Concepts for Kidney Allocation." OPTN (February 15). https://optn.transplant.hrsa.gov/news/feedback-requested-on-concepts-for-kidney-allocation/.

Organ Procurement and Transplantation Network (OPTN). United Network for Organ Sharing (UNOS). 2007. "Public Forum to Discuss Kidney Allocation Policy Development—Synopsis—Dallas, Texas, February 8, 2007." PDF on file with author.

———. 2009. "Kidney Transplantation Committee Report to the Board of Directors, June 22–23, 2009."

———. 2017. "Organ Transplantation: Report on Equity in Access—Deceased-Donor Kidney Allocation" (quarterly report). August 21. https://optn.transplant.hrsa.gov/media/2260/equity_in_access_report_201708.pdf.

Organisation for Economic Cooperation and Development (OECD). 2020. *Innovative Citizen Participation and New Democratic Institutions: Catching the Deliberative Wave.* Paris: OECD Publishing. DOI: https://doi.org/10.1787/339306da-en.

Park, Walter D., Joseph P. Grande, Dora Ninova, Karl A. Nath, Jeffrey L. Platt, James M. Gloor, and Mark D. Stegall. 2003. "Accommodation in ABO-Incompatible Kidney Allografts, a Novel Mechanism of Self-Protection against Antibody-Mediated Injury." *American Journal of Transplantation* 3(8): 952–60.

Partnership on Artificial Intelligence. 2019. *Report on Algorithmic Risk Assessment Tools in the U.S. Criminal Justice System.* https://partnershiponai.org/wp-content/uploads/2021/08/Report-on-Algorithmic-Risk-Assessment-Tools.pdf.

Passi, Samir, and Solon Barocas. 2019. "Problem Formulation and Fairness." In *Proceedings of the Conference on Fairness, Accountability, and Transparency* (January), 39–48. DOI: https://doi.org/10.1145/3287560.3287567.

Peixoto, Tiago. 2013. "The Uncertain Relationship between Open Data and Accountability." *UCLA Law Review Discourse* 60: 200.

Peter, Fabienne. 2017. "Political Legitimacy." In *The Stanford Encyclopedia of Philosophy* (Summer 2017 Edition), edited by Edward N. Zalta. https://plato.stanford.edu/archives/sum2017/entries/legitimacy/.

Pondrom, Sue. 2008. "New Kidney Allocation Policy Seeks Balance of Justice and Utility." *American Journal of Transplantation* 8(January): 263–64.

Porter, Theodore M. 1995. *Trust in Numbers: The Pursuit of Objectivity in Science and Public Life*. Princeton, N.J.: Princeton University Press.

——. 2020. "Preface to the New Edition." In *Trust in Numbers: The Pursuit of Objectivity in Science and Public Life*. Princeton, N.J.: Princeton University Press. (Originally published in 1995.)

Quigley, John M., and Steven Raphael. 2005. "Regulation and the High Cost of Housing in California." *American Economic Review* 95(2): 323–28.

Quinton, Wayne, David Dillard, and Belding H. Scribner. 1960. "Cannulation of Blood Vessels for Prolonged Hemodialysis." *American Society for Artificial Internal Organs Journal* (https://asaio.org/) 6(1): 104–13. https://journals.lww.com /asaiojournal/Citation/1960/04000/Cannulation_of_Blood_Vessels_for _Prolonged.19.aspx.

Rabin, Roni Caryn. 2021. "In a First, Surgeons Attached a Pig Kidney to a Human, and It Worked." *New York Times*, October 20. https://www.nytimes.com /2021/10/19/health/kidney-transplant-pig-human.html.

——. 2022. "Patient in Groundbreaking Heart Transplant Dies." *New York Times*, March 9. https://www.nytimes.com/2022/03/09/health/heart-transplant-pig -bennett.html.

Raji, Inioluwa Deborah, and Joy Buolamwini. 2019. "Actionable Auditing: Investigating the Impact of Publicly Naming Biased Performance Results of Commercial AI Products." In *Proceedings of the 2019 AAAI/ACM Conference on AI, Ethics, and Society* (January), 429–35. DOI: https://doi.org/10.1145/3306618 .3314244.

Raji, Inioluwa Deborah, Timnit Gebru, Margaret Mitchell, Joy Buolamwini, Joonseok Lee, and Emily Denton. 2020. "Saving Face: Investigating the Ethical Concerns of Facial Recognition Auditing." Cornell University, arXiv:2001.00964v1 [cs. CY]. Submitted January 3, 2020. http://arxiv.org/abs/2001.00964.

Raji, Inioluwa Deborah, Andrew Smart, Rebecca N. White, Margaret Mitchell, Timnit Gebru, Ben Hutchinson, Jamila Smith-Loud, Daniel Theron, and Parker Barnes. 2020. "Closing the AI Accountability Gap: Defining an End-to-End Framework for Internal Algorithmic Auditing." In *Proceedings Conference on Fairness, Accountability, and Transparency (FAT '20)* (January), 33–44, DOI: https://doi.org/10.1145/3351095.

Raji, Inioluwa Deborah, and Jingying Yang. 2019. "About ML: Annotation and Benchmarking on Understanding and Transparency of Machine Learning Lifecycles." Cornell University, arXiv:1912.06166v3 [cs. CY]. Submitted December 12, 2019; last revised January 8, 2020. DOI: https://doi.org/10.48550 /arXiv.1912.06166.

Rao, Panduranga S., et al. 2009. "A Comprehensive Risk Quantification Score for Deceased Donor Kidneys: The Kidney Donor Risk Index." *Transplantation* 88(2): 231–36.

Raz, Joseph. 1996. *Ethics in the Public Domain: Essays in the Morality of Law and Politics*, rev. ed. Oxford: Clarendon Press.

Reisman, Dillon, Jason Schultz, Kate Crawford, and Meredith Whittaker. 2018. "Algorithmic Impact Assessments: A Practical Framework for Public Agency Accountability." AI Now Institute (April). https://ainowinstitute.org/aiareport2018.pdf.

Rettig, Richard A. 1982. "The Federal Government and Social Planning for End-Stage Renal Disease: Past, Present, and Future." *Seminars in Nephrology* 2(2): 111–33.

———. 1989. "The Politics of Organ Transplantation: A Parable of Our Time." *Journal of Health Politics, Policy, and Law* 14(1): 191–227. DOI: https://doi.org/10.1215/03616878-14-1-191.

Richardson, Rashida. 2021. "Defining and Demystifying Automated Decision Systems." *Maryland Law Review*, forthcoming (written March 24, 2021). https://papers.ssrn.com/abstract=3811708.

Richardson, Rashida, Jason M. Schultz, and Vincent M. Southerland. 2019. "Litigating Algorithms 2019 U.S. Report: New Challenges to Government Use of Algorithmic Decision Systems." New York: New York University, AI Now Institute (September). https://ainowinstitute.org/litigatingalgorithms-2019-us.pdf.

Rieke, Aaron, Urmila Janardan, Mingwei Hsu, and Natasha Duarte. 2021. "Essential Work: Analyzing the Hiring Technologies of Large Hourly Employers." Washington, D.C.: Upturn (May). https://www.upturn.org/static/reports/2021/essential-work/files/upturn-essential-work.pdf.

Rieke, Aaron, David Robinson, and Harlan Yu. 2014. "Civil Rights, Big Data, and Our Algorithmic Future." Washington, D.C.: Upturn (September). https://bigdata.fairness.io/wp-content/uploads/2015/04/2015-04-20-Civil-Rights-Big-Data-and-Our-Algorithmic-Future-v1.2.pdf.

Roberts, William Clifford. 2001. "Boone Powell, Jr., MPH, FACHE: A Conversation with the Editor." *Baylor University Medical Center Proceedings* 14(1): 37–51. DOI: https://doi.org/10.1080/08998280.2001.11927731.

Roberts, William Clifford, and Göran Bo Gustaf Klintmalm. 2002. "Göran Bo Gustaf Klintmalm, MD, PhD: A Conversation with the Editor." *Baylor University Medical Center Proceedings* 15(3): 289–306. DOI: https://doi.org/10.1080/08998280.2002.11927855.

Robinson, David G., and Logan Koepke. 2019. "Civil Rights and Pretrial Risk Assessment Instruments." Pretrial Risk Management Project (December). https://www.safetyandjusticechallenge.org/wp-content/uploads/2019/12/Robinson-Koepke-Civil-Rights-Critical-Issue-Brief.pdf.

Robinson, David G., Hannah Jane Sassaman, and Megan Stevenson. 2018. "Pretrial Risk Assessments: A Practical Guide for Judges." *ABA Judges' Journal* (August 1).

Ross, Lainie. 2012. "Deceased Donor Kidney Allocation: Equity, Efficiency, and Unintended Consequences." Rotman Institute of Philosophy, November 2. https://www.youtube.com/watch?v=kz239hjiE74.

Ross, L. F., et al. 2012. "Equal Opportunity Supplemented by Fair Innings: Equity and Efficiency in Allocating Deceased Donor Kidneys." *American Journal of*

Transplantation 12(8): 2115–24. DOI: https://doi.org/10.1111/j.1600-6143.2012
.04141.x.

Rowe, Gene, and Lynn J. Frewer. 2000. "Public Participation Methods: A Framework
for Evaluation." *Science, Technology, and Human Values* 25(1): 3–29. DOI: https://
doi.org/10.1177/016224390002500101.

Russo, Mark J., David Meltzer, Aurelie Merlo, Elizabeth Johnson, Nazly M. Shariati,
Joshua R. Sonett, and Robert Gibbons. 2013. "Local Allocation of Lung Donors
Results in Transplanting Lungs in Lower Priority Transplant Recipients." *Annals
of Thoracic Surgery* 95(4): 1231–35. DOI: https://doi.org/10.1016/j.athoracsur.2012
.11.070.

Sanders, David, and Jesse Dukeminier. 1967. "Medical Advance and Legal Lag:
Hemodialysis and Kidney Transplantation." *UCLA Law Review* 15: 357–413.

Sandvig, Christian, Kevin Hamilton, Karrie Karahalios, and Cedric Langbort.
2014. "Auditing Algorithms: Research Methods for Detecting Discrimination on
Internet Platforms." Presented at the pre-conference "Data and Discrimination:
Converting Critical Concerns into Productive Inquiry" at the annual meeting
of the International Communication Association, Seattle, May 22. https://pdfs
.semanticscholar.org/b722/7cbd34766655dea10d0437ab10df3a127396.pdf.

Satel, Sally L., and Benjamin E. Hippen. 2007. "When Altruism Is Not Enough:
The Worsening Organ Shortage and What It Means for the Elderly." *Elder Law
Journal* 15(1): 153–204.

Schwamm, Susan. 2018. "Remembering Miriam Holman, a'h, on Her Sloshim." *The
Jewish Home*, February 28.

Scientific Registry of Transplant Recipients (SRTR). 2022. "Deceased-Donor Kidney
Transplant Rates among Adult Wait-Listed Candidates, by Race, 2006–2017."
Data provided directly to the author on February 18.

Scott, James C. 1998. *Seeing Like a State: How Certain Schemes to Improve the Human
Condition Have Failed.* New Haven, Conn.: Yale University Press.

Scribner, Belding H., R. Buri, J.E.Z. Caner, R. Hegstrom, and James M. Burnell. 1960.
"The Treatment of Chronic Uremia by Means of Intermittent Hemodialysis:
A Preliminary Report." *American Society for Artificial Internal Organs Journal* 6(1):
114–22.

Secondo, Donata, and Josh Lerner. 2020. "By the People, for the People: Participatory
Budgeting from the Bottom Up in North America." *Journal of Deliberative
Democracy* 8(2). DOI: https://doi.org/10.16997/jdd.148.

Selbst, Andrew D. 2018. "Disparate Impact in Big Data Policing." *Georgia Law
Review* 52: 109. DOI: https://doi.org/10.2139/ssrn.2819182.

———. 2021. "An Institutional View of Algorithmic Impact Assessments." *Harvard
Journal of Law and Technology* 35(1): 117. https://papers.ssrn.com/abstract=3867634.

Selbst, Andrew D., and Solon Barocas. 2018. "The Intuitive Appeal of Explainable
Machines." *Fordham Law Review* 87(3): 1085.

Selbst, Andrew D., danah boyd, Sorelle A. Friedler, Suresh Venkatasubramanian, and Janet Vertesi. 2019. "Fairness and Abstraction in Sociotechnical Systems." In *Proceedings of the Conference on Fairness, Accountability, and Transparency* (January), 59–68. DOI: https://doi.org/10.1145/3287560.3287598.

Senate of Australia. 2017. *Design, Scope, Cost-Benefit Analysis, Contracts Awarded, and Implementation Associated with the Better Management of the Social Welfare System Initiative.* Canberra: Senate of Australia, Community Affairs References Committee (June 21). https://www.aph.gov.au/Parliamentary_Business /Committees/Senate/Community_Affairs/SocialWelfareSystem/Report.

Sharp, Ann. 1995. *The Koala Book.* Pelican Publishing.

Sloane, Mona, Emanuel Moss, Olaitan Awomolo, and Laura Forlano. 2020. "Participation Is Not a Design Fix for Machine Learning." Cornell University, arXiv:2007.02423v3 [cs. CY]. Submitted July 5, 2020; last revised August 11, 2020. DOI: https://doi.org/10.48550/arXiv.2007.02423.

Smith, Graham. 2009. *Democratic Innovations: Designing Institutions for Citizen Participation.* Cambridge: Cambridge University Press.

Smith, J. M., S. W. Biggins, D. G. Haselby, W. R. Kim, J. Wedd, K. Lamb, B. Thompson, et al. 2012. "Kidney, Pancreas, and Liver Allocation and Distribution in the United States." *American Journal of Transplantation* 12(12): 3191–3212. DOI: https://doi.org/10.1111/j.1600-6143.2012.04259.x.

Sparrow, Malcolm K. 2015. "Measuring Performance in a Modern Police Organization." Washington, D.C.: U.S. Department of Justice, National Institute of Justice (March). https://nij.ojp.gov/library/publications/measuring-performance -modern-police-organization.

Stanley, Jay. 2017. "Pitfalls of Artificial Intelligence Decisionmaking Highlighted in Idaho ACLU Case." American Civil Liberties Union (blog), June 2. https:// www.aclu.org/blog/privacy-technology/pitfalls-artificial-intelligence-decision making-highlighted-idaho-aclu-case.

Stark, Luke, Daniel Greene, and Anna Lauren Hoffmann. 2021. "Critical Perspectives on Governance Mechanisms for AI/ML Systems." In *The Cultural Life of Machine Learning: An Incursion into Critical AI Studies*, edited by Jonathan Roberge and Michael Castelle. Cham: Springer International Publishing.

Starr, Sonja B. 2014. "Evidence-Based Sentencing and the Scientific Rationalization of Discrimination." *Stanford Law Review* 66(4): 803–72.

Starzl, Thomas E., Thomas R. Hakala, Andreas Tzakis, Robert Gordon, Andrei Stieber, Leonard Makowka, Joeta Klimoski, and Henry T. Bahnson. 1987. "A Multifactorial System for Equitable Selection of Cadaver Kidney Recipients." *JAMA* 257(22): 3073–75. DOI: https://doi.org/10.1001/jama.1987.03390220071023.

Starzl, Thomas E., Thomas L. Marchioro, and William R. Waddell. 1963. "The Reversal of Rejection in Human Renal Homografts with Subsequent Development of Homograft Tolerance." *Surgery, Gynecology, and Obstetrics* 117(October): 385–95.

Starzl, Thomas E., R. Shapiro, and L. Teperman. 1989. "The Point System for Organ Distribution." *Transplantation Proceedings* 21(3): 3432–44.

Stegall, Mark D. 2005. "The Development of Kidney Allocation Policy." *American Journal of Kidney Diseases* 46(5): 974–75. DOI: https://doi.org/10.1053/j.ajkd.2005.08.025.

———. 2009. "Developing a New Kidney Allocation Policy: The Rationale for Including Life Years from Transplant." *American Journal of Transplantation* 9(7): 1528–32. DOI: https://doi.org/10.1111/j.1600-6143.2009.02712.x.

Stegall, Mark D., Peter G. Stock, Kenneth Andreoni, John J. Friedewald, and Alan B. Leichtman. 2017. "Why Do We Have the Kidney Allocation System We Have Today? A History of the 2014 Kidney Allocation System." *Human Immunology* (special issue: "The New Kidney Allocation System (KAS): Perspectives from the Transplant Community Two Years Post-Implementation") 78(1): 4–8. DOI: https://doi.org/10.1016/j.humimm.2016.08.008.

Stein, Rob. 2011. "Under Kidney Transplant Proposal, Younger Patients Would Get the Best Organs." *Washington Post*, February 24. http://www.washingtonpost.com/wp-dyn/content/article/2011/02/23/AR2011022307207.html.

Stewart, D. E., A. R. Wilk, A. E. Toll, A. M. Harper, R. R. Lehman, A. M. Robinson, S. A. Noreen, E. B. Edwards, and D. K. Klassen. 2018. "Measuring and Monitoring Equity in Access to Deceased Donor Kidney Transplantation." *American Journal of Transplantation* 18(8): 1924–35. DOI: https://doi.org/10.1111/ajt.14922.

Stock, Peter G. 2009. "Balancing Multiple and Conflicting Allocation Goals: A Logical Path Forward." *American Journal of Transplantation* 9(7): 1519–22. DOI: https://doi.org/10.1111/j.1600-6143.2009.02715.x.

Su, Xuanming, Stefanos A. Zenios, Harini Chakkera, Edgar L. Milford, and Glenn M. Chertow. 2004. "Diminishing Significance of HLA Matching in Kidney Transplantation." *American Journal of Transplantation* 4(9): 1501–8. DOI: https://doi.org/10.1111/j.1600-6143.2004.00535.x.

Svarstad, Hanne, Hans Chr Bugge, and Shivcharn S. Dhillion. 2000. "From Norway to Novartis: Cyclosporin from Tolypocladium Inflatum in an Open Access Bioprospecting Regime." *Biodiversity and Conservation* 9: 1521–41, 22.

Szalavitz, Maia. 2021. "The Pain Was Unbearable. So Why Did Doctors Turn Her Away?" *Wired*, August 11. https://www.wired.com/story/opioid-drug-addiction-algorithm-chronic-pain/.

Teens Take Charge. 2020. "Title VI Complaint" (press release). November 16. https://www.teenstakecharge.com/statements-1/2020/11/16/press-release-announcing-title-vi-complaint.

Terzis, Gillian. 2017. "Austerity Is an Algorithm." *Logic Magazine*, December 1. https://logicmag.io/justice/austerity-is-an-algorithm/.

Thorarensen, Bjorg. 2011. "Constitutional Reform Process in Iceland: Involving the People into the Process." Presented at the Oslo-Rome International Workshop on Democracy, Viale Trenta Aprile, Rome, November 7–9.

Turing, Alan Mathison. 1948. "Intelligent Machinery." Reprinted in *The Essential Turing: The Ideas That Gave Birth to the Computer Age*, edited by Jack Copeland (Oxford: Clarendon Press, 2004).

Ubel, Peter A., Jonathan Baron, and David A. Asch. 1999. "Social Acceptability, Personal Responsibility, and Prognosis in Public Judgments and Transplant Allocation." *Bioethics* 13(1): 57–68. DOI: https://doi.org/10.1111/1467-8519.00131.

Ubel, Peter A., M. DeKay, Jonathan Baron, and David A. Asch. 1996. "Public Preferences for Efficiency and Racial Equity in Kidney Transplant Allocation Decisions." *Transplantation Proceedings* 28(5): 2997–3002.

U.S. Congress, House Committee on Ways and Means. 1972. *National Health Insurance Proposals: Hearings . . . 92-1, on the Subject of National Health Insurance Proposals.* Washington: U.S. Government Printing Office.

U.S. Department of Health and Human Services. Office of Inspector General. 1991. *The Distribution of Organs for Transplantation: Expectations and Practices.* https://oig.hhs.gov/oei/reports/oei-01-89-00550.pdf.

U.S. Department of Health and Human Services. Organ Procurement and Transplantation Network. 2013. "Board Approves Significant Revisions to Deceased Donor Kidney Allocation Policy." June 25. https://optn.transplant.hrsa.gov/news/board-approves-significant-revisions-to-deceased-donor-kidney-allocation-policy/.

U.S. Renal Data System. 2019. "U.S. Renal Data System 2018 Annual Data Report: Epidemiology of Kidney Disease in the United States." *American Journal of Kidney Disease* 73(3, suppl. 1): A7–A8. DOI: https://doi.org/10.1053/j.ajkd.2019.01.001.

U.S. Task Force on Organ Transplantation. 1986. *Organ Transplantation: Issues and Recommendations: Report of the Task Force on Organ Transplantation.* Washington, D.C.: U.S. Department of Health and Human Services, Health Resources and Services Administration, Office of Organ Transplantation.

Varner, Maddy, and Colin Lecher. 2021a. "How We Investigated NYC High School Admissions." *The Markup,* May 26. https://themarkup.org/show-your-work/2021/05/26/how-we-investigated-nyc-high-school-admissions.

———. 2021b. "NYC's School Algorithms Cement Segregation. This Data Shows How." *The Markup,* May 26. https://themarkup.org/news/2021/05/26/nycs-school-algorithms-cement-segregation-this-data-shows-how.

Veatch, Robert M. 1973. "Generalization of Expertise." *Hastings Center Studies* 1(2): 29–40. DOI: https://doi.org/10.2307/3527511.

Veatch, Robert M., and Lainie F. Ross. 2015. "The Role of the Clinician and the Public." In Veatch and Ross, *Transplantation Ethics,* 2nd ed. Washington, D.C.: Georgetown University Press.

Venkatasubramanian, Suresh. 2021. "It's about Time. . . ." Tweet by @geomblog, January 12, 2021. https://mobile.twitter.com/geomblog/status/1349058276118331392.

Vyas, Darshali A., Leo G. Eisenstein, and David S. Jones. 2020. "Hidden in Plain Sight: Reconsidering the Use of Race Correction in Clinical Algorithms." *New England Journal of Medicine* 383(9): 874–82. DOI: https://doi.org/10.1056/NEJMms2004740.

Wade, Nicholas. 1983. "Opinion | The Editorial Notebook; The Crisis in Human Spare Parts." *New York Times,* October 4. https://www.nytimes.com/1983/10/04/opinion/the-editorial-notebook-the-crisis-in-human-spare-parts.html.

Wald, Michael S., and Maria Woolverton. 1990. "Risk Assessment: The Emperor's New Clothes?" *Child Welfare* 69(6): 483–512.

Walzer, Michael. 1968. "A Day in the Life of a Socialist Citizen." *Dissent* (May/June). https://www.dissentmagazine.org/article/a-day-in-the-life-of-a-socialist-citizen.

Washington, Anne L. 2018. "How to Argue with an Algorithm: Lessons from the COMPAS-ProPublica Debate." *Colorado Tech Law Journal* 17(1): 30.

Weeks, Edward C. 2000. "The Practice of Deliberative Democracy: Results from Four Large-Scale Trials." *Public Administration Review* 60(4): 360–72.

Weimer, David L. 2010. *Medical Governance: Values, Expertise, and Interests in Organ Transplantation.* Washington, D.C.: Georgetown University Press.

Weimer, David L., and Laura Wilk. 2019. "Allocation of Indivisible Life-Saving Goods with Both Intrinsic and Relational Quality: The New Deceased-Donor Kidney Allocation System." *Administration and Society* 51(1): 140–69. DOI: https://doi.org/10.1177/0095399716647156.

Williams, Robert C., Gerhard Opelz, Chelsea J. McGarvey, E. Jennifer Weil, and Harini A. Chakkera. 2016. "The Risk of Transplant Failure with HLA Mismatch in First Adult Kidney Allografts from Deceased Donors." *Transplantation* 100(5): 1094–1102. DOI: https://doi.org/10.1097/TP.0000000000001115.

Williams, W. W., W. S. Cherikh, C. J. Young, P. Y. Fan, Y. Cheng, D. A. Distant, and C. F. Bryan. 2015. "First Report on the OPTN National Variance: Allocation of A2/A2B Deceased Donor Kidneys to Blood Group B Increases Minority Transplantation." *American Journal of Transplantation* 15(12): 3134–42. DOI: https://doi.org/10.1111/ajt.13409.

Wilson, Christo, Avijit Gosh, Shan Jiang, and Alan Mislove. 2020. "Auditing the Pymetrics Model Generation Process." https://cbw.sh/static/audit/pymetrics/pymetrics_audit_result_whitepaper.pdf.

Wolf, Christine T., Haiyi Zhu, Julia Bullard, Min Kyung Lee, and Jed R. Brubaker. 2018. "The Changing Contours of 'Participation' in Data-Driven, Algorithmic Ecosystems: Challenges, Tactics, and an Agenda." In *Companion of the 2018 ACM Conference on Computer Supported Cooperative Work and Social Computing,* Jersey City, N.J., November 7–9377–84. CSCW '18. DOI: https://doi.org/10.1145/3272973.3273005.

Wolfe, R. A., K. P. McCullough, and A. B. Leichtman. 2009. "Predictability of Survival Models for Waiting List and Transplant Patients: Calculating LYFT." *American Journal of Transplantation* 9(7): 1523–27. DOI: https://doi.org/10.1111/j.1600-6143.2009.02708.x.

Wolfe, R. A., K. P. McCullough, D. E. Schaubel, J. D. Kalbfleisch, S. Murray, M. D. Stegall, and A. B. Leichtman. 2008. "Calculating Life Years from Transplant (LYFT): Methods for Kidney and Kidney-Pancreas Candidates." *American Journal of Transplantation* 8(4p2): 997–1011. DOI: https://doi.org/10.1111/j.1600-6143.2008.02177.x.

Wong, Pak-Hang. 2020. "Democratizing Algorithmic Fairness." *Philosophy and Technology* 33(2): 225–44. DOI: https://doi.org/10.1007/s13347-019-00355-w.

Yang, Ke, Julia Stoyanovich, Abolfazl Asudeh, Bill Howe, H. V. Jagadish, and Gerome Miklau. 2018. "A Nutritional Label for Rankings." Presented at SIGMOD'18, Houston, June 10–15.

Zarembo, Alan. 2018. "In a Turf Battle for Organs, a Policy Review Rattles the National Transplant System." *Los Angeles Times*, January 3. https://www.latimes.com/nation/la-na-organ-transplant-20180103-htmlstory.html.

Zhang, Baobao. 2021. "Public Opinion toward Artificial Intelligence." *Oxford Handbook of AI Governance*. OSF Preprints. October 7. DOI: https://doi.org/10.31219/osf.io/284sm.

Zhang, Yukun, and Longsheng Zhou. 2019. "Fairness Assessment for Artificial Intelligence in Financial Industry." Cornell University, arXiv:1912.07211v1 [stat. ML]. Submitted December 19, 2019. http://arxiv.org/abs/1912.07211.

Zimmerman, Annette, Elena Di Rosa, and Hochan Kim. 2020. "Technology Can't Fix Algorithmic Injustice." *Boston Review*, January 9. http://bostonreview.net/science-nature-politics/annette-zimmermann-elena-di-rosa-hochan-kim-technology-cant-fix-algorithmic.

Zuckerman, Ethan. 2017. "Mistrust, Efficacy, and the New Civics: Understanding the Deep Roots of the Crisis of Faith in Journalism." Knight Commission Workshop on Trust, Media, and American Democracy, Aspen Institute (October). https://dspace.mit.edu/handle/1721.1/110987.

Zuloaga, Lindsey. 2021. "Industry Leadership: New Audit Results and Decision on Visual Analysis." HireVue (blog), January 11, 2021. https://www.hirevue.com/blog/hiring/industry-leadership-new-audit-results-and-decision-on-visual-analysis.

Index |

Note: tables and figures are listed in **boldface**.

ABO antibody barrier, new drugs and, 74–75
Accenture, auditing of algorithms by, 47
Access to Transplant Score (ATS), 100; development, 108; effect of geography on, 100
accountability of algorithms, as inadequately addressed, 2
ADA. *See* Age Discrimination Act
Administrative Procedure Act, on community voice in algorithms, 37
African Americans. *See* racial bias/ discrimination
AFST. *See* Allegheny Family Screening Tool
Age Discrimination Act (ADA), 20/80 proposal compliance with, 92–94
Alcorn, James, 73–74, 106
Algorithmic Accountability Act of 2019 (U.S.), 44
Algorithmic Fairness and Opacity Group (AFOG), 143n113
algorithmists, 46
algorithms: definition of, 1, 4–5; as easier to adopt than to govern, 2; false image of objectivity, 1–2, 4;

growing movement to reject, 50–51; importance life decisions made by, 1; increasing use of, 3; machine-based, *versus* bureaucratic algorithms, 6; shaping of perception by, 51; as Turing machines, 4; types of organizations using, 1. *See also* prediction, data-driven
algorithms, poor: characteristics of, 26; as common, 110; consequences for real people, 27; examples of, 10–20, 26; and moral decisions made without thought, 110
Allegheny Family Screening Tool (AFST), 47–49; and best practices for algorithmic governance, 47, 50; biases embedded in, 50; correcting for biases in, 48–49; ethical analysis of, 48; scholarship on, 48; and shared understanding via shared infrastructure, 123–24; study on community engagement, 49
Alwall, Nils, 144n8
ambulance dispatch algorithm, choice of alternative to, 51
American Medical Association Code of Medical Ethics, 77–78